Father

Edward P. Vargo, S.V.D.

7-11-74

RAINSTORMS
AND
FIRE

EDWARD P. VARGO

RAINSTORMS
AND
FIRE

RITUAL IN THE NOVELS OF JOHN UPDIKE

NATIONAL UNIVERSITY PUBLICATIONS
KENNIKAT PRESS · 1973
PORT WASHINGTON, N. Y. · LONDON

Library of Congress Catalog Card No. 73-83271
ISBN: 0-8046-9053-7

Manufactured in the United States of America

Published by
Kennikat Press, Inc.
Port Washington, N.Y./London

CONTENTS

RAINSTORMS
AND
FIRE

1

THE SUBSOIL OF REALITY

For the past fifteen years, critics have been praising John Updike for his elegant style. So much so that any review of his last few books feels incomplete unless it includes at least perfunctory obeisance to this given. His language has been called poetic, magical, incandescent, bejewelled with brilliant baroque metaphors and similes.[1] William Peden has described his short stories as, at their best, "a triumph of the art of the usual; Updike possesses a genius for recording, as it were, the flicker of the eyelid which becomes an epiphany, and his small apartments, automobiles stuck in the snow, and mildly frustrating Sunday afternoons which make his characters reflect that 'this was the sort of day when you sow and not reap' are sharply observed and brilliantly recorded."[2]

Just as consistently, many critics have fallen into the habit of complaining about the preciousness of his style and the commonplace quality of his subject matter. Of late this has taken the form of waiting for the "Great Novel" that Updike is bound to write while deciding that the latest addition to his canon does not qualify. William Peden has judged the least successful of his stories "to be trivial rather than significant, and more dull than delightful."[3] While grudgingly admitting good patches of prose in *The Centaur,* a good number have still considered it too self-conscious and "lushly poetical."[4] To Norman Mailer, who feels that Updike "could become the best of our literary novelists if he could forget about style and go deeper into the literature of sex," Updike's style "smells like stale garlic."[5] Richard Stern has claimed that Updike's "inability to stop fondling detail" has hindered his development of consistent narrative skill: "Concern for the richness of minutiae may be a writer's chief gift, but if he works in the narrative convention whose strictest term is that nothing shall be written which does not advance and enlarge the narrative, he must exercise the gift with especial caution."[6] More severely, Richard Gilman has branded Updike as an "author of preternaturally scintillant but thin and arrested fiction . . . in which rococo states of consciousness and refined conditions of memory come more and more to replace imaginative event and action." Through his constant movement "from event to embroidery, from drama to coy details," Updike has, in the opinion of Gilman, evaded "the supreme task and burden of literature: the appropriation and transfiguration, in one way or another, of suffering, struggle, conflict, disaster and death."[7]

Such criticism continues today, with even greater finality. Paul Theroux determines Updike's real deficiency as a writer to be "an obsession with surfaces he is unable to penetrate." *Rabbit Redux* is "the shabby outrage of an imagination damaged by indulgence." "His verbal skill, grown derelict, has delivered him into a glibness that cannot admit compassion or true observation."[8] These objections about lack of depth, flawed moral vision, and manipulation of detail rather than genuine human involvement, have been voiced too frequently and too seriously to be passed over lightly. It will be one of my objectives in the following chapters to face these difficulties.

A few of the earlier critics latched onto Updike's apprenticeship with the *New Yorker* from 1955 to 1957 to explain the weaknesses found in his stories. Thus, Pamela Hansford Johnson described *The Poorhouse Fair* as "New Yorkerishly freakish in theme."[9] Granted, the novels and stories of Updike do bear a resemblance to the stereotype of the *New Yorker* story, especially on the point of technique. They generally follow a realistic pattern that finds touches of tragedy and even heroism under commonplace surfaces. They are dependent on observation rather than invention. They develop by implication rather than direct statement, by revelation rather than narrative summary. They display an "immense virtuosity in using details—using brand names, gestures, turns of phrase, patterns of taste, all pregnant trivialities—to *make* the surfaces commonplace."[10] Still, these similarities should not blind one to the manner in which Updike goes beyond the stereotype.

How John Updike views his vocation as a creative writer is made clear in the essay "The Sea's Green Sameness," written in 1960 and reprinted in his most recent collection *Museums and Women* (1972). Using the sea as the basic metaphor for his topic, Updike seeks to discover what new element he can contribute to human knowledge of the sea. No longer can he conceive legends about the origin of any of its qualities, such as its saltiness, for the explanation of these qualities now belongs in the realm of science. Nor is there any point in attempting to explain the essence of the sea, for that is the realm of philosophy. What he can transmit to human beings is the esthetic experience of the sea's aliveness. By putting his head in the sand and closing one eye, he receives a vision of the sea as a tremulous wall that beckons him to press his body against its perpendicular surface and feel "the answer of another heart beating" against his own. Although his vision disappears when he opens both eyes, he seems to hear in the sound of the surf the sea's encouragement for him to repeat the attempt in his mind again and again. The performance of this challenge assimilates his role to that of primitive magicians and priests: "I have reverted, in my art, which I gaily admit I have not mastered, to the first enchanters, who expected their nets of words to imprison the

weather, to induce the trees to bear and the clouds to weep,
and to drag down advice from the stars." He is to be a myth-
maker, a poet who brings inanimate things of nature to
participation in the life of men, one who realizes the inter-
connection of all things in this world. But he does not expect
the forces of nature to obey his words; he does not live in the
world of the early Greeks. "All I expect is that once into my
blindly spun web of words the thing itself will break: make an
entry and an account of itself. Not declare what it will do. . . .
I wish it to yield only on the point of its identity. What is it?
Its breath, its glitter, its greenness and sameness balk me.
What is it? If I knew, I could say."[11] This suggests Updike's
understanding of his task as a quest for the unseen and
elusive ambiguity behind life, as a search for the means to
help his readers experience the transcendent realities of life.

Updike's acceptance of ambiguity as a fact of human
existence explains the low-key, apparently unresolved con-
clusions to his novels, which have disturbed some critics. In a
conversation at Schenectady's Union College, he presented his
literary stance in this way:

I do see each book as a picturing of actual tensions, conflicts,
and awkward spots in our private and social lives. My books
feed, I suppose, on some kind of perverse relish in the fact that
there are insolvable problems. There is no reconciliation between
the inner, intimate, appetites and the external consolations of
life. You want to live forever, you want to have endless wealth,
you have an endless avarice for conquests, crave endless freedom
really. . . . But there is no way to reconcile these individual
wants to the very real need of any society to set strict limits and
to confine its members. *Rabbit, Run,* which is a book much on
my mind lately, I wrote just to say, that there is no solution.
It is a novel about the bouncing, the oscillating back and forth
between these two kinds of urgencies until, eventually, one just
gets tired and wears out and dies, and that's the end of the
problem.[12]

And yet his role as writer is not just to bounce us back and
forth between tensions. Through his writing he wants to bring
into focus what we ordinarily do not see, for lack of distance

or too much distance. "I describe things not because their muteness mocks our subjectivity but because they seem to be masks for God. . . . There is, in fiction, an image-making function, above image-retailing."[13] The reality behind the immediately apparent is the crucial thing. In searching for the elusive identity, Updike is moving more and more from pointillism as technique to pointillism as philosophy. In "Midpoint," the long poem which epitomizes his attitude toward his art in the first half of his life, Updike insists that a pattern of dots cannot be seen for an ordered picture until we discover the right distance from which to view it. Particles in nature, like pointillistic images in time, are not always what they seem to be. Any particular point in time, especially if sharply conceived, is a position from which other points in past or future can be recognized more clearly.[14] His faith in the concrete and the irreducible—telephone poles, female bodies, the minutest detail, the word, the atom—is inextricably meshed with his desire to achieve a new creation through his imagination—the recognition of the interconnectedness of all things, the bringing into focus of the divinity present in every particle of the universe.

Unless we are willing to take this as the author's *donnée,* we will tend to put Updike's work down as critically inferior when in reality we are simply reacting against the kind of world he has created. In an illuminating essay, Michael Novak has analyzed what I feel to be a major difficulty for many of the critics in their approach to Updike's work:

Updike's sensibility, however, is specifically Christian—an alert, open, human, sensual Calvinism; a tension of the spirit stung by the pressure of death, uncommonly driven by passions of sensual and sexual nostalgia. Updike's inner world is not Catholic. It is almost wholly Platonic: his art is ever bitten by the pain of memory. His vision forces itself to press through the hard, defined realities of toothpaste tubes, wooden shingles, sea coral, and exquisitely described female nakedness to a world more real. So deep is Updike's confidence in that distant world that the hard, glorious shapes of this one are no danger to him; his exquisite control of sensual detail springs from a consciousness whose source is elsewhere. His radical dualism makes myth and symbol his necessary tools, familiar, warm and restful in his hand.

It is difficult for the Jewish sensibility, and for the hard, pragmatic, secular sensibility, of our critical establishment, to enter this delicately hung, delicately balanced cave where flame-tinted shadows dance and reel and the really real intermingle.[15]

Only after we admit the validity of the world he presents in his novels, like it or not, can we begin to make judgments about whether his style and subject matter fuse into one meaningful vision or not.

As a religious writer, Updike's investigation of the "intrinsic problem in human existence" centers chiefly upon the alienation, uprootedness, and disharmony of modern man's situation in the world, and upon man's struggle for personal freedom in this context.[16] One cause for man's disjointedness, as he has viewed it in "The Sea's Green Sameness," is that the world is naturally split into two halves: "the ego and the external object." The incarnation of this ego—"that omnivorous and somehow pre-existent 'I'—in a speck so specifically situated amid the billions of history"—has always been a source of wonderment for him. "Why was I I? The arbitrariness of it astounded me; in comparison nothing was too marvellous."[17] Naturally connected with this insecurity about his existence is man's fear of his non-existence, of death:

Might it not simply be that sex has become involved in the Promethean protest forced upon Man by his paradoxical position in the Universe as a self-conscious animal? Our fundamental anxiety is that we do not exist—or will cease to exist. Only in being loved do we find external corroboration of the supremely high valuation each ego secretly assigns itself. This exalted arena, then, is above all others the one where men and women will insist upon their freedom to choose—to choose that other being in whose existence their own existence is confirmed and amplified.[18]

The terror of death is a repeated motif in the short stories and novels; the individual's sense of alienation is a major theme in *The Centaur;* the "exalted arena" where men and women will insist most upon their freedom of choice is explored in *Couples.*

In answer to the anxieties of existence, Updike investigates the human values implicit in love, nostalgia, and awareness of the concrete details of our environment. As human love has already been shown to affirm us in life, so it also aids in retaining our past:

What is nostalgia but love for that part of ourselves which is in Heaven, forever removed from change and corruption? A woman, loved, momentarily eases the pain of time by localizing nostalgia; the vague and irrecoverable objects of nostalgic longing are assimilated, under the pressure of libidinous desire, into the details of her person. Freud says she is our mother. But the images we hoard in wait for the woman who will seem to body them forth include the inhuman—a certain slant of sunshine, a delicate flavor of dust, a kind of rasping tune that is reborn in her voice; they are nameless, these elusive glints of original goodness that a man's memory stores toward an erotic commitment. Perhaps it is to the degree that the beloved crystallizes the lover's past that she presents herself to him, alpha and omega, as his Fate.[19]

In the following chapters, we will see in greater detail how the characters in the novels depend upon human love or upon the reliving of the past to overcome the fear of death. In passing on, however, we ought to note that the theme of memory, introduced in the epigraphs of *The Same Door* and *Pigeon Feathers,* pulls together the short stories in these two collections. Its significance is suggested by the question which Walter asks at the end of "The Astronomer": "What is the past, after all, but a vast sheet of darkness in which a few moments, pricked apparently at random, shine."[20] It is in these shining past moments that we must seek the meaning of our present condition, for "memory does more than recall; it becomes so impressive by creating a presence. It has a sacramental power. Memory, working with open honesty and at points of beauty, resurrects."[21] In story after story, then, a tension between two worlds is resolved by the action of memory. In "Walter Briggs," for example, Jack finally remembers a name out of the past that has been eluding him all day, and he achieves a renewed communion with his wife, a sense of wholeness, a link between the past and the present, the visible and the unseen.[22] Nor should we forget that the "deliberate recapturing of something no longer possessed is a distinctive mark of human ritual."[23]

The elaborate concern that Updike devotes to the details of his stories flows more from an appreciative awareness of their deeper significance than from a shallow preoccupation with style. He reveals a special feeling for the physical objects around him which may be a result of having been raised in Pennsylvania Dutch country: "Shillington bred a receptivity to the supernatural unrelated to orthodox religion. This is the land of the hex signs, and in the neighboring town of Grille a 'witch doctor' hung out a shingle with a qualified M.D. I was struck recently, on reading Frazer's contemptuous list of superstitions in *The Golden Bough,* by how many of them seemed good sense."[24] This same aura of the nostalgic and the supernatural is brought out in the "Foreword" to *Olinger Stories:* "The surrounding land is loamy, and Olinger is haunted—hexed, perhaps—by rural memories, accents, and superstitions."[25] Details speak to Updike, affirm goodness, stabilize his world:

And in fact there is a color, a quiet but tireless goodness that things at rest, like a brick wall or a small stone, seem to affirm. A wordless reassurance these things are pressing to give. An hallucination? To transcribe middleness with all its grits, bumps, and anonymities, in its fullness of satisfaction and mystery: is it possible or, in view of the suffering that violently colors the periphery and that at all moments threatens to move into the center, worth doing? Possibly not; but the horse-chestnut trees, the telephone poles, the porches, the green hedges recede to a calm point that in my subjective geography is still the center of the world.[26]

Details also serve a religious function of praise. Updike makes this clear at the end of "Fanning Island," where he had sketched a potential novel: "This is the outline; but it would be the days, the evocation of the days . . . the green days. The tasks, the grass, the weather, the shades of sea and air. Just as a piece of turf torn from a meadow becomes a *gloria* when drawn by Dürer. Details. Details are the giant's fingers. He seizes the stick and strips the bark and shows, burning beneath, the moist white wood of joy."[27] Finally, in a reminiscence on a pop art exhibit in New York, Updike has shown that even the most apparently meaningless details of life can lead him to communion with God: "Our impression . . . was of an art that, able at last to relent in its fierce, long battle with pictorial convention, was giving God, God the maker of unmade things, the glory. The world is full of blatant trash—industrial, mental, visual. Perhaps the time has come to give this trash the homage that Nature in all her aspects deserves."[28]

In an essay that resonates with the point I am making, Melvin J. Friedman has written of Flannery O'Connor's preoccupation with physical objects to reveal the sacred. A stone is still a stone, but for the religious man it is also transmuted into a supernatural reality. The illogical reverence with which *Wise Blood*'s Hazel Motes treats things like his "glaring blue" suit and "stiff black broad-rimmed hat" and black Bible and "silver-rimmed spectacles" and "high rat-colored car" illustrates one way in which immediate reality can take on the dimensions of cosmic reality. While his hearing aid is merely a functional commonplace object to Rayber in *The Violent Bear It Away,* for Tarwater, with his perverse sensitivity to the sacred, it becomes a miracle box with special powers.[29] Although Flannery O'Connor's Catholic and Bible Belt vision conditions the response of her characters to the sacred in the physical objects around them quite differently from the way John Updike's Protestant and suburban vision operates, both novelists are concerned with a similar religious interpenetration of the sacred and the profane.

We know that John Updike was raised a Lutheran, that he is a Congregationalist by convenience, and that he has felt branded with the cross despite his light exposure to Christian doctrine as a child: "And a brand so specifically Lutheran, so distinctly Nordic; an obdurate insistence that at the core of the core there is a right-angled clash to which, of all verbal combinations we can invent, the Apostle's Creed offers the most adequate correspondence and response." The very core lies in the first article: belief in the existence of God; once that is accepted, the rest, including the appearance of the God-man in "the form of a Syrian carpenter," "follows as water flows downhill."[30]

Even here he reveals that his approach to Christianity is a search for an answer to the anxieties of existence that have been pointed out above, but his dialectic comes into sharper focus in a highly sophisticated review of Karl Barth's *Anselm: Fides Quaerens Intellectum.* On several occasions, Updike has mentioned the personal meaning and support that he has found in Barth;[31] here he acutely makes a distinction between the nature of Barth's faith and Anselm's, despite Barth's implication that there is none. For one thing, Anselm believed that he had truly discovered a rational basis for faith, whereas Barth in his paraphrase cannot do without the conditional, "if he exists," that emphasizes the essentially irrational basis of faith. Today's man must depend on "Jahweh's unappealable imperatives" to span the gap between *credere* and *intelligere.* Nine centuries of repeated disbelief have forced the medieval theologian without the sense of crisis to become the modern theologian of crisis. In his final evaluation of Barth's argument, then, Updike recognizes the intimate bond that can grow between faith and the awareness of man's condition: "The understanding that faith seeks is, for Barth, fundamentally an understanding of what man and religion are *not.* Anselm's proof—'a model piece of good, penetrating, and neat theology'—interests him in its rigorous negativity, its perfect independence of natural phenomena, and the 'key' it holds for him is, possibly, that it proves nothing—probes, that is, the nothingness from which rises the cry for God."[32]

The existence of God which is debated in this review is the substratum on which man's immortality is grounded in Updike's fiction. The nothingness of death constantly returns as a major anxiety, which is for the most part resolved by the hope of a resurrection. This is the point where religion and art join in his work, "that point at which a story becomes a sacramental symbol of an archetypal resurrection. . . . What lies behind these epiphanies and esthetic experiences is that Resurrection which occurred in an unseen world to which memory, confession, and beauty can unite us . . ."[33]

Modern American novelists who come closest to sharing with Updike in this hope of some kind of rebirth are J. D. Salinger and Flannery O'Connor. But where hope and affirmation are present in significant American novels since 1945, it "is the kind of affirmation found in such novels as Heller's *Catch-22* and Kesey's *One Flew Over the Cuckoo's Nest*— the defiant assertion of one's humanity in the face of overwhelming forces that dehumanize and destroy."[34] Less defiant and more transcendental, Updike is out of this mainstream.

In "Pigeon Feathers," we have an entirely convincing and moving description of an adolescent's first religious doubts and a reaffirmation of his belief in an afterlife. Having stumbled across a passage in H. G. Wells in which Jesus and Christianity are presented as frauds, David is bothered by the possibility that this may be true. If so, then death will be a total annihilation, the end of everything. Such a vivid vision of the horror of death overwhelms David as he sits in the outhouse that he desperately needs some physical affirmation, some nod or gesture to reveal to him that faith is true, that man will have a resurrection, that heaven exists. His search for this visible sign occupies the remainder of the story.

At first, he wants Christ to touch his hands in reassurance in the darkness of his bedroom. "Not hard or long: the faintest, quickest grip would be final for a lifetime." But even if Christ touched him, could he be certain of His infinitely gentle touch? From the Lutheran minister at his catechetical class he receives the answer that Heaven exists only as the goodness of Lincoln exists. From his mother he elicits her belief that God is a creation of Man. All the answers that human beings give to the boy simply confirm his growing horror of death and his fear that dying means "never moving or seeing or hearing anything ever again." He wants to hang onto the Christian promise of resurrection as an act which gives shape to life, as that which "made every good and real thing, ball games and jokes and pert-breasted girls, possible."[35]

Unable to reach human satisfaction, David searches for the confirmation of his belief in any sign whatsoever. First he finds some comfort by mixing in a crowd, for surely someone there must hold the truth. "The sight of clergymen cheered him; whatever they themselves thought, their collars were still a sign that somewhere, at some time, someone had recognized that we cannot, *cannot,* submit to death. The sermon topics posted outside churches, the flip, hurried pieties of disc jockeys, the cartoons in magazines showing angels or devils—on such scraps he kept alive the possibility of hope."[36] In giving comfort to his dog Copper, in stroking him, in the sure intricate folding of Copper's ears, in his hairs, even in their smell, David somehow seeks the sign that seems to elude him elsewhere. Finally, while burying the pigeons that his mother had ordered him to kill, he closely examines all the details of their beautiful feathers and receives a visible sign, a sacramental revelation of invisible truth. Handling the dead pigeons, David recognizes the nod or gesture he had been searching for. Through all of his body, he feels the certainty "that the God who had lavished such craft upon these worthless birds would not destroy His whole Creation by refusing to let David live forever."[37] The Christian paradox in operation here is that through the killing of the pigeons, through this act of destruction, David is saved. The close contemplation of the birds, made possible by death, leads him to an insight that reaffirms his shaken faith.

Inseparable from this resurrection-theology is the joy, the spirit of play, the awareness of the intrinsic blessing of each moment of life that is expressed in "Lifeguard." Here a seminarian converted into a lifeguard for the summer complements his theological studies with "the texts of the flesh." Once he has mounted his chair ("it is as if I am climbing into an immense, rigid, loosely fitting vestment"), he views man's relation to the sea before him as a parable for life. "We struggle and thrash, and drown; we succumb, even in despair, and float, and are saved."[38]

His chief meditations, however, are upon the people for whose lives he is responsible. The arrival of the old sets him thinking of the onrush of death. The young girls stir his lust and turn his thoughts to life-giving intercourse, to the rescue and redemption that is experienced through love. But the major activity of his mind is an attempt to conceive the life after death, the immortality, that "this immense clot gathered on the beach" will share with him. The conception is beyond his ability.

On Sunday mornings, this crowd of people exasperates him most. Puzzled by their apparent neglect of worship, by noon he imagines them "gathered by the water's edge in impassioned poses of devotion" through the blurred vision of his fatigue. Now he gains the insight that "the single ever-present moment that we perpetually bring to our lips brimful" is "our most obvious possession, our most platitudinous blessing." An appreciation of this fact can lead only to exultant joy in life: "Be joyful is my commandment. It is the message I read in your jiggle. Stretch your skins like pegged hides curing in the miracle of the sun's moment. Exult in your legs' scissoring, your waist's swivel. Romp, eat the froth; be children. I am here above you; I have given my youth that you may do this. I wait."[39] Accepting the joy in every moment will make of it a praise of God, like the milkman's "chains slogging a tune on his stout tires: glory be," in "The Crow in the Woods."[40] Still, the lifeguard senses a bittersweet irony. Although the tides of time inevitably pull men to the horizons of death, and the seminarian-lifeguard is in readiness for the moment that he hears the call for help, it has not yet come.

What should be apparent from the analysis of these last two stories is that Updike's religious concerns have also influenced his literary technique. In attempting to create metaphors that make transcendent realities like immortality and resurrection conceivable, he has fused the spiritual with the physical, presenting us with a heightened, or better, a sacramental understanding of the material universe. To invest the familiar objects and gestures of everyday experience with religious meaning, he has had to attune himself to the significance of the least details. Structurally, the maintenance of spiritual tensions has sometimes led to static physical appearances, devoid of much action, as in "Lifeguard." His writings then take on the character of illuminated moments, of prayer. They become a "liturgy of life," a dirge for the passing of time and a canticle of praise for Nature in all its forms. His attempts to visualize the experience of the transcendent, to bring it within our focus, have led him into a sophisticated use of ritual, of which the three basic elements are pattern, myth, and celebration.

On the sensory level, consequently on the most obvious level, ritual is the performance of an easily defined pattern: a repeatable form, usually consisting of language as well as gesture. The popular idea of ritual does not progress beyond this notion of an action which is done over and over again without any thought and without any significant meaning. There is a subtle connection, however, between this human principle of recurrence and the repetitions that make time intelligible to man. The sun rises and sets to measure the day; the moon waxes and wanes to measure the month; the seasons go through their cycle to outline the year; birth and death delimit a life. Rituals cluster around these cyclical movements and, by imitation, extend beyond them.[41] To mention only two examples, *The Poorhouse Fair* operates within the pattern of one day, and the plot of Willa Cather's *My Antonia* takes on resonance from the natural cycles of the year, of life, of cyclic cultural evolution toward higher civilization.

Some examples that emphasize the element of pattern are the recurrent acts of symbolic communication, such as baptisms, weddings, funerals, or the liturgical holidays of the churches. College yells, crowd chants like that before the basketball game in *The Centaur,* the echolalia introduced into prayer to increase the sense of meditation, the device of the catalogue: these also follow the form of simple patterns of repetition.[42] A vignette like "In Central Park," with its simple cataloguing of unrelated images, evokes by accumulation a lyric view of New York City slowly being resurrected from the last days of winter.[43] In this sense of pattern, the paths produced by the packing of human feet, driving an automobile, acts of human kindness, even churchgoing without faith "represent a spontaneous ritual of human beings giving shape to their lives."[44]

The chief function of ritual as pattern is to sustain whatever belief man has and to make it meaningful by a "rehearsed attitude." Sentiment also demands outward expression, or it will die. "We need certain patterns of action which signify the way we look at things, the respect in which we hold them, and which allow us to manifest our feelings without first having to organize and work through a complex of ideas and feelings."[45] An outstanding exemplar of this human need is Rabbit Angstrom.

When one relates pattern to the workings of the novel, as E. M. Forster does in his essay "Pattern and Rhythm," it can apply to any element—a character, a scene, a gesture, a word, but most significantly to the plot. Usually it will pull the novel into a unity; it will catch the novel's "scattered statements in a net, make them cohere like a planet, and swing through the skies of memory."[46] The language remarkably foreshadows Updike's own preoccupation with his "blindly spun web of

words," with the stars as signs of religious permanence, with
the mysteries evoked by nostalgia. In dealing with the smaller
elements within his works, Updike reveals his belief that
pattern is enjoyable in itself. Nonessential though it might be,
especially when concerned with purely decorative effects, it
certainly adds to the joy of human existence. It activates
human imagination. Updike's light verse, poems like "A
Wooden Darning Egg" in which he extols "the skilled match-
ing of natural and man-made patterns which carpentry
demands," novels like *The Poorhouse Fair* and *Couples* in
which he praises the "patterned" workmanship of skilled
carpenters, novels like *Rabbit Redux* in which he expresses
nostalgia for the extinction of the linotypist in the face of
cheaper and more efficient processes, all glory in pattern for
its own sake.[47] But Updike also conceives of pattern on the
level of plot in terms similar to Forster's "hour-glass or grand
chain" for Henry James' *The Ambassadors* and Percy
Lubbock's *Roman Pictures*. To the amusement of some, he has
spoken of *Rabbit, Run* as a "pattern of Zs." *Of the Farm*
resembles an "X". More wildly, *The Centaur* is shaped like a
"sandwich" and *The Poorhouse Fair* like a "gladiola."[48] Shape
is a primary concern for him.

When critics have complained about the coyness of Updike's
details and his lack of caring for the concerns of real life, they
may be simply responding to his exuberance for pattern. The
rigid pattern which can expand and enrich and unify a novel
can also eviscerate it, as Forster has acutely noted. "It may
externalize the atmosphere, spring naturally from the plot, but
it shuts the doors on life and leaves the novelist doing exercises, generally in the drawing-room. Beauty has arrived, but
in too tyrannous a guise. . . . To most readers of fiction the
sensation from a pattern is not intense enough to justify the
sacrifices that made it, and their verdict is 'Beautifully done,
but not worth doing.' "[49] As this complaint is being brought
against John Updike today, so it has been brought against
Henry James in the past. If we are willing to care about the

world which James has circumscribed for us in his novels, we are in a better position both to judge and to enjoy what he offers. I suggest a similar dynamic for an approach to Updike. Let us enter his world before we dismiss it as irrelevant.

Beyond pattern lies the second basic element of ritual: myth, which expresses the rational level of experience. To say this is, however, misleading. Too often myth is still understood as a primitive attempt at philosophical explanation for the phenomena of nature, now discredited by the advance of science. In the first place, myth is a dramatic human tale, a narrative which is a product of the human imagination. Since the content of myth is generally the supernatural, or at least the preternatural, myth does "set itself off from the real world as we ordinarily perceive it. But that is not because it is *less* than ordinarily real but because it is far *more* than ordinarily real. . . ."[50] Myth views what has always existed and always will exist: the timeless problem of life and death. Myth speaks of what *really* happened, whether this was in the time of the gods or in our own mythic childhoods, and becomes the paradigmatic model for actions in the present.[51]

So, then, the function of myth is not merely to resurrect a primeval reality in narrative form, but also to serve as a dynamic guide for mankind's present life and activities. This is precisely where myth is linked with ritual. Ritual as pattern, pre-logical and pre-verbal, is incompletely human. Its rhythms, deeply felt but unanalyzed, link man with plants and animals to a biological dependence on the natural cycle. The interaction of myth with these rhythms is a distinctively human action by which man is able to make his life more meaningful in a larger sense.[52]

While not all of Updike's writings reflect the rhythmic patterns of ritual, the vast majority of them have myth as their structural principle. This should be evident in his constant return to events of childhood or of the past in general. When the re-enactment of the mythic childhood dramatizes the disharmonies or the neurotic disturbances that the character feels in his present life, when the myth aids the character in reconciling the clash of inward and outward forces of his present life, as in *The Centaur,* then the stage is set for the flowering of ritual in celebration.[53]

This third element, on the emotional level of experience, is an intense moment which brings into play the affectivity that is inherent in the intelligible pattern. Celebration is the existential initiation or achievement of an exaltation through the union of past and present, of the sensual, emotional, and rational. It cures the dissociation of sensibility, the splitting of intellect and feeling. Because the experienced harmony or exaltation may be felt in varying degrees, even to the point of communion with the ultimate, with total Being, the chief function of celebration may be considered the externalization of man's religious feelings and the tangible embodiment of the transcendent. The effect should be similar to this description by Ernst Cassirer: "The men who celebrate such a festivity, who perform their magical dances, are fused with each other and fused with all things in nature. They are not isolated; their joy is felt by the whole of nature and shared by their ancestors. Space and time have vanished; the past has become the present; the golden age of mankind has come back."[54]

In some of its aspects, this celebration sounds suspiciously similar to the Joycean epiphany, "an event in which an encompassing whole is mediated to us through a particular object or action."[55] Updike's short stories usually do lead to some type of illumination or epiphany. When this esthetic experience is more than a moment of brilliant stasis, when it transcends the secular or reveals the eternal value of the transitory in such a way as to give a character strength for future action, it would be more accurate to call this epiphany celebration, an element of the larger operation of ritual.

Everything that I have been saying about ritual and Updike's use of it can be demonstrated by an analysis of the final two stories in *Pigeon Feathers.* It is from the germ discovered in these central, experimental stories that my conception of ritual in all of Updike's writings has grown. While these stories delineate the operation of ritual as an attempt to make the transcendent conceivable, they also portray some of the basic themes that will be discussed in the novels.

In "The Blessed Man of Boston, My Grandmother's Thimble, and Fanning Island," Updike outlines three potential novels that could develop from three unrelated experiences in his past. While hurrying from Fenway Park after a ball game, having joined the "Occidental panic" of the crowd, Updike recognizes in a Chinese man who remains in his seat—immobile and smiling—"the happy man, the man of unceasing and effortless blessing." A flood of details and images rushes in upon him as parts of the huge novel he could write about this man: "all set sequentially down with the bald simplicity of intrinsic blessing, thousands upon thousands of pages; ecstatically uneventful; divinely and defiantly dull."[56] In the details lies the power of praise.

When the narrator trips over his wife's sewing basket, the "stemless chalice" of his grandmother's old thimble returns him to the mythical days of her life and places upon him the "necessary and holy" task of re-creating her life in text. He even prays before beginning: "O Lord, bless these poor paragraphs, that would do in their vile ignorance Your work of resurrection."[57] He recalls how she acted when his grandfather died. Since the narrator himself had just come home with his new wife, his mother and father weakly tried to go on with the matter of welcome, but his grandmother stayed upstairs with his dead grandfather. From her action he had gained the insight "that we have no gestures adequate to answer the imperious gestures of nature."[58] He also recalls how she used to hover over him as he prepared for his adolescent social-sexual excursions into town. He would communicate his joy to the whole family in the dramatic gesture of lifting her suddenly like a child and twirling her: "I was carrying her who had carried me, I was giving my past a dance, I had lifted the anxious caretaker of my childhood from the floor, I was bringing her with my boldness to the edge of danger, from which she had always sought to guard me."[59] Through the details of his various recollections, he hopes to sing the uniqueness of this woman and to stave off the terror of obliteration that came over him when he picked up this keepsake from his grandmother.

Finally, the story on Fanning Island is to grow out of an image for the human condition from Pascal and the discovery of signs of habitation on an uninhabited island. The narrator re-constructs the stranding of a company of men on this island. They devour the body of the bravest man, the first to die, sacramentally gaining strength from it. They repeat the rituals of their former way of life: combat, the building of shelter, the harvesting, sex, worship, and burial of the dead. In the end, with the question, "for what had we been brought here?" still unanswered, the narrator is the only one alive.[60] Although the story seems to point toward despair in a meaningless universe, even this story, had the writer energy to fill in its details, would have been full of joy, a song of praise for life.

Through the four sections of "Packed Dirt, Churchgoing, A Dying Cat, A Traded Car," Updike employs the gestures and concrete details of everyday existence to create images of hope, love and faith for a technologically oriented audience. Each of the sections portrays a moment of communion, a ceremony that brings joy or understanding into life. In "Packed Dirt," David Kern, an older, less religious version of the David in "Pigeon Feathers," reflects on the patches of bare earth that are smoothed by the passing of human feet in small towns. In their sight he is reassured, "the passive fruit of ceremony."[61] In the reliving of paths from his childhood, he is nostalgically pleased. In this sign of an active victory won by men, he is made proud. When he sees a path made by children's feet on the harsh cut into his land by bulldozers preparing a new road, he rejoices in its accidental nature, its element of grace. The impress of human feet on earth reminds him "of John Dewey's definition of God as the union of the actual and the ideal," of our continued ability to see the world not only as an enemy, but as a holy playmate: "As our sense of God's forested legacy to us dwindles, there grows, in these worn, rubbed, and patted patches, a sense of human legacy—like those feet of statues of saints which have lost their toes to centuries of kisses."[62]

"Churchgoing" continues this theme of the world as a place of play, of liturgy, not of work. David asks what could be more delightful, taken purely as a human reaction, than "to sit and stand in unison and sing and recite creeds and petitions that are like paths worn smooth in the raw terrain of our hearts?" Three anecdotes—taking the collection at Lenten services with his father, finding the hushed shelter of a Greenwich Village church "like one of those spots worn bare by a softball game in a weed-filled vacant lot," participating in a tedious service on a Caribbean Island—lead to the climax: "God made the world, Aquinas says, in play."[63] Placed in counterpoint to the world of men and nature outside the church walls, the liturgy seems irrelevant, especially in the contrast of the transcendent blue of the sea and sky with the exhausting service on the island. "The churches do not seem to understand symbol and ceremony any longer. They are as technological and dry as the cities of cement. They do not relate us to the earth."[64] Sadly, in a mechanized world that has lost its connection with nature, even the divine liturgy goes dry.

In "A Dying Cat," the interest moves from our relation to the earth to the question of death itself. In England now, David comes across a dying cat on the road while his wife awaits the birth of their first child. He does it an act of kindness, by the ceremony of putting it at the side of the road, off the pavement and upon the earth. His glove is stained a sacramental "wine-brown."[65] Death mingles with new life.

Finally, in the largest section, "A Traded Car," through

his reminiscences on the meaning and soul that his old car had acquired, David finds a symbol, a ceremony, to explain the meaning of immortality. The movement of the story is much the same as in "Pigeon Feathers": a specific incident triggers an intense horror of death, which is dispelled in just as gratuitous and unexpected a manner as it began. At a dance, David and another woman are sexually attracted to each other, but at most she strokes his erect thumbs. Unable to sleep that evening, David recalls a Sunday school dictum that leads him to think that his soul has been judged: "To feel a sin was to commit it; to touch the brink was to be on the floor of the chasm. The universe that so easily permitted me to commit adultery became, by logical steps each one of which went more steeply down than the one above it, a universe that would easily permit me to die." David becomes convinced that he will be "eternally forgotten," and responds just as he had in his adolescence. "The dark vibrating air of my bedroom seemed the dust of my grave; the dust went up and up and I prayed upward into it, prayed, prayed for a sign, any glimmer at all, any microscopic loophole or chink in the chain of evidence, and saw none." So intense is his fright—"Each second my agony went unanswered justified it more certainly: the God who permitted me this fear was unworthy of existence. Each instant my horror was extended amplified God's non-existence"—that he must awake his wife and gain reassurance from her.[66]

The next day his mother tells him on the phone that his father is dying. Deciding to drive home from Boston, he picks up a hitchhiking sailor who serves as an image of America, fattened "on our unprecedented abundance of milk and honey, vitamins and protein. He had that instinctive optimism of the young animal that in America is the only generatrix of hope we have allowed ourselves; until recently, it seemed enough."[67] Crossing the Pennsylvania border, however, he enters a different country. Eating on Mennonite land, he feels in the waitresses "that old sense, of Pennsylvania knowingness—of knowing, that is, that the truth is good. They were the innkeeper's daughters, God had given us crops, and my wagon was hitched outside."[68] At home, he drinks a ceremonial glass of wine with his mother as she mentions his father's loss of faith. On his visit with his father, David wants to express his need and love for him, but here ceremony fails: "there were no words, no form of words available in our tradition." When a somewhat apprehensive girl from the Lutheran Home Missions asks the patient for routine religious information, his father tells her what a wonderful woman she is for her work, "and she left the room transformed into just that. As a star shines in our heaven though it has vanished from the universe, so my father continued to shed faith upon others."[69]

The law of continuity goes on: new paths for the old, a life for a death, fresh faith for the lost. That night David drives home to Boston. Observing the Pennsylvania landscape at sunset, he senses "the same quality—perhaps of reposing in the certainty that the truth is good—that is in Pennsylvania faces. It seemed to me for this sunset hour that the world is our bride, given to us to love, and the terror and joy of the marriage is that we bring to it a nature not our bride's," the nature of technology and science.[70] As the night wears on, though, David loses his connection with the world around him; his soul and the moving car fuse:

I had been driving forever, furniture, earth, churches, women, were all things I had innocently dreamed. And through those aeons my car, beginning as a mechanical spiral of molecules, evolved into something soft and organic and consciously brave. I lost, first, heart, then head, and finally any sense of my body. In the last hour of the trip I ceased to care or feel or in any real sense see, but the car, though its soul the driver had died, maintained steady forward motion, and completed the endless journey safely. Above my back yard the stars were frozen in place, and the shapes of my neighbors' houses wore the wonder that children induce by whirling.[71]

In the patterned experience of long-distance driving, David gains a conception of what immortality will be like. He discovers a meaningful ceremony to bring him into communication with the transcendent, with an immutable heaven and an ecstasy-filled earth. Again he escapes the horror of annihilating death in the hope of renewed life.

Sad to say, the car in which David had this significant moment of light will be traded in, "dissolved back into the mineral world from which it was conjured, dismissed without a blessing, a kiss, a treatment, or any ceremony of farewell."[72] The major conclusion that Updike must draw is that "we in America need ceremonies." No longer can we be satisfied with a pragmatic, secular, animal optimism to feed our hope. We need ceremonies such as these in order to recover the hope that arises from the transcendent, the hope that has been smothered in the "milk and honey, vitamins and protein" of a materialistic world.

In *Celebration in Postwar American Fiction,* Richard Rupp has viewed ceremony as Updike's way to interconnect the things of heaven and earth, as his protagonists' way to create a festive world and heal fear and isolation: "The poorhouse with its band, its home-made candy, and its patchwork quilts is a gesture toward the continuity of things; the vitiation of all ceremonies disconnects Rabbit from wife, home, and God; the filial pieties of George Caldwell and his son are a source of life and renewal for them. In each case the ceremonial action . . . proceeds from an individual belief that the act is possible. The chief significance of Updike's fourth novel, *Of the Farm* (1965), is the doubt that ceremony is still possible."[73]

My own presentation of the uses and the significance of ritual in the novels of John Updike is, I believe, further developed and specified than Richard Rupp's. *The Poorhouse Fair* cannot be discussed without considering the notion of sacred time. In *Rabbit, Run,* the external aspects of ritual become apparent: the need for repetition and the need for celebration. All the elements of ritual—pattern, myth, and celebration—merge in *The Centaur* to bring George and

Peter Caldwell to a new reality. *Of the Farm* illustrates the notion of sacred place. *Couples* and *Rabbit Redux* focus upon the desperate search for ceremonies to bring wholeness into a desacralized and dehumanized world.

As we discuss these novels chapter by chapter, there ought to emerge a picture of the kind of religious writer that Updike is. The "yes, but" quality of his vision ought to stand clear. He himself has given the outline: "Yes, in *Rabbit, Run,* to our inner urgent whispers, but—the social fabric collapses murderously. Yes, in *The Centaur,* to self-sacrifice and duty, but—what of a man's private agony and dwindling? No, in *The Poorhouse Fair,* to social homogenization and loss of faith, but—listen to the voices, the joy of persistent existence. No, in *Couples,* to a religious community founded on physical and psychical interpenetration, but— what else shall we do, as God destroys our churches?"[74]

In these novels, ritual serves to fulfill the great desire of capturing the past, to make the present meaningful through connection with the past, to overcome death, and to grasp immortality. For John Updike, ritual leads to resurrection, to a foretaste of eternal life. In a decadent society, however, in a society that has lost all sense of the transcendent, ritual degenerates into an empty form, to fill the void with meaningless, unthinking activity. Or it must discover new patterns, new myths, new ways to reintegrate man and to celebrate his vital yearning for the transcendent. *Couples* and *Rabbit Redux* are both an end and a beginning.

2

SACRED TIME: *THE POORHOUSE FAIR*

In "The Happiest I've Been," the last of the short stories in Updike's first collection, *The Same Door,* the narrator (a *persona* of Updike himself) speaks of the bond that he feels with Neil Hovey, the friend with whom he is going to drive to Chicago. What he feels most important about their friendship is that each has lived with grandparents. "This improved both our backward and forward vistas; we knew about the bedside commodes and midnight coughing fits that awaited most men, and we had a sense of childhoods before 1900, when the farmer ruled the land and America faced west. We had gained a humane dimension that made us gentle and humorous among peers but diffident at dances and hesitant in cars."[1] This humane dimension and sense of the past are very much in evidence in Updike's first novel, well-constructed and well-modulated, *The Poorhouse Fair.* In the respect and gentleness with which Updike presents the vegetal existence and various senilities of the weak and helpless poorhouse characters, there is a sharp contrast to his contempt for the garish superficialities of the world outside these walls.

The three chapters of *The Poorhouse Fair* move through the morning, afternoon, and evening of the third Wednesday of August of some future year, the day of the annual fair at the Diamond County Home for the Aged. Just as neatly, the three chapters treat of the final preparations for the fair, the apparent cancellation because of the afternoon rain, and the occurrence of the fair itself. My own analysis will follow this same progression in order to demonstrate how the various elements of this novel lead to the culminating ritual action of the annual celebration.

In the first chapter, a strong sense of time is established through the constant attention paid by various characters, notably by Hook and Conner, the prefect, to the development of clouds in the sky above. From the clearness of the early morning to the thunderclouds that burst over the scene at noon, time becomes a very visible and physical presence. Under this threatening sky, the values and reflections of Hook and Conner, both passive spectators to the preparations—the one by reason of age, the other by force of circumstance—gradually become apparent to us.

While the dew is still on the ground and the women are already setting up their tables, we meet the three basic characters among the old men: thoughtful nonagenarian Hook; passionate, sputtering Gregg; and the sensual, painfearing Lucas. At the very outset, Gregg is beginning to remove the name tags from the chairs on the porch in rebellion against what he considers Conner's dehumanizing regimentation. His ensuing actions are just as impulsive. He jumps over the poorhouse wall to bring a hurt and diseased cat onto the grounds. On returning with food taken from the kitchen for the cat, he confronts Conner with a rash verbal attack, becomes frightened by his own audacity, and is immensely relieved when he understands that Conner will not discipline him for his misdemeanor. Finally, after obscenely taunting Ted, the young driver who delivers the soft drinks, he concocts a wild plan to escape from the poorhouse in Ted's truck.

Lucas' chief action in this chapter, aside from poking his infected ear with a matchstick, is to volunteer to visit Conner in his cupola office and ask the reason for the name tags. Hook, the former schoolteacher, has a certain distaste for both of these men. Gregg, who has been trailing him of late, he views as a recalcitrant student who abuses the fatherly attention that his teacher might show to him. He also senses in a vague way that Gregg seeks from him "elevated forms of thought to shape and justify the confused rage he felt toward the world that had in the end discarded him."[2] Lucas he dislikes for another reason, for his detachment from the other inmates and for his apparent unwillingness to sever "the strings of the outer world" (9).

More than any other character, Hook represents a living connection with the past; he consistently relates the things around him to the values and experiences of his past. His first reaction to the name tags is to remember that "in the days when certain honors were allowed him," he had desired "the dignity of the middle initial" (3-4). As he looks over the small hills of New Jersey from the porch, he recalls the idyllic days when he had walked on a path beside the Delaware River beyond those hills on his way to teach school. Convinced that modern workmen cannot compare with those of the past, Hook meticulously, almost reverently, describes for Gregg and Lucas the craft of carpenters before the days of wire nails. In doing so, he reveals a value that recurs later in the novel: a respect for the individuality of the materials that is a hallmark of fine, manmade items.

As he wanders through the booths being prepared by the others, Hook continues this characteristic juxtaposition of past and present in both thought and word. In his banter with Mrs. Jamiesson, he mimics a friend from normal school, Horace Frye, forty years dead. While she drives a tack into the table, he recalls the sure strokes of carpenters in his youth. Coming to two men stringing bulbs, he looks over the town of Andrews in the distance and remembers how untamed this country was before the present homes were built on it. However, what triggers his most vivid reminiscence of the past, specifically of his own childhood, is the quilt that Amy Mortis is displaying for sale:

The violet ground, the five yellow ovals around a blue five-point star, within a brown square, again and again, were too much like his childhood bedspread for belief—the very dusty grape tone, the nameless flowers seen so squarely from above. In the confused way of recollections from that time he saw himself as a child wandering among the rectilinear paths of the pattern, searching for the deeper-dyed thread that occasionally, in the woven cloth, would arch above the others. In the rough-walled room lit by kerosene, the wick kept thriftily low, he saw the coverlet waiting for him; it was evening, he was a child. His parents were down below; his father's voice shook softly up the stairs. He felt no great resentment, for as a serious-minded child he feared the dark but knew that he must sleep, when the time came each day. Studying the cloth Hook felt the small condensed grief—that the past was so far, the end so near—secreted safe within his system well up and fill his head so exactly the thin arcs of his eyes smarted with what they contained (27-28).

For a moment, memory has the power to stop time. Hook enters into a mythic past. But he snaps out of this revery, and enters into a discussion with Amy on how Mendelssohn, the former prefect, would have responded to the quilt. What Amy loved in him was the dignity (so like McKinley) blended with kindness, and the dramatic way in which he said grace. Inevitably, they compare the days of McKinley and Bryan to the modern welfare state in which they live. Basically in agreement with Amy, Hook still attempts to see the good in the present: " 'Were Mark Hanna still running the country, good lady, our kind would be dead long past.' " In response, quick-tongued Amy cuts him down: " 'If we had any sense we'd let the Lord take us and start us off fresh' " (29-30).

This pragmatic view of death, coupled with the unsettling sense of death's proximity that had accompanied Hook's reminiscence on his childhood quilt, disturbs his normal morning calm. He had already been somewhat jarred by Gregg's flippant and angry remark about heart attacks if the chairs were removed, "for death, to his schoolteacher's mind, was a bell that must find the students with their noses to the desks" (5). The preparation for the fair had helped to gladden Hook, but now Amy's "speaking so plainly of death stirred the uglier humors in him. In the mid-mornings of days he usually felt that he would persist, on this earth, forever. . . . Amy, with her sharp short view, had disrupted the customary tide of his toward-noon serenity" (37). The feeling of dread that comes over Hook on this occasion is one of the factors that saves his nostalgia from spreading into sentimentality.[3] But Hook's recollections also serve a very important function; they create an atmosphere of a mythic past, of sacred time. His nostalgia "provides a reality beyond the moment" in answer to the terror of oncoming death.[4] In his unconscious attempts to re-live the golden age of his youth, to sustain life by a re-creation of past experiences, Hook is in a sense trying to make eternity touch time.[5] Thus Hook's reflections, by their fusion of past and present, introduce the possibility of ritual action into the novel.

In contrast to Hook's finding comfort in memory and in the worn paths of routine, Conner seeks happiness in a self-imposed scheme that only alienates him from his subjects of three years' standing. His physical movements more or less parallel Hook's in this first chapter, but his reflections reveal that he lives in a universe vastly different from that of the old people. In a remembrance of how Mendelssohn looked in his coffin, Amy Mortis sees a loving and saintly man; Conner only sees a heavy drinker and pompous old man who "had in part thought of himself as God" (14). For Conner, there is no God. Where Hook can sense the impending storm in the clear morning sky, Conner is deaf to Nature: "The slats of light from the east and south windows, broken into code by the leaves and stems of the plants on the sills, spoke no language to him. He had lost all sense of omen" (14). Where Gregg views the name tags as an affront to his human dignity, Conner's intention had been to give the inmates a sense of property and dignity. Feeling that his morning's routine has been soiled by Lucas' visit to inquire about the name tags, disturbed by a crank-letter he had received that morning, convinced that Hook is plotting against him, Conner, the man of logic and good intentions, believes that he is always ungratefully misunderstood: "The sculptor has his rock and the saint the silence of his Lord, but a man like Conner who has vowed to bring order and beauty out of human substance has no third factor; he is a slave, at first, to gratitude" (16).

Partly because he thinks that Hook is walking around the grounds like the proprietor, and partly because he is infected by "the aura of holiday, the general dislocation of duties," Conner descends the stairs from his cupola office and ineffectually tries to be of some assistance (41). Noticing a few clouds, he feels some concern for unblemished weather, for anything less would be taken as a judgment against him on this "one day of profit and celebration" (41). He eventually finds his way to the table of Amy Mortis, who he gently insists should move out of the sun. She refuses in her blunt fashion: " 'You expect us to give up the old ways, and make this place a little copy of the world outside, the way it's going. I don't say you don't mean well, but it won't do. We're too old and too mean; we're too tired' " (43). He loses by her silent comparison of his detached, medical interest in her with Mendelssohn's more human and personal interest.

Still, there is one moment when Conner comes close to communication with these people. Moving from Amy to Hook, he asks if the old man had seen a cat wandering on the grounds. The thought of its suffering leads Conner, who hates pain, to the reasonable conclusion that it should not be be alive. When Hook suggests that some children might torture it, and when Gregg threatens to wring its neck, Conner draws back: "The idea sickened Conner, children soaking the dying animal with kerosene. He lacked most men's tolerance for cruelty, their ability to blur and forget rumors of it. He wondered if Gregg were ugly enough to make good his

insane threat" (52). But when he realizes that Gregg only
wanted to feed the cat, Conner melts in kindness. Attempting to communicate his affection and humility to Gregg at
this moment, he only succeeds in relieving Gregg of the fear
of punishment for trespassing in the kitchen.

One reason for Conner's inability to communicate on a
human level is his philosophy of life. His utopian vision can
end only in a dehumanized, antiseptic world, where there is
no pain and no aging. Striving for neat patterns, Conner has
no regrets when his assistant, Buddy, carries out his orders
and kills the cat:

He wanted things *clean;* the world needed renewal, and this was
a time of history when there were no cleansing wars or sweeping
purges, when reform was slow, and decayed things were allowed
to stand and rot themselves away. It was a vegetable world. Its
theory was organic: perhaps old institutions in their dying could
make fertile the chemical earth. So the gunshot ringing out,
through a discord, pleased the rebel in Conner, the idealist, anxious to make space for the crystalline erections that in his heart
he felt certain would arise, once his old people were gone (64).

He refuses to accept the inevitable movement of the world
towards entropy. In all aspects of life—the political situation,
the economic condition, the maturity of the physical universe
—everything is in a process of settling, of stagnating. Everything is moving towards greater homogeneity as well as in-
creased disorganization. Conner expends his energy at the
poorhouse in trying to convert the disordered system of this
messy world into an ordered one, not realizing that his dislike of dirt and passion for order have developed into an
antipathy to life itself. He is searching for "the appropriate
motive which will transform motion into direction," but his
drive for "uniform motion" will only accelerate the entropy
which he hopes to counter.[6] He cannot understand that, in
the last analysis, life and death transcend order and control.
Victory is always on the side of disorder.

Conner is unwilling to cast aside his "dynamic vision: that
of Man living healthy and unafraid beneath blank skies,

'integrated,' as the accepted phrase had it, 'with his fulfilled possibilities' " (65). The state of equilibrium, or "perfect adjustment to the prevailing ethos of the world," is an ideal which he maintains at "the loss of any distinct inner reality he might have had."[7] While Conner gains sympathy through his clumsy kindnesses and his fear of nature's indiscriminate wastings, he loses sympathy for the imposition of his rigid patternings upon these old people who understand life's complexity much better than he does. After Conner returns to the safety of his office in the morning, thunder punctuates his thoughts of a godless happiness under a blank sky in such a way that we are again reminded of the distance between his views and a mythic time: "Then a cumbersome tumble and crash resounded, and Conner witnessed an appearance of the phenomenon which two millennia before had convinced the poet Horace that gods do exist: thunder from a clear sky" (66).

The dichotomy between the values of the past and present, as reflected in Hook and Conner, is strengthened by further associations. The Victorian house that serves as poorhouse is a visible sign of the craftsmanship of another era's carpenters. Even a description of the windows in the cupola office, a former music room, juxtaposes modern insensitivity to past art: "The metal supporting the Venetian blinds muddled the stately lines, and the semi-circles, each fitted of five pieces of hand-worked wood, peeked above the manufactured horizontals like the upper margin of a fresco painted where now an exit has been broken through the wall" (21).

The kind of world that Conner dreams of, a world of physical beauty and rational order, finds its external symbolization in the young people, Buddy and Ted. As Conner has no sense of omen, so Buddy has no sense of festal days; he resents Conner's drifting from the office because of the activities below. "He protested aloud, 'What do these people want a holiday for, every day is a holiday for them?' " (55). When Ted comes upon this scene in his truck, he views it as "death's

realm" and recalls a horror movie in which a colony of skeletons live on young flesh. But he dispels this horror from his
mind by fantasies of the girl that he will meet in Newark at
noon and of the parodic adolescent rite he had recently experienced: not allowed to touch his girl (she belongs to the
Newark Nuns), he had knelt before her beautiful bare belly
with his hands folded on his chest.

What has been established in the first chapter is the creation of a tension between mythic time and the desacralized
time of the modern humanist. In the second chapter, this
tension is developed and verbalized in the confrontation between Hook and Conner. From lunch until the abatement of
the rain, actual time seems to stand still, and the symposium
on heaven takes place in a kind of eternal present.

Before joining the inmates in their common room, Conner
peers through the blurring rain from the porch to assess the
damage done to the stone wall by Ted's truck. His mind,
however, is still preoccupied with the letter that he had
received in the morning: *"Yr duty is to help not hinder these
old people on there way to there final Reward.* Their final
reward, *this* was their final reward. How much longer before
people ceased to be fools? . . . When would they all die and
let the human day dawn?" (78). In this frame of mind, he
will meet his subjects.

Meanwhile, the presence of Mendelssohn is very much
alive in the dining hall. While the people linger after their
meal, Amy Mortis pictures how he would have them singing
and praying and preparing for death. So vivid does the
image of Mendelssohn become to the community consciousness that they all look toward the empty dais to see how his
ghost would posture in this situation:

As the songs grew more religious the rims of Mendelssohn's eyes
grew redder, and he was dabbing at his cheeks with the huge
handkerchief he always carried and was saying, in the splendid
calm voice that carried to the farthest corner and to the dullest
ear, how here they all lived close to death, which cast a shadow
over even their gaiety, and for him to hear them sing was an

experience in which joy and grief were so mixed laughter and
tears battled for control of his face; here they lived with Death
at their sides, the third participant in every conversation, the
other guest at every meal—and even he, yes even he—but no.
Today was not the day for talk of bad health. As the Preacher
said, To every thing there is a season, and a time to every purpose under Heaven. This was the day intended for rejoicing.
Though for the moment the rain had obscured the rays of the
sun, in another hour these rays would break forth again in the
glory of their strength and from all the points of the compass
people in the prime of their lives, carrying children in their arms,
would come to this famous fair (80).

A realization that the fair is a stay against death, a wistful
yearning for the sense of celebration that Mendelssohn could
arouse in the community, puts a religious patina on the fair
itself. It is into this atmosphere that the unbelieving Conner
steps, feeling obliged to present himself to these elders as
their guide.

  While the conversation shifts from Civil War politics to
religion, Conner fumbles at the fireplace. Finally, the blind
Elizabeth Heinemann, who has become somewhat excited by
Conner's presence, asks him whether we shall see in the
Afterlife. Of course, Conner cannot believe such a thing.
With the dissolution of the eyes, vision must also cease. Sur-
prisingly, Elizabeth agrees. As she explains her position, the
atmosphere, already sanctified by the memory of Mendelssohn, shifts toward the other world of eternity and myth:
"there was a smoothness in the discharge of her inner ac-
cumulations that compelled the silence sacred performances
ask" (97). When she was a child, Elizabeth believed that the
least concrete detail of earth would be visible in Heaven.
Now she believes that "Heaven will be, how can I say, a
mist of all the joy sensations have given us. Perfumes, and
children speaking, and cloth on our skin, hungers satisfied as
soon as we have them. Other souls will make themselves
known like drops of water touching our arms" (98-99). The
loss of her sight has attuned her to the magic of the human
presence that she had previously detested, to the music of

speech, and to the feel of others' emotions to which sight had
blinded her. After a gentle rebuke from Hook for her unwillingness to accept the blessing of renewed vision, she tear-
fully insists on her resignation to her present situation but still
holds fast to her conception: "No. Isn't it absurd? Mr. Conner thinks so. What Heaven can there be for our eyes when
vision separates, and judges, and marks differences for envy
to seize on? Why are we taught as children to close our eyes
to pray?" (100).

Elizabeth's opinion sparks others. Tommy Franklin presents a faltering, disappointing view of Heaven right here on
earth, a reconstruction of his mythic childhood. For Mrs.
Jamiesson, Heaven is a place where she of the long jaw will
be beautiful and her handsome but harsh mother will not be.
Amy Mortis will lose her goiter. Egged on by Elizabeth,
Conner finally offers his picture of what Heaven is like: a
bland earthly utopia with no disease, no oppression, no
hunger for power, with clean cities, atomic power, lengthened
life-spans, work and love. " 'The factors which for ages have
warped the mind of man and stunted his body will be de-
troyed; man will grow like a tree in the open. There will be
no waste. No pain and above all no *waste*. And this heaven
will come to *this* earth, and come soon' " (107). But when
Conner tells the inmates that their generation will not share
in this Heaven, Mrs. Mortis sums up their attitude with a
spry, "to hell with it" (108).

Hook, who had joined in the general laughter at Conner's
expense, points out to Conner that the annihilation of evil
will not follow the elimination of pain. Elizabeth's blindness,
Mrs. Jamiesson's ugliness, his own weak health in youth have
worked to humanize them, to make them sensitive to other
values in life, so that Hook can say that " 'looking back I
perceive a mar-velous fitting together of right and wrong,
like the joints the old-time carpenters used to make, before
everything was manufactured metal and plastic' " (110).
Virtue itself, obedience to God's commands, has the firmness

and workability of wood; Conner's bitterness is his own will-ful work.

Naturally, Conner cannot accept obedience to God's com-mands as the source of peace of mind and happiness. Nor can he accept the evidence for the existence of God that Hook sees in the Creation around him and in conscience, the inner spokesman, so he proceeds to devastate these proofs by his logic. Hook understands that creatures are more than their skeletons, stars are more than balls of fire. This man of faith senses that there are mysteries beyond man's geo-metric patterns and logical propositions. But for Conner, there is no meaning behind the universe. He simply cannot believe that the things of earth were made by "a young car-penter in Syria" (113). The universe is merely the product of the chance combinations of various elements in endless time. " 'There is infinitely more nothing in the universe than anything else' " (113). Likewise, for Conner, there is no inner spokesman because science has been unable to locate man's soul.

Because Hook is increasingly appalled by the cruelty of the experiments mentioned by Conner, the prefect thinks that he has finally and inevitably shaken Hook's faith. In reality he has not. Hook knows the value of belief, knows that death does not cancel life but gives meaning to it. Con-ner is smug because he thinks he has achieved a state of equilibrium in which he holds the answer to every question. He has failed to understand that, as long as an individual is not a closed system, he need not and cannot be in a state of equilibrium. The old people may take in decreasing amounts of food and sensory data because of the natural running down of old age, but Conner takes in decreasing amounts of information about the reality of existence be-cause he has shut himself off from ways of knowing to which the old people remain open. It is the sense of his own per-sonal entropy that he projects over the world around him. As a matter of fact, he has turned himself into an "isolated system."[8] Hook's final remarks in the discussion are an indictment of Conner's foolish activity and faithlessness: " 'There is no goodness, without belief. There is nothing but busy-ness. And if you have not believed, at the end of your life you shall know you have buried your talent in the ground of this world and have nothing saved, to take into the next' " (116).

Although Conner had entered the room with the intention of clarifying his position as guide and had been certain that he had devastated Hook's arguments, in the end he realizes that he has lost completely. They had all become furious: "He stood in such an ambiguous relation to these people, between that of a shepherd and that of a captive, and his quarrel with Hook had produced such a darkness, that he spoke blindly, uncertain even of whether he lingered among them in the hope of making himself clear, or merely to avoid the appearance of a retreat. One retreat had taken place: they had withdrawn from him" (119). Lightning flashes through the room; other inmates begin to drift in from other parts of the house. Time loses its mythic quality and resumes its inevitable progression: "It was as if the world had been holding its breath while Hook and Conner debated its condition, and now resumed bumping onward" (121).

While the dialogue has not disturbed Hook's faith, it has heated his blood and leads him to a conclusion that blossoms forth only at the end of the novel. Conner, on the other hand, withdraws into fantasies where he is the center of adulation. In particular, he imagines himself cavorting with near-naked men and women at an idyllic seashore, as he listens to the melodies of the band. Central to this daydream is the attitude that there is "no fear here, no dread of time" (124). While the old people have included death and passing time in their myth of life, Conner can conceive happiness only in terms that ignore or side-step these inevitabilities. Even his fantasies emanate from the control of pure intelligence. Everything in life must follow perfect, immovable plans—plans that destroy the past and human pluralism through their simple, geometrical forward progression, that attempt to control the future so perfectly that it need not be lived at all.[9] Conner's rationalistic humanism, placed against the values of the old, leads to dehumanization.

What the second chapter adds to the sense of mythic time that was already established in the first chapter is an increasing sense of celebration, despite the apparent setback to the fair. Even Conner feels heavenly presences that perdure through the rain: "In the volume of space above the lawn, set like a table for a feast, the impression was not of vacancy but of fullness; the feast was attended" (78-79). The community's evocation of the spirit of Mendelssohn grows out of the special mood that has captured the people: "Today was what weather could not change, a holiday. They remained seated at the small white tables, enjoying the corporate existence created by the common misfortune of having their fair washed away" (79). For a short period, during the interim between the debate and the band's playing, this sense of celebration seems on the verge of collapse; "a gust of irresponsibility had swept into the room, as if the fair were, rather than an awaited holiday, an annual humiliation from which they were this year to be delivered" (122-123). But, with the return of fair weather, the corporate sense of celebration is intensified: "The inmates of the house, already united in expectation of the holiday, had passed as a group through two turns of fortune: the rain, and the rain's abatement, which last joined them together in a mood of raucous, cruel exhilaration quite unlike the sweet and moderate expectation of the morning" (127-128).

In the third chapter, then, the elements of mythic time and celebration find their culmination in the ritual stoning of Conner and in the ritual of the fair itself. One of the first things that Conner feels obliged to do after the rain is to tidy up the stones that have fallen from the old wall at the entrance, lest he be accused of negligence by the townspeople. Just as he had vaguely felt presences in the rainy air, now he experiences elements of a vestigial ritual: "Stones were man's oldest companions; handling them, the first civilized act. The subconscious commemoration roused by the abrasion on his hands and the pull on his forearm muscles made Conner feel brisk, purged, central: there was a widespread anthropolatry in things of which he was the focus" (130). In all his fantasies Conner is the center of things, a god or a messiah. This mood is soon disturbed, however. When Gregg deliberately throws a few stones at him, the other gatherers spontaneously follow his lead (131). Conner senses the people's presence as "magical and menacing," but the menace is only psychological, a wound for his vanity. The attackers accompany their weak, harmless throws at pudgy Conner with laughter at the realization of what they are doing (133).

Updike himself has spoken of this scene as a latter-day version of the stoning of St. Stephen, the first martyr of the Christian Church, and there are some obvious parallels between the two stories. Both men are commissioned to care for older members of the community. Both men stir controversy by entering into debate over religious issues; the early Christian Stephen with non-Christian Jews, the non-believing Conner with latter-day Christians. Both men are considered blasphemers by their opponents. Both Stephen and Conner are stoned at least partly because of emotions aroused by their speeches. The response of both is to forgive the stoners. The basic irony of the parallel lies in the reversal of sympathies; in *The Poorhouse Fair,* the self-proclaimed nonbelieving messiah becomes at best a scapegoat, but certainly not a martyr. Still another dimension which the Stephen parallel introduces into the novel is the implication that entropy is operating within the world's religious forces as well as within its socio-economic and political forces. The energetic early Christian vision with which Stephen challenged Judaism has run to seed in the reduced paradisal vision of Conner. His earthbound non-belief is entropic to religious belief.

For the inmates of the poorhouse, however, the stoning has become a satisfying communal action through which they have temporarily purged their resentments against Conner. During the remainder of the day, the event colors their thoughts and conversation. Gregg, Lucas, and Hay describe Conner's appearance in terms of a mock-Christ: "he wheeled like a bird with a foot in a trap, his arms spread winglike and his mouth open like he wanted a worm put in it" (141). Amy Mortis reflects upon the motives behind her participation: boredom and her anger over Conner's roughshod treatment of Hook (142). Gregg had expressed the seething frustrations of his life in the poorhouse: "He had shown there were rights. Unable to keep his feet still he danced over the plaza of dirt, kicking chips of wood and poking his fist against the deteriorating wooden walls of sheds. Sons of screwed-up f. faced white-faced bitches. Gregg was happy, proud, happy; he had never before dreamed that such intense innocent pleasure existed anywhere in old age" (145). Conner himself, highly embarrassed but retaining "the conviction that he was the hope of the world," recognizes the ritual nature of the stoning as he broods over the incident in his office: "He realized, suddenly and clearly, that the dozen guilty had acted for all" (156, 158).

In contrast to the burlesque use of ritual in this episode, the fair is a ritual to recapture the past. All the items that are for sale—the old-fashioned candies of Mrs. Johnson, the quilts of Amy Mortis, the charms that Tommy Franklin has carved out of peachstones—exude the smell of the past. What modern men sense in the items, the closeness to nature that men of a former era experienced through their craftsmanship, is emphasized in an authorial comment integrated into a conversation between Amy and an antique dealer from Trenton: "There was a keen subversive need, at least in the cities, for objects that showed the trace of a hand, whether in an irregular seam, the crescent cuts of a chisel, or the dents of a forge hammer" (145). The visitors "came to the fair to be freshened in the recollection of an older America, the America of Dan Patch and of Senator Beveridge exhorting the Anglo-Saxons to march across the Pacific and save the beautiful weak-minded islands there, an America· of stained-glass lampshades, hardshell evangelists, Flag days, ice men, plug tobacco, China trade, oval windows marking on the exterior of a house a stair landing within, pungent nostrums for catarrhal complaints, opportunism, churchgoing, and well-worded orations in the glare of a cemetery on summer days" (158-159).

It is not only for the gewgaws of an earlier age that these visitors come; they also come to hear the quaint, old-fashioned concepts. For one such participant, a middle-aged man, Hook expounds on the "invisible goals" that once gave purpose to man's activities, on the degeneration of the times, on the modern world's lack of virtue, of "a manliness from which comes all life" (160). "Every sentiment of Hook's was as precious to him as a piece of creamware or a sewing bird to the antique dealer from Trenton" (159). Through their annual visitation of the fair, these people from the "outside world" attempt to find some healing remedy for their fragmented lives. They are a people who have lost all "heart," who have only physical health, or their daily concerns of power, sex, or money. They live in a world of pleasure-seekers, where "the people continued to live as cells of a body do in the coffin, for the conception 'America' had died in their skulls" (159).

Still, this society is not completely without hope. As long as its members can perform acts of kindness like the visit of the nurse Grace and her friends to the west wing, this society is not entirely dehumanized. As long as the townspeople continue to participate in the annual healing ritual of this fair, they will in some tenuous way maintain some connections with tradition that will bring wholeness into their lives. In the words of Kenneth Hamilton, "whether they knew it or not they received a much more basic refreshment of the heart, because they had come out of the sphere of the merely contemporary—life in the meaningless flux of passing moments—into the sphere of history, where events are stamped with purpose and are integrated into significant patterns."[10]

This is the aspect of ritual that comes forth strongly in this final chapter. Through the juxtaposition of the many commonplace details and the fragments of various conversations, Updike stitches together an intricate pattern that is much like the old-time quilts. The events of this fair form a pattern that reflects the glory of nature and the joy of human existence despite the drabness of the modern world. It is a pattern that allows for the unpredictability and profusion of nature that is stifled by Conner's simplistic, rigid plans to control life. To summarize with another citation from Kenneth Hamilton, "Pattern is what Updike gives us—a hundred years of America in stone and wood, sky and grass, argument and reverie, laughter and curses."[11] Through this pattern, the past is re-enacted, and hope is found for the future.

While the visitors, with their physical health and their lack of "heart," find in the fair a connection with the past, the old people, with their broken-down bodies and their retention of ancient values, achieve through this celebration a renewed sense of resurrection. Several times during this day Hook had been grappling with the inescapable presence of death. The consciousness of his life's end returns to him after the stoning of Conner and during a walk through the fair grounds; "his angel wrestled with the gloom that overcame him customarily in the late afternoon, when the sun's rays, growing oblique, commenced to turn golden" (142). Becoming preoccupied with his own thoughts, he envisions his entire life as a long walk, nearly ended, "across easy and firm meadows into the doubtful terrain of stony foothills, or from another aspect down a long smooth gallery hung with the portraits of presidents of the United States" (143). Death was waiting for him at the end of the path. By the time Hook reaches a row of horse chestnuts along the western wall, he is so taken up in his inner world that the physical details around him are transformed into a religious atmosphere, perhaps associated with death: "Slowly Hook proceeded down the nave of the cathedral that had resulted, whose high roof released spatterings of water coagulate as wax and admitted, in the gaps between shifting leaves, bits of light, cool yet unquiet, like the flames of clustered candles" (144). But the sound of voices leads him to focus upon the children and young women who are entering the poorhouse gates in procession. Through them, his forebodings of death are overcome by a renewed sense of life: "It seemed a resurrection of his students, and he sensed that he would never leave them, never be abandoned by this parade" (144).

Amy Mortis, the lover of death, comes to the notion of resurrection through her recollections. Although she sells all her quilts, she still feels that the fair is not as good as it was in the days of Mendelssohn. "Mendelssohn, Mendelssohn in his beautiful knobbed casket, a carnation in his lapel, legs pillowed in satin, can we believe that he will never rise? Grass returns. Perfectly preserved his blind lids stretch above the crumbled smile. The skin that life has fled is calm as marble. Can we believe, who have seen his vital nostrils flare expressively, revealing in lifting the flaming septum, the secret wall red with pride within, that there is no resurrection? That bright bit of flesh; where would such a thing have gone?" (180-181). This image has been haunting her all day; now Amy, who desires death so much, affirms eternal life in a way that the young people of this novel, with their worship of bellies and breasts, cannot.

Finally, night comes, and the fair ends. Awakened by phlegm rising in his throat, Hook paces his room and recalls his encounter with Conner during the past day. The weakness and the vulnerability of the prefect cry to Hook for help. He feels that he must find some word to unite them, to make his own values live and to give strength to Conner: "He stood motionless, half in moonlight, groping after the fitful shadow

of the advice he must impart to Conner, as a bond between
them and a testament to endure his dying in the world. What
was it?" (185). The novel ends in ambiguity because there
is no facile manner in which to bridge the gap between the
world and values of Hook and of Conner.

In overview, *The Poorhouse Fair* may be considered a
ritual because of its cyclical nature. Changes in the weather
and the rhythms of the sun and moon, day and night, limit
and to a large extent determine the action of the novel. Hook
reflects the rhythms of nature in his changes from serenity
in mid-morning to gloom at dusk. Gradually, the cycle of
Hook's moods becomes an image for the cycle of moods
from childhood to old age, just as the shift from morning to
night becomes a natural metaphor for man's movement from
birth to death—and to new life beyond. The concentric manner in which these cycles enfold each other is reminiscent of
the overlapping cycles in Willa Cather's *My Antonia*. There,
Jim Burden's sensibility penetrates the action of the novel
with the movement of the seasons which determine the flow
of life for the Nebraska pioneers, with the development of
Antonia's life through girlhood and into the fruition of
motherhood, and with the pattern of struggling against the
elements of nature, taming the land, moving to the city,
looking back to the East for education and sophistication
which is paralleled in Jim's own life and in America's move
westward across the continent.[12] Both novels build meaning
in concentric circles.

The Poorhouse Fair resonates with other modern novels,
too. Updike himself has compared it to John Barth's first
novel, *The Floating Opera*. Both end "with a kind of carnival, a brainless celebration of the fact of existence."[13] Still
another novel to incorporate a carnival into its action for a
celebration of life is John Knowles' *A Separate Peace*. When
the season of winter is running down, "enfeebled by the
absence of challenge," Phineas and Gene Forester devise the
Devon Winter Carnival of games and prizes to fill in a dull

Saturday. Not only the cider, but the youthful exuberance of the boys turns the day into a Dionysian revel. Phineas, leg in cast, dances on a tabletop out of his joy for life, recapturing "his magic gift for existing primarily in space." Gene surpasses himself in the mock-decathlon because of "this liberation we had torn from the gray encroachments of 1943, the escape we had concocted, this afternoon of momentary, illusory, special and separate peace."[14] Both carnival and fair are rituals that create a magic moment to counter the signs of death in a lingering winter and vanishing adolescence or in old age and a tired civilization.

The celebration is unequivocal, one of utter abandonment to the joy of the moment, for the boys in *A Separate Peace*. In *The Poorhouse Fair,* the celebration is tempered by severe doubts and shadows.[15] Has the link between generations been permanently severed? Has the wisdom of the ages become incommunicable? Is belief in an afterlife *really* the answer to the chaos of life on earth? With this novel, John Updike joins those other American novelists concerned with the various disintegrations arising from entropy and our patterned response to it: Thomas Pynchon in *V.,* Stanley Elkins in *A Bad Man,* Joseph Heller in *Catch-22,* James Purdy in *Eustace Chisholm and the Works,* William Burroughs in *Naked Lunch.*[16]

Where Updike differs from other novelist-entropologists is in his religious stance. As a ritual response to the fears of passing time and death, *The Poorhouse Fair* accepts historical time for what it is and, in the acceptance, transcends it. On the one hand, to promote his vision of physical beauty and rational control over life, Conner must ignore or devalue the effects of time. He would like to live in an "atemporal mythical instant."[17] Ironically, the inmates are the ones who achieve this instant through the reactualization of the past. Through their recollections of the past, through their correlation of the present with the past, they suspend the flow of profane time and project themselves into a mythical sacred time. Through the acceptance of history and tradition, they come to the realization of the joy and sense of celebration with which the moments of the present should be lived. Through the annual re-enactment of the past at the fair, they also renew their belief and hope in life itself.

One final comparison should be made, to suggest a possible inspiration for this first novel by Updike and to show how he has imprinted his own unique concerns upon his source materials. *The Poorhouse Fair* bears striking resemblances to *Concluding,* by Henry Green, whom Updike has claimed to be one of the great influences upon his writing.[18]

The three chapters of *Concluding* move through the morning, afternoon, and evening of a summer day in an undetermined future year, the annual celebration of Founder's Day at the all-girl Institute to train State Servants. These three chapters treat, in general, the preparations for the evening dance, the disappearance of two inmates, Mary and Merode, which nearly threatens a cancellation of the dance, and the dance itself. The English welfare-state which is satirized in the actions of the Institute's directors, regulation-conscious Miss Edge and Miss Baker, is much like the rationalistic American welfare-state in which Conner operates. Under the guise of achieving a more efficient administration of her Institute and regardless of the personal harm that she may inflict upon the seventy-six-year-old Mr. Rock, Miss Edge is determined to acquire the cottage in which he lives upon the premises, despite the fact that it was awarded to him for his lifetime when the State confiscated the rest of the estate. Playing the role of God, Miss Edge even feels that one of her responsibilities is to provide the girls with memories: " 'It is a minor function, of course, in a great Place like this, but we must send them out so they can look back on the small pleasures shared.' "[19] For this reason, she favors the tradition of the annual dance, which is described as "a soft ritual beneath azalea and rhododendron."

In both novels, the directors, ensconced in their sanctum-like offices, brood over poison-pen letters. Mr. Rock in his old man's fears, foibles, weaknesses and charm is a remarkable prototype of Mr. Hook. But the two novels differ in ultimate intention and tone. In *Concluding,* we relish the humor of Mr. Rock's conversations, which are usually at cross-purposes by reason of his deafness or his pretense of it; the pathos of his thirty-five-year-old granddaughter Elizabeth, who is conducting an affair with Sebastian Birt, a young master at the school, while recuperating from a nervous breakdown precipitated by overwork in the service of the State; the high-handedness of Mrs. Manley, Merode's aunt; the deviltry of Moira; the preposterous hilarity of Miss Edge's marriage proposal to Mr. Rock; the odd lovableness of Mr. Rock's pets—Alice the cat, Ted the goose, and Daisy the pig. Green has produced a novel that touches lightly upon the surface of things and gently mocks the attempt to destroy human relationships generally accepted by the society for which he writes. Updike, less subtly, feels obligated to act as prophet, to remind an America which is losing its sense of tradition of the dangerous path which it is walking. To some superficial borrowings from Green of characterization, structure and technique, he has added a strong sense of the inevitable passage of time, an overriding fear of death, and an emphasis upon the need for ceremonies to retain our connection with the past and our hope of continuing life.

3

THE MAGIC DANCE: *RABBIT, RUN*

With the summary statement, "Futility, however accurately described, remains futility," one critic has condemned *Rabbit, Run* for its ineffectual characters and its "depressing emptiness."[1] Yet this so-called exercise in futility has given us one of the most perduring and controversial characters in all of Updike's writing. In any discussion of *Rabbit, Run*, the questions of style, plot, structure, and total significance inevitably return to the elemental question, "Do you like or dislike Harry Angstrom?" The response is generally clear cut: Harry is either a completely insensitive, irresponsible cad, or a saint and the only man of integrity in the entire novel.

Critics like Sister Tate, Gerry Brenner, and Larry Taylor have focussed upon Rabbit as an anti-hero and consequently stress his sin or irresponsibility. Sister Mary Judith Tate, for example, elaborates on *Rabbit, Run* as "a kind of grotesque allegory, on one level relating the dalliance of a lustful boy-man; on the other level first revealing and then shattering the modern 'myth' that happiness and freedom are synonymous with concupiscence and irresponsibility."[2] To her, the entire story is essentially an allegory of regression in which Rabbit kills the seed of faith within himself and runs from

his own self-hood. Sister Tate gives a good exposition of the
novel's door and wall images as symbols of the lack of communication between characters, but in her focus upon *Rabbit,
Run* as an allegory against sin, she has downplayed the sin-
cerity and anguish of Rabbit's search for meaning.

Gerry Brenner and Larry Taylor agree that a return to
nature, such as Rabbit's drive to cast aside all external pre-
scriptions and to follow only his physical impulse, ends in
destruction. Larry Taylor in particular reacts against those
critics who have de-emphasized Rabbit's role as anti-hero,
who present Rabbit as a sympathetic hero on a quest, who
treat his quest as philosophically valid and theologically significant. Such critics, Larry Taylor feels, fail to recognize
that Rabbit is morally worse than any other character in the
novel. He has an intelligence and sensibility which make him
singularly responsible for his actions. The evil that happens
to him, as well as to those around him, is not the result of
"external circumstances" over which Rabbit has no control.
Rather, the evil flows from the hardness of his own heart,
a result of his own willful moral acts. Rabbit's main sin is
that "he has left undone those things he ought to have done,"
such as caring for his wife and children. Anyone who feels
compassion for Rabbit more than for his family is being
morally sentimental and has missed the anti-pastoral satire
in the development of the "return to nature" motif. The
pathos and the satire fuse into one vision.[3]

While Taylor's exposition is a healthy corrective to a certain kind of moral mushiness, I feel that he has too easily
excused the other characters in the novel to make his point
about Rabbit. Moreover, in treating the "return to nature"
theme solely as satire, he has chosen to ignore the sacral
dimensions of the world which Updike has created in this
novel. Robert Detweiler, on the other hand, has been able
to place Rabbit's failure in relation to the middle-class
Protestant American society in which he lives. Detweiler
realizes that Rabbit's quest is a search for God, a religious

crisis that ends in a loss of faith because Rabbit cannot locate "the missing third dimension—the transcendent." Using Niebuhr's analysis of religious crisis, Detweiler interprets Rabbit's actions as exercises in self-deception, which stem from his vanity or moral, intellectual, and religious pride. His pride covers his insecurity as a person. From this point of view, Rabbit's love for sport and his forays into sex become a retreat from guilt into sensuality, "an effort to escape from the confusion which sin has created into some form of subconscious existence." But Rabbit does not sin alone; he is the product of " 'a society which, because it will not come to terms with its evil, cannot find the redemption of love.' " His failure is his community's as well.[4]

In contrast to these essentially moralistic interpretations, which stress Rabbit's loss of faith or irresponsibility or pride, David Galloway has presented Rabbit as a saint of the existential order. Where Sister Tate took the words of the Mouseketeer, "Know thyself," as the central theme of the novel, Galloway takes the words of Tothero about "the sacredness of achievement" as the central theme. Where Detweiler compared the philosophy of *Rabbit, Run* to Niebuhr's, Galloway compares it to Camus's. Rabbit's rejection of family and responsibilities, his break with conventional ethics and systems, his search for values, his desire to express universal compassion, "to embrace the very soul of man"—all are elements of his sainthood. Galloway even explains Rabbit's lack of commitment to individuals or any particular system through a saint's absolute, all-consuming devotion to a higher ideal. Under such an interpretation, the ending becomes a kind of triumph: "Harry doubts that he can succeed, but Tothero has emphasized for us the fact that achievement can come even in defeat. For the saint, it is the struggle, not the success of the struggle, which is significant."[5]

But the God affirmed in *Rabbit, Run* is not representative of traditional Christianity, and the epigraph from Pascal's *Pensées* is seen "as a testimony to the spiritual struggle of

man and not as a testimony to the struggle of Christian man."
What Rabbit becomes for Galloway is a humanist saint who
rejects "formal Christianity because it is not religious enough.
. . . Rabbit remains true to a standard of good by which he
attempts to live, and the intensity of his loyalty to this standard can only be described as 'religious.' Everything in his
world is in flux, but his intention is, in the presumed absence
of God, to impose order and value on this flux."[6]

Other critics have also canonized Rabbit by the use of
inversion in the manner of Jean Genêt and other absurdists.
J. A. Ward has concluded that Rabbit is a man of inverse
piety in this manner: "Since all attempts to find order and
all social postures are shown to be absurd, illogic becomes
logic, irresponsibility becomes responsibility, and escape becomes discovery."[7] John K. Hutchens has considered Rabbit
more amoral than immoral, "an unanointed saint punished
because in all tenderness he is inclined to love everybody,
and in ignorance to wound cruelly those whom he loves and
who love him."[8]

My difficulties with the "saintly" critics stem from a conviction that they have imposed their own universe upon this
novel before savoring the full flavor of Updike's creation.
Irresponsibility does not really become responsibility in this
novel. There are enough clues given to recognize a "good"
and a "bad" against which to measure Rabbit's own subjective
responses as well as those of the other characters. And to
speak of sainthood in Hutchens' terms is to make of it a sentimentality. A man who loves everybody tenderly is more in
love with love itself, like the Duke Orsino in *Twelfth Night,*
and probably shares no true intimacy with any particular
person. A man who continues to wound others cruelly out
of ignorance is at best an innocent child, still unaware of
the evil within himself. A saint is an adult who knows his
own capacity for evil but chooses to act otherwise. Hutchens
highlights weaknesses rather than strengths in Rabbit.

Finally, Galloway's interpretation puts Rabbit into a context where man can find meaning only within himself. This brand of existentialism, originating in Heidegger, leads Galloway to a distortion of Pascal's meaning in the epigraph. For Pascal, self-knowledge does not lead to the truth, as Galloway suggests; only a realization that we need God's grace and forgiveness does. Rabbit's problems and limitations arise within the context of Protestant America. In considering Rabbit as a saint, Galloway tends to treat him as an essence rather than an existence within this particular society. Rabbit's fear of nothingness is tinged with Christian existential concerns; it flows from his vague awareness of having fallen from grace; it is a Kierkegaardian dread.[9]

The attempt to categorize Rabbit as hero or anti-hero is, as the controversy suggests, a futile exercise. He is neither and he is both. Rabbit is basically an ambivalent middle-class American Christian living in a similarly ambivalent world. He is strong in potential but weak in action. He gains sympathy for his earnest desire for the Something Beyond but gains contempt for his callous disregard of wife and children and Ruth. He equates freedom with saying *no* to distasteful responsibilities, but he senses that true liberation demands a *yes* to Something. He refuses to follow a straight line of action that would lead him to significant changes and discoveries. Instead he zigzags from action to action without consequence. His basic flaw is his ambivalence, his inability to focus upon a reality and carry through: " 'Rabbit' has no focal point—no clearly conceived object outside of himself (either man or reason or god) with which he can affirm the reality of his own existence either in affinity for or in rebellion from. . . . He also has no alternative internal focal point—no sense of his own selfhood either in the process of becoming or as having crystallized."[10]

That Rabbit is on a quest is hardly the question. True, the quest is severely hampered by his refusal to accept any guidance except that of his own uneducated intuition. Still, Rabbit fits the pattern of the modern literary quester, who "suffers temptations both of flesh and spirit. He sins, and feels guilt, and strives mightily for expiation. Unlike the holy man and knight, however, the modern quester has no fixed order or system to guide him; all that he has is himself and his ability to live." The transcendent value of what he seeks is love of man and responsibility to self and for others. Sex may be a part of the quester's self-discovery or his substitution for God, "but sex without love (accepting responsibility) is sin, the punishment is loss of the way."[11]

Thus, there is some success in modern quests. Love sets Cass Kinsolving's house on fire and restores his sanity. Love forces Holden Caulfield to distinguish the real and the unreal among the values of American life. Love rescues Moses Herzog from depression. Love urges Frank Alpine to become his lover's father in Malamud's *The Assistant*. Love impels Henderson to save the baby at the airport. Love drives Randle P. McMurphy to offer his life in Ken Kesey's *One Flew Over the Cuckoo's Nest*. But Harry's quest fails for lack of love. The dream dissipates under the test of day-to-day living, and he joins other failures like Kit Moresby in Paul Bowles' *The Sheltering Sky*, George in Sinclair Lewis' *Babbitt*, the homosexual hero in John Rechy's *City of Night*, and the entire group in *Couples*.[12]

As a *running* quester, Harry Angstrom fits into a long American tradition. "The escape from culture itself" is apparent in the figure of Cooper's Natty Bumppo, Melville's Ishmael, Twain's Huckleberry Finn, and Thoreau himself in *Walden*. The protagonist who finds himself in opposition to the values of his society literally flees from it. "During the nineteenth century . . . he could still run away *from* but also *to* something: from the settlement to the frontier, from slavery to freedom, from land to sea, to the river, or to the Pond." With no geographical escape from society, running in the twentieth century becomes either a criminal activity or an inward exploration of the self. The runner, like those in Fitzgerald, Salinger, Kerouac, and Updike, either freely chooses to run, or he is compelled to run because he has committed some "sin" against the system, as for example Ellison's Invisible Man. In his quest for a new identity, he may desert like Babbitt or Yossarian or Harry Angstrom. At the same time, he searches for an "environment in which he can perform at his best," like the Invisible Man or Holden Caulfield or Harry. But wherever he goes, the modern running quester cannot evade the question, "Who are you?" For Harry, the question remains unanswered at the end of *Rabbit, Run,* at the end of *Rabbit Redux,* perhaps forever. He continuously moves in a pattern of disentanglement from society followed by attempted reintegration.[13]

Closer to home, Harry Angstrom is remarkably similar to Conner of *The Poorhouse Fair.* Both are fastidious, tidy men who like cleanliness and dislike the waste and litter engendered by nature. Both men court blankness, Conner in his vision of blank skies and Rabbit in his search for the hole without the accompanying net. Neither realizes that ideal perfection leads only to death. Both reject the healing patterns of actual existence for their own private patternings, Conner for the crystalline structures of his mind and Rabbit for the shapeless rhythms of instinct and biological necessity. Both men are ambivalent characters, meant to stir our sympathy and our disgust. Considering each man within the environment that circumscribes him, however, I see Conner as basically an unsympathetic character and Rabbit as basically a sympathetic character.

My further analysis of *Rabbit, Run* will concentrate on the repeated patterns in Rabbit's life and on his reasons for returning to these patterns. The patterns which he uses to achieve a sense of religious celebration are those which constitute the liturgy or the concrete religion of Rabbit. As has been suggested already, the basic weakness of his liturgy lies in the absence of any definitive myth behind the patterns. While Rabbit has more religious feeling than any other major character in the novel, he is unable to integrate it with any paradigmatic myth that will actually help him achieve harmony with himself and communion with the transcendent in any consistent and meaningful manner.

The most meaningful experience that Rabbit ever had in his life was high-school basketball. Basketball, by its very nature and by its character as a game, lies in the same area of life as the liturgy. Like any ritual or liturgy, it has an easily defined basic pattern which is repeatable and geared to producing the same effect each time. Likewise it includes a sense of celebration, the reaching of intense moments which spontaneously bring our affectivity into play. An exaltation can be achieved or at least attempted through the union of body, emotions, and intellect, all reaching toward one goal. Significantly, in man's play-activities, he freely accepts his own rules; in his work, "the rules are set by actuality itself, by 'life,' by the way things are."[14]

When Rabbit joins the boys in their alley game at the beginning of the novel, he feels a certain lifting of his spirits, a connection with past exaltation. In sinking a variety of shots, "he feels liberated from long gloom" because "his touch still lives in his hands."[15] But this is the only time that Rabbit actually plays basketball in the course of the novel; now he can do nothing but relive the experiences of his high-school days, like Tom Buchanan, the ex-football hero in *The Great Gatsby*. After he ceases his struggle with the net of roads that thwart his first flight from home, as he effortlessly follows the roads back to Brewer, Rabbit enters upon the same sensations of peace and unreality that he used to feel toward the end of a basketball game: "The last quarter of a basketball game used to carry him into this world; you ran not as the crowd thought for the sake of the score but for yourself, in a kind of idleness. There was you and sometimes the ball and then the hole, the high perfect hole with its pretty skirt of net. It was you, just you and that fringed ring, and sometimes it came down right to your lips it seemed and sometimes it stayed away, hard and remote and small" (37). So important is this old sensation to

Rabbit that he attempts to explain it to Ruth, Margaret, and Tothero around the table in the Chinese restaurant: "And there are just a couple dozen people sitting up on the stage and the game isn't a league game so nothing matters much, and I get this funny feeling I can do anything, just drifting around, passing the ball, and all of a sudden I know, you see, I *know* I can do anything" (65). While he relives the exhilaration of that moment, Rabbit cannot understand the lack of enthusiasm in the others, why they cannot feel what was so special. To the detriment of those who depend upon him, Rabbit has made the sense of exaltation that he experienced on the courts the norm by which to measure the worth of elements in his adult life. For this reason he has deserted Janice; in their life together, he found it impossible to achieve the same kind of joy he felt in basketball (105).

Although Rabbit can no longer achieve exaltation through basketball (except in his memory), there is one moment in the novel, at the climax to the first major portion, when he does regain that lost sense of celebration through sport, through a game of golf with Eccles. On the way to the golf course, while Eccles is presumably leading Rabbit to recognize his guilt and return to Janice, Rabbit expresses his belief in an unseen world, in a transcendence with which he must find communion: " 'Well I don't know all this about theology, but I'll tell you. I do feel, I guess, that somewhere behind all this'—he gestures outward at the scenery; they are passing the housing development this side of the golf course, half-wood half-brick one-and-a-half-stories in little flat bulldozed yards with tricycles and spindly three-year-old trees, the ungrandest landscape in the world—'there's something that wants me to find it' " (127). Thrown off balance by the gibes of Eccles on the golf course, Harry finds that his normal touch with objects is not with him. He begins to talk to the clubs as if they were women, and he feels in the entire scene around him "an almost optical overlay of presences" (131). When Eccles insists on eliciting from Rabbit a definition of this "thing" in which he believes (" 'What is it? What *is* it? Is it hard or soft? Harry. Is it blue? Is it red? Does it have polka dots?' "), Rabbit begins to realize that "underneath all this I-know-more-about-it-than-you heresies-of-the-early-Church business he really wants to be told about it, wants to be told that it is there, that he's not lying to all those people every Sunday" (133). So angered does he become by Eccles' prodding that Rabbit brings all his energy and concentration to bear upon the ball before him:

Very simply he brings the clubhead around his shoulder into it. The sound has a hollowness, a singleness he hasn't heard before. His arms force his head up and his ball is hung way out, lunarly pale against the beautiful black blue of storm clouds, his grand-father's color stretched dense across the east. It recedes along a line straight as a ruler-edge. Stricken; sphere, star, speck. It hesi-tates, and Rabbit thinks it will die, but he's fooled, for the ball makes this hesitation the ground of a final leap: with a kind of visible sob takes a last bite of space before vanishing in falling. "That's *it!*" he cries and, turning to Eccles with a smile of ag-grandizement, repeats, "That's it" (133-134).

Through the union of his intellectual concentration and his emotional energy and his bodily coordination, Rabbit gains at this moment the exaltation, the sense of celebration, the sense of the transcendent which Eccles so desperately wants but is unable to attain. Movement in a straight line and the timeless quality of the stars in space fuse. By his recognition of cosmic dimensions in the golf ball, Rabbit feels the "some-thing beyond."

This is the type of celebration that Rabbit is attempting to recapture in his sexual activities. That he is searching for the same kind of communion and harmony that he achieved in his high-school basketball games is especially apparent in the description of his first night with Ruth. On the way to her apartment, he realizes that "she wants him to be content with just her heavy body, but he wants whole women, light as feathers" (75). Once inside her apartment, he grabs her in a crushing embrace with "no love in it, love that glances and glides along the skin, he is unconscious of their skins, it is her

heart he wants to grind into his own, to comfort her completely" (75). This same urge for complete communion per-
sists as his passion increases: "it is not her crotch he wants,
not the machine; but her, her" (78). In all that follows, in his
insistence that she use no contraceptives, in his removal of her
makeup, in the rubdown that he gives her, Rabbit is performing a rite of preparation for the total experience that he
desires. Through their twists and turns, Rabbit feels that he is
finding in her a friend in his search. At the moment of climax,
it seems that he will achieve his end: "She feels transparent; he
sees her heart" (84). Still, in the sexual experience that is the
most satisfying of the entire novel, that comes closest to a
true celebration, Rabbit cannot reach the wholeness for which
he yearns. His night with Ruth is only a temporary illusory
escape. "He looks in her face and seems to read in its shadows
a sad expression of forgiveness, as if she knows that at the
moment of release, the root of love, he betrayed her by feeling
despair. Nature leads you up like a mother and as soon as she
gets her little price leaves you with nothing" (84-85).

I have suggested that this experience is a ritual, a patterned
response by which Rabbit tries to touch the transcendent. His
other sexual activities can also be seen as ritual acts, but not
in this same sense. The fellatio that he forces upon Ruth may
be considered a ritual act of atonement which he demands of
her because he felt a wall arising between them, because he
felt her slipping away from him in the restaurant. It is a crude
power-play, an act of humbling by which he intends to make
her his once again, quite in character with his emotional
immaturity. During the act he did experience "that strange
floating feeling of high pride," but in the end he feels only
shame (191). His sexual demand upon Janice during her con-
valescence from childbirth, more than any other act in the
novel, seems like mere animal lust, a routine release. Yet even
here the spiritual is confused with the physical. During the
preceding week, in which he had controlled himself out of
gratitude and pride in Janice, Rabbit had in a way been

worshipping her (234). On this Sunday night, and all during that day, the lust which had been making him so restless is the afterglow of the religious feeling that he had felt in church that morning. Rabbit moves very easily between the religious and the sexual.

It should also be noted that the two kinds of ritual actions mentioned so far, sex and basketball, are inseparably connected in Rabbit's mind. While sitting in the hospital waiting room, he recalls the furtive sex that he used to have after basketball games with one of his high-school girlfriends, Mary Ann. Although Rabbit's inability to find meaning in his present life and his rebellion against the middle-class values of his suburban universe find much of their motivation in his disgust with the utter banality of modern life, Rabbit's disintegration has also been abetted by his loss of Mary Ann and the possibility of achieving integration through her:

He came to her as a winner and that was the feeling he missed since. In the same way she was the best of them all because she was the one he brought most to, so tired. Sometimes the shouting glare of the gym would darken behind his sweat-burned eyes into a shadowed anticipation of the careful touchings that would come under the padded gray car roof and once there the bright triumph of the past game flashed across her quiet skin streaked with the shadows of rain on the windshield. So that the two kinds of triumph were united in his mind. She married when he was in the Army; a P.S. in a letter from his mother shoved him out from shore. That day he was launched (198).

There are still other ways in which Rabbit relates the material things of this earth to his conviction of an unseen world. The most obvious of these is the meaning that he finds in the symbols of the Christian liturgy. The cigarette which Eccles gives him in the waiting room of the hospital has the effect upon Rabbit of "a wafer of repentance" (196). As he envisions the labor of Janice, his guilt leads him to see childbirth itself as a ritual cleansing of sin, as a baptism, "the smell running everywhere along the white-washed walls, of being washed, washed, blood washed, retching washed until every surface smells like the inside of a bucket but it will never come

clean because we will always fill it up again with our filth"
(196). In the first days after Janice and Rebecca June come
home, "the presence of the baby fills the apartment as a little
casket of incense fills a chapel" (232).

But the most powerful such metaphor, one with a certain
literal force, is the stained glass church window across from
Ruth's apartment. Its sacramental significance for Rabbit is
immediately apparent when he first sights it from Ruth's
window: "Lights behind its rose window are left burning, and
this circle of red and purple and gold seems in the city night
a hole punched in reality to show the abstract brilliance burning underneath" (80). He feels gratitude to its builders and
later that night, as depression begins to envelop him, "its
childish brightness seems the one kind of comfort left to him"
(85). Rabbit develops another little pattern in his life by
regularly turning to the brilliantly lit window to keep his vague
belief in the transcendent, as he does on the night Eccles calls
him back to Janice and on the night of his second flight from
Janice (191, 269). In the end this simple sign of spiritual
reality fails him. After his final rejection by Ruth, he again
turns to "what once consoled him by seeming to make a hole
where he looked through into underlying brightness." Only
now he sees nothing but an unlit window, "a dark circle in a
stone facade" (306).

In the people who go to Sunday services, Rabbit finds still
another predictable pattern to bolster his beliefs. Upon
awakening in Ruth's bed and watching the people gather
around the church below, he is pleased, reassured, and led to
prayer. When Ruth challenges his belief in God, he clings to
the thought that these people have put on their best clothes as
"a visual proof of the unseen world" (90). After his return
to Janice, he decides to go to church not only because he has
a certain affection for Eccles, but also "because he considers
himself happy, lucky, blessed, forgiven, and wants to give
thanks. His feeling that there is an unseen world is instinctive
and more of his actions than anyone suspects constitute

transactions with it" (234). He too dresses in his best clothes
and joins those heading for church. He feels that there is a
rightness that goes beyond physicalities, a liberation from
them, an invisible meaning behind the visible world, a realm
of mystery reserved for him:

> He hates all the people on the street in dirty everyday clothes,
> advertising their belief that the world arches over a pit, that death
> is final, that the wandering thread of his feelings leads nowhere.
> Correspondingly he loves the ones dressed for church; the pressed
> business suits of portly men give substance and respectability to
> his furtive sensations of the invisible; the flowers in the hats of
> their wives seem to begin to make it visible; and their daughters
> are themselves whole flowers, their bodies each a single flower,
> petaled in gauze and frills, a bloom of faith, so that even the
> plainest, sandwiched between their parents with olive complexions
> and bony arms, walk in Rabbit's eyes glowing with beauty, the
> beauty of belief, he could kiss their feet in gratitude; they release
> him from fear (234-235).

Filled with an overwhelming joy and feeling that he moves
"in a field of flowers," Harry is in a mood of resurrection by
the time of his actual participation in the Episcopalian liturgy.
But discordant notes enter. Despite the secular patterns that
lead him to the transcendent, Harry finds this religious pattern
of worship meaningless. He misses the familiar Lutheran
liturgy of his youth. This service is too patterned, too canned,
too cursory. The collection takes too large a place. Eccles
seems like a remote "Japanese doll in his vestments." His
contortions during the sermon are disagreeable, and Harry
does not listen much. Its message of death to our old life to
gain a new life in Christ does not sit well on Rabbit: "Harry
has no taste for the dark, tangled, visceral aspect of Christianity, the *going through* quality of it, the passage *into* death
and suffering that redeems and inverts these things, like an
umbrella blowing inside out. He lacks the mindful will to walk
the straight line of a paradox. His eyes turn toward the light
however it glances into his retina" (237).

All the patterns that have been discussed to this point fail
Rabbit in his search for communion with the transcendent.

He is out of physical condition to play basketball; he cannot depend on a consistent game of golf. He feels despair in the act of sex. He cannot expect the stained-glass window to be constantly lit. He is not willing to accept the penitential aspects of the Christian liturgy. However, by the communion with nature that he experiences in the garden of Mrs. Smith, he comes closest to the type of religious celebration for which he searches. Through the insight that he gains into the nature of flowers, their spiritual quality, their innocence, their ability to symbolize the intangible and invisible aspects of life, Rabbit also comes to the understanding of death that leads to his final action in the novel.

Even before the gardening episode, flowers loom large in Rabbit's consciousness. When he saw the "actual living flowers innocent in the window" of the Texas brothel, he was tempted to run away (45). The town of Brewer itself is colored "an orange rose flowerpot red" (17); by night there shines in it an enormous neon sunflower (72). Ruth's lips are a wet flower to his kisses (80). In bed she is "like the bell of a big blue lily slipped down on his slow head" (85). In his affection for Ruth, he proudly tells her that he made her bloom (108). Later, when Rabbit leaves Ruth, she views their relationship in the same light: "All she wants is what she had a minute ago *him* in the room who when he was good could make her into a flower who could undress her of her flesh and turn her into sweet air Sweet Ruth he called her and if he had just said 'sweet' talking to her she might have answered and he'd still be within these walls" (193).

One might say that all of this is simply metaphor, not ritual. True enough until the gardening episode, where the metaphor takes on the character of ritual. The cycle of nature is felt in the rhythm of the opening sentences: "Sun and moon, sun and moon, time goes. In Mrs. Smith's acres, crocuses break the crust. Daffodils and narcissi unpack their trumpets. The reviving grass harbors violets, and the lawn is suddenly coarse with dandelions and broad-leaved weeds."[16] As Rabbit works the earth, he senses in the new life around him the mysterious presence of God as well as the ever recurring pattern that makes him feel so comfortable in games or the sexual act: "He loves folding the hoed ridge of crumbs of soil over the seeds. Sealed, they cease to be his. The simplicity. Getting rid of something by giving it. God Himself folded into the tiny adamant structure, Self-destined to a succession of explosions, the great slow gathering out of water and air and silicon: felt without words in the turn of the round hoe-handle in his palms" (136). As Rabbit watches the flowers go through their Spring cycles, they take on the personality and brainless beauty of women that he has desired. Finally, in the queen of this garden, in the rhododendron, Rabbit discovers the same sacramental truth that he had found in the church window across from Ruth's. With Mrs. Smith on his arm, he gazes at "a small rhododendron clothed in pink of penetrating purity, a color through whose raw simplicity, as through stained glass, you seem to look into the ideal subsoil of reality" (139).

Harry finds a short-lived happiness and harmony in this garden. But with his return to Janice, he must quit this job for a more lucrative one at his father-in-law's used car lot. In saying his farewell to Mrs. Smith, he admits the exaltation that he achieved through his closeness to the earth by describing his work in the garden as "sort of like Heaven" (222). At the same time, he had unwittingly brought to Mrs. Smith a victory over death, a kind of resurrection: "All winter I was fighting the grave and then in April I looked out the window and here was this tall young man burning my old stalks and I knew life hadn't left me. That's what you have, Harry: Life" (223).

Once Harry is away from the garden, however, when he seriously attempts to conform to the attitudes of the people around him, he loses the sense of communion with the transcendent and the joyful hope that he had momentarily recaptured in his gardening. In a moment of discouragement, he fatalistically views life as a brainless movement toward death.

Because he fears death so much more immediately than Conner does, he is less capable of building illusionistic fantasies against inevitable entropy: "He feels the truth: the thing that had left his life had left irrevocably; no search would recover it. No flight would reach it. It was here, beneath the town, in these smells and these voices, forever behind him. The best he can do is submit to the system and give Nelson the chance to pass, as he did, unthinkingly, through it. The fullness ends when we give Nature her ransom, when we make children for her. Then she is through with us, and we become, first inside, and then outside, junk. Flower stalks" (225).

Up to this point, my emphasis has been almost entirely on Rabbit's dependence upon ritualistic patterns in his search for communion with the transcendent. However, no ritual is truly complete without the myth or mystery that underlies it, as its motive force and anchor of belief. For Rabbit, the mystery that drives him on his quest is his refusal to accept death as the end of everything. The experiences that we have already considered have given Rabbit at least partial confirmation of the truth of his conviction. The sky, which becomes part of the Barthian "inconceivable heaven" in *The Centaur,* is still another visual proof to him that God exists and that man can go beyond earthly life. Yet, although the movement of his mind into the outer space of transcendence produces an airy feeling in him, the consequent detachment from earth, the possible folly of his belief, frightens him. After climbing up Mt. Judge with Ruth on their first Sunday together, he looks over the city before him and reflects:

His day has been bothered by God: Ruth mocking, Eccles blinking—why did they teach you such things if no one believed them? It seems plain, standing here, that if there is this floor there is a ceiling, that the true space in which we live is upward space. Someone is dying. In this great stretch of brick someone is dying. The thought comes from nowhere: simple percentages. Someone in some house along these streets, if not this minute then the next, dies; and in that suddenly stone chest the heart of this flat prostrate rose seems to him to be. He moves his eyes to find the spot; perhaps he can see the cancer-blackened soul of an old man mount through the blue like a monkey on a string. He strains his ears to hear the pang of release as this ruddy illusion at his feet gives up this reality. Silence blasts him. Chains of cars creep without noise; a dot comes out of a door. What is he doing here, standing on air? Why isn't he home? He becomes frightened and begs Ruth, "Put your arm around me" (112-113).

Very conscious of the space that envelops his skin, Rabbit feels that he is disengaged, floating in it without anchor whenever he is frightened, but in his joy, in the consciousness of his health and temporarily reformed life, he finds this space, "even the antiseptic space in the hospital corridors, delicious" (214). In all of his personal difficulties, Rabbit cannot rid himself of the idea that somewhere in the closed space of the nets and traps and little deaths of his daily life, he would find the opening into the space above. Somewhere there is something better than listening to crying babies or cheating in used-car lots (270). Because he has this conviction of an unseen world, of a space above which is the true space in which we live, the concretization of his transcendent yearnings and of his desire for freedom from life's psychological and physical realities naturally takes on the form of passing through or going beyond the hole—whether it be athletic, sexual, or religious.

Nonetheless, the feeling of something beyond the sky, in the space above, never becomes defined. It remains just that: a vague feeling that Rabbit stubbornly and instinctively follows. He cannot tolerate a tension between freedom and responsibility; it must be all or nothing, black or white. When he opts for freedom without responsibility in fleeing from Janice, his deeper instincts tell him that he is right; "he feels freedom like oxygen everywhere around him," and "the clutter of the world has been vaporized by the simple trigger of his decision" (49-50). In explaining his actions to Eccles or Janice or Ruth, he insists on his own importance, on his own emotions, regardless of others: "All I know is what feels right."[17] Even at the very end, Rabbit is unable to break out of the isolation into which his belief has led him: "Funny, how what makes you move is so simple and the field you must move in is so crowded. Goodness lies inside, there is nothing outside, those things he was trying to balance have no weight. He feels his inside as very real suddenly, a pure blank space in the middle of a dense net" (306). Momentarily Rabbit experiences the weightlessness man feels in space. Briefly he escapes the trap of matter.

Rabbit's insight into the necessity of transcendence for complete human living breaks down because he cannot cope with the real world around him. There is no way for man to escape the ultimate trap of matter and its disintegration. Only by facing that reality can man transcend it. Where George and Peter Caldwell in *The Centaur* are able to develop a sacralized universe through the paradigmatic use of myth, and consequently are able to go on living in a desacralized milieu, Rabbit does not have the inner strength for such action. At times he does reach out to those around him for assistance, but in the end he must reject it. As Robert Detweiler has pointed out, "Rabbit's tragedy is not only that he has no inner resources but that none of the natural and social institutions of his environment are able to help him. . . . Neither marriage, parenthood, vocation, school, nor church can provide him with a good reason for living or with a reason for taking up the responsibilities that each of them offers."[18] In relation to Rabbit's groping after his spiritual vision, the solutions and explanations offered to him by the other characters in the novel are traps leading to spiritual death, manifestations of "the prison of an entirely secular way of life, with its promises of salvation through social and economic success."[19]

At the very beginning, as he pauses to observe Jimmy the Mouseketeer on TV, he reveals his belief that the entire system of American life is rotten: "We're all in it together. Fraud makes the world go round. The base of our economy" (10). With this view, he cannot quite accept the dictum, "know thyself, boys and girls." Neither can he accept the pragmatic advice of the gas-station attendant as he flees his home in the night, although it contains enough truth to unsettle him, to make him lose his "airy feeling"; "decide where you want to go and then go: it missed the whole point and yet there is always the chance that, little as it is, it is everything" (36).

The Springers offer a purely secular, economic solution to life, and Tothero offers his clichés. At first he implies that Rabbit's desertion dissolves his responsibilities. In the Chinese restaurant he expounds that "the heart is our only guide" (52), and that "a boy who has had his heart enlarged by an inspiring coach can never become, in the deepest sense, a failure in the greater game of life" (61). Despite all his talk about "the sacredness of achievement," however, Tothero himself is just a bloated mixture of bravado, shame and conceit (67). Later, when Tothero, recently recovered from his stroke, comes to extend his sympathy to the bereaved Harry, his blind hypocrisy is revealed in his mouthings of an earthbound morality: of how Rabbit refused to listen when Tothero told him to return to Janice, to conform, and above all, to avoid suffering (279). In Tothero's world, God does not exist, nor does a moral code above man. " 'Right and wrong aren't dropped from the sky. We. We make them' " (279). Rabbit cannot accept this view of life any more than he could accept Ruth's mocking, cynical unbelief on an earlier occasion. "Tothero's revelation chilled him. He wants to believe in the sky as the source of all things" (280).

As a minister, Eccles should have a body of beliefs to underlay Rabbit's innate need for pattern and celebration. But Eccles is more concerned with his social ministry of reconciliation on a human level than with his vocation as prophet of the transcendent, as exemplar of faith's viability in a secular world. On his first meeting with Harry, Eccles prods and probes with the technique of an amateur psychologist in his attempt to get Harry to bare his soul. At any rate, Harry agrees to another session on the golf course. There, as has been seen, Eccles reveals his own need to discover stays for

his faith, while Harry finds direct confirmation of his belief
in the beyond. Eccles' inadequacies become most apparent,
however, in a series of house calls through which he attempts
to repair the marriage bond of Harry and Janice. When he
is confronted by Mrs. Springer's sarcasm and disapproval for
his methods, he realizes what a faithless man he is. "With
his white collar he forges God's name on every word he
speaks. He steals belief from the children he is supposed to
be teaching. He murders faith in the minds of any who really
listen to his babble. He commits fraud with every schooled
cadence of the service, mouthing Our Father when his heart
knows the real father he is trying to please, has been trying
to please all his life" (154). He begins to feel that in his
meetings with Harry on the golf course, "they are together
engaged in an impossible, startling, bottomless quest" (168).
But when he visits the Lutheran Pastor Kruppenbach, he is
castigated for his ineffectual meddling and reminded that his
true role is to be hot with Christ, to burn people with the
force of his belief (171). Nor does Eccles gain much support for his efforts from his scoffing, Freud-parroting wife
Lucy.

Kruppenbach's lecture on the role of the ministry deserves
more attention, for it reveals an unflinching faith that could
have fleshed out Harry's vague belief in the Beyond. First
of all, dogmatic Kruppenbach damns Eccles for acting as "an
unpaid doctor," trying to smooth out all the problems in
people's lives, or as a policeman with no other sanction but
his human good nature. His role is not to ape the secular
servant of man's needs, but to view human misery from the
perspective of God, and above all, to spend much time in
prayer, so that he will be prepared to comfort his people with
the strength of Christ in their times of need: " 'In running
back and forth you run from the duty given you by God, to
make your faith powerful, so when the call comes you can go
out and tell them, "Yes, he is dead, but you will see him
again in Heaven. Yes, you suffer, but you must love your

pain, because it is *Christ*'s pain" ' " (171). Nothing else can justify a minister's existence: he must put on Christ, he must live the life of Christ, he must be such a visible witness to the truth of Christ, that through him, Christ speaks to and lives for the people: " 'Make no mistake. There is nothing but Christ for us. All the rest, all this decency and busyness, is nothing. It is Devil's work' " (171). Eccles is just as much on the run as Harry; he is just as caught up in busy work as Conner.

The validity of Kruppenbach's indictment is underlined by Eccles' inability to provide Harry with comfort after the death of his child. On the day before Rebecca's funeral, after Harry's talk with Tothero, more than any other time Harry feels like pleading with Eccles for a confirmation of his belief in "the thing behind everything." The only answer he receives is: " 'Harry, you know I don't think that thing exists in the way you think it does' " (280). Sensing how this reply has deflated Rabbit, Eccles then attempts to give him a more meaningful response: " 'We must work for forgiveness; we must *earn* the right to see that thing behind everything. Harry, I *know* that people are brought to Christ. I've seen it with my eyes and tasted it with my mouth. And I do think this. I think marriage is a sacrament, and that this tragedy, terrible as it is, has at last united you and Janice in a sacred way' " (281). For the next few hours, Rabbit clings to this belief, though Eccles' words are really unfelt formulas which Harry must eventually reject for the belief that he truly feels in his heart. So Eccles fails. If he could have combined Kruppenbach's faith with his own humanistic feeling, he would have possibly helped Rabbit to a resolution of his crisis.

At the moment in his life when he feels most oppressed by his sin and guilt, while he is waiting for the birth of his second child, Rabbit judges his life to be "a sequence of grotesque poses assumed to no purpose, a magic dance empty of belief" (198). But is it really so? Has he not rather been a man "in search of the Happy Isles, the Grail, grace, the goal-net, a heaven of alfalfa or rhododendrons?"[20] He believes in the sky, the thing beyond, God, the one with whom he seeks communion. He has experienced that transcendence and tries to recapture it in his daily life. He is convinced that life is not worth living, is not truly human, unless it finds room for the life of outer space, our true place of living. Put conversely, he cannot accept death in the manner that people around him do, as the end to human living.

So Rabbit's life is not really empty of belief, but the belief is vague, undeveloped, and disengaged from ordinary human responsibilities. In its wake Harry leaves a line of grieving parents, suffering women, and dead children, all of whom Updike treats with a fair degree of impartiality and insight. At the same time Updike develops an extensive vocabulary of constriction to chart Harry's panic.[21] Harry is obsessed by a fear of death, whether this be actual physical death or the death of freedom and manhood, so strong that it determines his actions and is reflected in the recurring images of the door and wall, the net and trap. His life with Janice, the road on which he attempts to escape, Eccles' handshake and his probing conversations, his brief discussion with Harrison in the restaurant booth, the barbs of his own mother, his Sunday afternoon with Janice and Rebecca, his job for MagiPeel or for Mr. Springer: all are part of the same trap. Wherever he turns, he feels hemmed in by walls. The forces that inclose and thwart him affect him like a net in which he is hopelessly entangled. The "red lines and blue lines" of his road map become the threads of a net at which he must tear and claw. He feels the attempts of his family to trace him "as a net of telephone calls and hasty trips, trails of tears and strings of words, white worried threads shuttled through the night and now faded but still existent, an invisible net overlaying the steep streets" (40). Even the ceiling above his bed at home "is mottled with an unsteady network of veins like the net of yellow and blue that mottled the skin of his baby" (276).

All these traps and nets are merely the metaphors for Rabbit's fear of death, the force that drives him to yearn for the transcendent and to attempt grasping it in a ritualistic way. When he considers external circumstances and objects in themselves, he can only see death in them. For instance, when he suspects that Eccles views his flight from Janice as immature, he categorically states that in his opinion maturity and death are the same thing (106). When he tries to explain to Janice why he ran from her, he can only say that he had to because "you get the feeling you're in your coffin before they've taken your blood out" (215). Waiting for Janice to return from the hospital, he tries to blot Tothero and Ruth from his mind because both remind him of death. Their "mute dense presences" keep crowding him (230-231).

In the dream that comes to him on the night before Rebecca June's funeral, Rabbit's conscious preoccupations about death resolve themselves in a cosmic rite. The locus is a sporting field. He is alone. Two discs identical in circumference, one a dense white, the other transparent, move toward each other in the sky and touch. At that touch, which frightens Rabbit, a voice booms over a loudspeaker, "The cowslip swallows up the elder." When the weaker disc eventually puts the stronger into total eclipse, the cosmic nature of his dream bursts forth upon Rabbit: "He understands: 'the cowslip' is the moon, and 'the elder' the sun, and that what he has witnessed is the explanation of death: lovely life eclipsed by lovely death" (282). So excited does he become that he feels impelled to be the evangelist of this truth. Upon awakening, however, he realizes that he has nothing to tell the world; the old pain and oppression return to him. Yet the vision of death as the absorption and continuation of earthly life in a new, beautiful form is crucial to the liberation that Rabbit experiences at the funeral itself.

This liberation already begins when his mother absorbs Janice in her grieving embrace, much as the two discs merged in his dream. From that point on, Harry is taken into a mood of religious celebration, in which the outer world has an increasing irrelevance (290). His liberation finds its completion through his participation in the Christian rite of burial. As Eccles recites Christ's promise of resurrection and everlasting life for those who believe, Rabbit remembers that his daughter has not been baptized. While the words of the liturgy take on meaning, life and possibility for Rabbit, he is aware that they remain unfelt formulas for the people around him, including false-voiced Eccles. But the irrevocability of his daughter's death overwhelms Rabbit with grief during Eccles' final words at the funeral home about Christ as the Shepherd who cares for his lambs (291). For the moment, his exaltation is flawed.

At the cemetery, the liturgy continues, and Rabbit's exultant conviction that Rebecca has ascended into Heaven fills the words of Eccles' oration with life: "Give us Grace, we beseech thee, to entrust the soul of this child to thy never-failing care and love" (292). The Grace comes to Rabbit; he feels a harmony and unity of purpose in all of existence at this moment: "He feels them all, the heads as still around him as tombstones, he feels them all one, all one with the grass, with the hothouse flowers, all, the undertaker's men, the unseen caretaker who has halted his mower, all gathered into one here to give his unbaptized baby force to leap to Heaven" (292). The vision is reminiscent of Rabbit's ecstatic moment on the golf course. As the casket is lowered into the grave, Eccles offers a final prayer for those who mourn, who should be "casting every care on thee." His blessing merges with a breath of wind and the smell of flowers. The liturgy is over.

Because he has given his daughter to Heaven and has cast all his care on Christ, Rabbit feels full of strength. At last he has found the hole through which to move toward the beyond. Death has become for him a matter of joy in new life rather than a cause of fear and mourning. But he alone has received this Grace, this gift of vision. His childishly brutal remark to Janice is an instinctive reaction to his realization that she is still earthbound, unwilling to cast her guilt on Christ, an impediment that blocks his communion with the transcendent (293). When he sees that none of the group are ready to join him in truth, that they form a wall against him, he understands that they are the truly dead. Apropos to Rabbit's attitude are these remarks by Karl Barth: "All life must be measured by Life. An independent life aside from Life is not life but death. We are engaged in life's revolt against the powers of death that inclose it. We cannot longer allow ourselves to be *wholly* deceived by the theories with which those powers have surrounded themselves and by the facts which seem to point to their authority. There is something fundamental in us that denies these powers."[22] Rabbit has no way to communicate his vision to these people and no way to assure himself that it is valid. To sustain his own life, he runs.

This running is the final ritual action of Rabbit. It is something that he had learned in his basketball days. Part of Tothero's threefold plan to prepare his boys for winning, together with the elegance of strategy and the will to achieve, was physical conditioning. In a loose manner, his plan includes the three elements of ritual. Throughout the novel, from the time that he gets winded in the alley basketball game to his final flight down the streets of Brewer, Harry is running. Usually, an exhilaration is connected with this brainless pattern. When Rabbit first escapes from Janice, he experiences a wonderful "washed feeling inside" (23). Even though the net of circumstances gradually enfolds him, until after midnight he is convinced that the mere external action of flight will maintain his exaltation, that he will be able to slough off all thought of conditions behind him and achieve a state of perfect, lasting bliss.[23]

Similarly, in his flight from the cemetery, Rabbit is at first exultant, in the sheer joy of action buoyed up by the reminiscence of dodging down a basketball court (294). As he enters deeper into the woods and senses their mystery and menace, "the hushed, deathly life of the woods," he is overcome by fear (295). When he loses his way and stumbles across the ruins of a deserted house, his fear changes to "a clangorous horror, as if this ruined evidence of a human intrusion into a world of blind life tolls bells that ring to the edges of the universe" (296). The presences of those who lived here loom before Harry, and, in a moment of religious awe, he has another confrontation with the transcendent: "He obscurely feels lit by a great spark, the spark whereby the blind tumble of matter recognized itself, a spark struck in the collision of two opposed realms, an encounter a terrible God willed" (297). He seems to hear a voice that drives him to run. He finally strikes the mountain road, and he seems entered on a new life.

Instinctively, he returns to Ruth, but his life with her is dead, too. For all the love and security that Rabbit feels he can offer Ruth, she can see nothing but death in everything that he has touched and calls him "Mr. Death himself" (301). Rejected by Ruth, Rabbit has nowhere to turn, not even to the Church window across the street. Guilt and responsibility threaten to block his way. Thoroughly afraid and at a loss for what to do, Rabbit does regain some sense of the goodness that lies inside. The only thing to do is run, submit to the familiar, unthinking pattern and hope to discover the opening through the dense net that seems to surround him. For the moment at least, it succeeds in leading him out of fear and insecurity into a quiet peace and ecstasy: "his hands lift of their own and he feels the wind on his ears even before, his heels hitting heavily on the pavement at first but with an effortless gathering out of a kind of sweet panic growing lighter and quicker and quieter, he runs. Ah: runs. Runs" (306-307). Rabbit's flight has for him the same significance that Mircea Eliade claims it had in archaic religions; flight becomes "an appropriation of the condition of the spirit."[24]

In Rabbit's environment, the great secularization, from which all other secularizations flow, is the inability to see in death anything more than the concrete end of earthly life. With the deprivation of spiritual significance for death, all other vital experiences, including birth, sexual union, work, and play, become desacralized and lose their ritual character of uniting man with the cosmos. As Mircea Eliade has stated, "For the nonreligious men of the modern age, the cosmos has become opaque, inert, mute; it transmits no message, it holds no cipher."[25] While Rabbit, like every other character in this novel, is a product of Western materialism, he alone, for all his crudity, immaturity, and irresponsibility, has been able to recognize the sacred aspects in human life, and to believe in God and the resurrection from the dead.[26] He alone has been able to understand that death is a rite of passage from earth to heaven.

Underlying Rabbit's final insight about death is the implicit belief that there can be no distinct dichotomy between the secular and the divine. He instinctively shares the view expressed by Karl Barth:

We must return to that reserve maintained by the divine over against the human—though it must now have become clear to all that the separation of the two cannot be ultimate, for then God would not be God. There *must still* be a way from there to here. And with this "must" and this "still" we confess to the miracle of the *revelation* of God. . . . Once we are conscious of the life in life, we continue no longer in the land of the dead, in a life whose forms unhappily allow us to miss the very meaning of life—that is, its connection with its creative origin. We perceive the Wholly Other, the eternity of the divine life; and we cannot escape the thought that for us also eternal life can alone be called and really be "life." The Wholly Other in God—itself resisting all secularization, all mere being put to use and hyphenated—drives us with compelling power to look for a basic, ultimate, original correlation between our life and that wholly other life. We would not die but live. It is the living *God* who, when he meets us, makes it inevitable for us to believe in our own life.[27]

As Barth points out, even men like Isaiah and Jonah had to prove their devotion to the holy by daring to relate it directly to the secular life of man. In this sense, Rabbit is also a prophet. With his gift of life, with his stubborn insistence that there is something beyond material existence which wants him to find it, Rabbit dares to profess belief in a transcendence that is denied by everyone else.

But by no means do I want to canonize Rabbit. While he fights the external circumstances that threaten to swallow him, while he is sometimes open to the motions of Grace, he also wreaks havoc by the hardness of his heart. In deserting his family, he selfishly ignores the physical and emotional hardships which his absence will inflict upon Janice and his son Nelson. He refuses to consider the possible consequences of living with Ruth and is even blind to the fact that he has made her pregnant. To some extent, he is responsible for the death of Rebecca by his impulsive second departure from Janice. Even at the end, he casts his responsibilities for Ruth and Janice upon their parents; his duty to Nelson he more or less evades (305). He is simply unwilling to walk the straight line of a paradox, to accept the going through quality of Christianity or the purgative aspect of suffering. In many ways, he is a most unimpressive character.

He is truly a man caught in the middle. "Harry can feel as though he has fallen out of the given world at the same time as he realizes he cannot escape from it; at once alienated and trapped."[28] Unlike Robert Jordan in Hemingway's *For Whom the Bell Tolls,* he has no "fear-purged, purging ecstasy of battle" into which to throw himself and be cleansed. Unlike Jordan, he deliberately seeks but fails to achieve the experience of the transcendent in sexual intercourse. It comes to Jordan as an unexpected gift in his two encounters with Maria, where time stood still and the earth moved and the two became one with the cosmos.[29]

Harry sometimes clings to the material world in which he lives; at other times he pulls into a private ideal world. By the end of the novel, though, he has gained an insight into the meaning of death that could lead him out of his tortured ambivalence, if he chose to walk the straight line of the Christian paradox instead of zigzagging across his life. Insight alone is not enough. Temporary exaltation is not enough. Aimless running will not maintain the moment forever. The option which he refuses is to take that last leap into the space of faith and uncertainty.

As *Rabbit Redux* reveals ten years later, Harry will continue to temporize. He will try to follow both the "right" way of others and his own "good" way.[30] He will return to Janice and slip back into the conventions of the System, even accepting some of its values. Passively, he will continue to follow his instincts, to do what satisfies him, even though this will inevitably lead him to inexcusable selfishness and an inordinate concern for sensuous pleasure and panic and a consciousness of sin. Still, unimpressive slow-learner that he might be, Harry Angstrom has the right to search for the significance of his uniqueness.[31] And just as much as anyone else, he deserves our attention. Even if he fails.

4

THE NECESSITY OF MYTH IN *THE CENTAUR*

In a brief essay entitled "Ulysses, Order, and Myth," T. S. Eliot noticed that the first reaction of the critics to James Joyce's use of the *Odyssey* had been to treat it "as an amusing dodge, or scaffolding erected by the author for the purpose of disposing his realistic tale, of no interest in the completed structure." For Mr. Eliot, however, Joyce's "mythical method" offers the modern author a technique for giving shape and significance to the apparent anarchy and meaninglessness of contemporary history. "Manipulating a continuous parallel between contemporaneity and antiquity" helps make "the modern world possible for art."[1]

Inevitably, when *The Centaur* was published, it was compared to *Ulysses,* in the cubism of its opening scene as well as in the father-son relationship of George and Peter Caldwell.[2] On the point of Updike's "mythical method," however, many of the critics expressed dismay in terms similar to the first reaction to *Ulysses.* George Steiner, for example, admitted that the Homeric myth in Joyce "acts from inside as a central impulse of shape and wit," but he saw the myth in Updike as merely an obtruding "allegoric scaffold."[3] With accusations that he is too literal-minded or fundamentalist in his use of myth, other critics bemoaned Updike's ruining a perfectly good, poignant story through his desire for novelty or false grandeur. Even Granville Hicks, generally amiable to Updike, felt that in this case he has overreached himself "to find a contemporary parallel for every god in the pantheon."[4]

Still, some of the critics felt that Updike had definitely succeeded in his attempt to integrate myth and reality. J. A. Ward was convinced that in *The Centaur* "the craft and the vision are completely of a piece," that from the blend of mythic and topical elements, two major effects emerge: the creation of comic surprises and a "preternatural view of the actual." "In effect," said Ward, "the mythic plane eliminates the temporal and spatial plane, even while problems of time and space most engage the minds of Caldwell-Chiron and Peter-Prometheus."[5] Not only is the mythic parallel artful, but it is also necessary to take us beyond the confines of the immediate, to objectify the implicit religious intuition which the characters feel throughout the novel. Because the religious content of Greek mythology is alien to moderns, this mythology can be used for Updike's own purposes, without having the tenets of any institutionalized belief attached to it.[6]

How then are we to understand the use of myth in *The Centaur?* Are we to take it as a brilliant *tour de force,* as Ward suggests, one which presents us with a valid religious insight behind the surface story? Or are we to see it as a brilliant display of technique which is flawed by the introduction of an essentially arbitrary, pointless, and self-conscious myth?

It seems to me that the entire controversy surrounding Updike's use of myth in *The Centaur* has centered on the simple facts that he does not employ myth as some critics desire, and that his world-view is unacceptable to them. To compare him to James Joyce or Ezra Pound on these points is unfair, for the implicit presumption is that Updike's intention in the use of myth is (or should be) the same as Joyce's or Pound's. John Updike himself has stated that the mythol-

ogy of *The Centaur* is meant to be comic, a sign of Caldwell's estrangement from the "powers" of Olinger, and "a
quality of Peter's remembering, in which these childhood
events have become mythical."[7] In writing *The Fixer,* a
triumphant book about a folk hero, Bernard Malamud was
trying to move from history to mythology. Here the movement is from personal history to personal mythology. If the
myth sometimes jangles, so does life.[8]

One should view the mythological index which Updike has
so unfortunately inserted at the end of this novel in the light
of the statements above. Highly berated, offered as a proof
of the pointless character of the myth, this index is also a
final indication of the omnipresence of the myth element
throughout the world of this novel. Certainly, it is not necessary for us to trace the allusions page by page in order to
gain the meaning or the vicarious experience of the novel.
The index may be a piece of pretentious and naive display
on the part of Updike; more likely, it is one of the comic
elements of the novel, a spoof on allegorical novels and on
"the critics-with-keys." With greater success Updike has done
something similar in the burlesque of bibliographies at the
end of *Bech: A Book.*

In the novel proper, the literal use of referents from Greek
mythology achieves its comic effect through the bizarre juxtaposition of the activities of the ancient gods with those of
modern men, as, for example, in the easy metamorphosis of
three garage mechanics into gabbling Cyclopes, or in the
conversion of Caldwell's walk down the school corridor into
the clatter of hooves. The use of the myth is also a natural
metaphor for Caldwell's estrangement, for his persistent conviction that the townspeople's poses and actions of superior-
ity with him are an attempt to keep him in his place, to
remind him, as it were, that he is merely human in contrast
to their divinity: "And this was the way with all these
Olinger aristocrats. They wouldn't take any money but they
did take an authoritative tone. They forced a favor on you

and that made them gods."[9] While my emphasis rests on the
spirit of myth which infuses all of Peter's memories with a
new and deeper significance, these comic and ironic overtones should not be disregarded. Larry Taylor has done just
that in arguing for *The Centaur* as a "pastoral elegy."[10]

With myth as a central element in the structure of this
novel, *The Centaur* takes on the character of a complete
ritual in itself. The entire narration is a patterned ceremony
of word and action in which Peter celebrates his former
experiences with his father. Where Harry Angstrom of *Rabbit, Run* is unable to discover a specific myth that can incorporate and fructify his sense of the transcendent, Peter has,
in the life and actions of his father, a myth that enables him
to face the transcendent questions of time, life and death.
Through his re-living or re-enactment of the myth, Peter
gains the possibility of renewed strength for his present life.
The relationship of the adult Peter to his father is analogous
to the Christian's relationship with Christ through the ritual
of the Mass. In a sense, George Caldwell is Peter's redeemer;
through his sacrifice, Peter lives. This sacrifice, offered during
Peter's adolescence, continues to bear fruit for Peter in the
present through its ritual re-enactment.

Behind this view of *The Centaur* as a meaningful ritual is
my conviction that the entire novel is presented to us as the
experience of Peter, reliving three days in his life with his
father, while he lies beside his black mistress in varying states
of wakefulness or sleep. Certainly, chapters II, IV, and VIII,
the chapters in which the realistic elements predominate, are
the first-person narration of Peter to his mistress. Chapters
I, III, VI, and IX, filled with a free-flowing irrationality, with
illogical shifts from fact to myth, with the types of associations that can be expected of an artist, may be considered
the dreams that come to Peter between his periods of narration, or the meanderings of Peter's semi-conscious mind.
Chapter V, the obituary for Peter's father, may be seen in
the same light. Only chapter VII remains. Although this

chapter is apparently a simple pastiche of set pieces viewed by some omniscient narrator, within the context of the whole these can be understood as a series of memories reconstructed in the mind of Peter, as he lies awake in bed. The entire novel is a fusion of the dreams and reveries and actual narration of Peter. That this experience takes on the character of a rite for Peter will become evident in a moment.

It is only at the beginning of the second chapter that we become aware of the presence of the elder Peter and his mistress: "My father and my mother were talking. I wake now often to silence, beside you, with the pang of fear, after dreams that leave a sour wash of atheism in my stomach. . . . But in those days I always awoke to the sound of my parents talking, voices which even in agreement were contentious and full of life" (46-47). The very subject matter suggests that Peter has just awakened from a nightmarish dream of the chaos that reigned at the end of his father's science lecture. The transition from chapter III to chapter IV contains the same suggestion, with the last sentence of the former trailing off, and the first sentence of the next chapter returning to the directness of first-person narration. Then, it is not until the eighth chapter that Peter directly addresses his mistress, once again in terms that reveal their shifts in consciousness: "My love, listen. Or are you asleep? It doesn't matter" (265). Finally Peter warns her that his story is coming to a close, but not before the weariness that he felt in the original experience overtakes him in the telling (268, 282).

Nor does Peter finish before he makes an important confession to his mistress. What he lives for now is the life that he shares with her. Still he misses the sense of participation in the inconceivable heaven that he had in his father's house: "When we make love sometimes you sigh my name and I feel radically confirmed. I am glad I have met you, glad, proud, glad; I miss only, and then only a little, in the late afternoon, the sudden white laughter that like heat lightning bursts in

an atmosphere where souls are trying to serve the impossible.
My father for all his mourning moved in the atmosphere of
such laughter" (269). Peter is a professed atheist, a secular
humanist who feels that he can find fulfillment in human
love, yet he looks at his life of "half-Freudian half-Oriental
sex-Mysticism" and wonders, *"Was it for this that my father
gave up his life?"* (270). In this question lies the reason for
viewing the entire narration of *The Centaur* as a ritual action
of Peter. For in the retelling of these events, in the celebration
of his three-days communion with his father, Peter is also
searching for a "paradigmatic pattern" to bring renewed hope
and meaning into his present life. How this liturgical attitude
is reinforced by the details of the novel remains to be seen.

The natural place to begin an extended discussion of *The
Centaur* as ritual is with the epigraph from Karl Barth:
"Heaven is the creation inconceivable to man, earth the creation conceivable to him. He himself is the creature on the
boundary between heaven and earth." Commentators like
David D. Galloway have used this epigraph to justify an
interpretation of *The Centaur* as an image of man divorced
from God and standing on his own rights as a human being
in an absurd universe.[11] For Karl Barth, on the contrary,
inconceivable heaven and conceivable earth are not two
opposing worlds, "not a reality in themselves, which are
understandable and explicable in terms of themselves, but
they, with man in the centre, as the meaning of their existence,
derive *from God,* belong to God."[12]

Man exists not on the boundary between God and creation, but on a boundary within creation itself: between the
visibilia et invisibilia, the conceivable and inconceivable, the
humanly attainable and the humanly transcendent. "Within
creation as well we are faced by an inconceivable mystery,
by depths of being which may alternately terrify and delight
us." Included in that part of creation which is conceivable
to man, in the earth, is everything of man's human and
spiritual capacity, all that he can conceive intuitively, even

the world of reason or ideas. So then man is a creature who lives in a world of constant tension and delicate balance. Because he can see, hear, understand, and dominate his environment, "he is the essence of a free being in this earthly world. And the same creature stands beneath heaven; and in the face of the *invisibilia,* of what he cannot conceive or dispose of, he does not dominate but is completely dependent."[13]

Neither is this the complete picture. For the whole of creation, heaven and earth in union, constitutes a single, mighty *signum* of the covenant between God and Man: "Since within this world there really exists an above and a below confronting one another, since in every breath we take, in every one of our thoughts, in every great and petty experience of our human lives heaven and earth are side by side, greeting each other, attracting and repelling each other and yet belonging to one another, we are, in our existence, of which God is the Creator, a sign and indication, a promise of what ought to happen in creation and to creation— the meeting, the togetherness, the fellowship and, in Jesus Christ, the oneness of Creator and creature."[14]

The Barthian world-view outlined above is implicit in *The Centaur* and offers the substratum from which specific rituals grow. In the remainder of this chapter, I shall demonstrate how the ordinary elements of human life on this conceivable earth are brought within the sacral sphere, how elements of the inconceivable heaven affect the life of man on earth, and how rituals grow out of this sacral atmosphere to enrich the lives of George Caldwell and his son Peter.

Even the language and metaphors in which the most insignificant and banal activities of this earth are expressed reflect the formal rites of religion. The disorder in Caldwell's classroom is not merely chaotic, but a "furious festal noise" (4). As Caldwell limps down the school corridor with the arrow scraping on the floor, the sounds that emanate from the classrooms—fused voices chanting French, singing the national anthem, discussing problems of social science—affect him almost as some ritualistic chant (4). When he reaches Hummel's garage, he sees that the various items that are strewn about are not simply realistic elements of the picture, but "like the outpouring of a material hymn to material creation" (10). To Caldwell the girls' locker room is sacred (20), to Peter, Penny's crotch is sacred (120); even Doc Appleton's office takes on the aura of a sanctum (129-130). A farewell by Peter's grandfather becomes a benediction (69). Moreover, Caldwell is capable of achieving communion with the things of earth through the simplest experiences. The sense of wholeness that comes to him after a tooth is pulled puts him into a mood of praise and religious celebration: "Abruptly he feels absurdly grateful for all created things, . . . for the sounds of Kenny restoring his tools to the sterilizer bath, for the radio on the shelf filtering a shudder of organ music through its static."[15]

One of the novel's moments of communion, between Caldwell and the French teacher, Hester Appleton, takes place simply through a ritualistic sharing of a phrase and a poem that have special significance for them. Even Hester's mere pronunciation of French gives George a certain comfort, so he asks her to say something for him in a moment of dejection. She responds with a formula that she has lived by: *"Dieu est très fin."* In response, Caldwell shares with her a poem that he used to recite in Passaic thirty years ago. While not a great poem (it contains an image of God's Providence and of time's forward flow), to Caldwell this had been a happy poem. The shared formulas bring the two of them together for that moment (194-195).

But the best example of an earthly action seen in terms of a ritual that unconsciously draws its participants into a mystery is the basketball game. As the students enter the gymnasium, the stereotyped character of their conversations creates the atmosphere of an in-group (225). The use of language to produce the sense of a community sharing in a mystery is emphasized even more strongly when the cheer-leaders lead the students in the pre-game rites. Peter actually feels a certain kind of ecstasy, the experience of being "sucked down into another kingdom," as the word *Olinger* is spelled out in the form of invocation-response (227).

A major metaphor by which Updike connects both Cald-well and Peter with the earth is the *tree,* which has its roots deep in the earth. Caldwell's recollection of surprising Vera Hummel, the girls' physical education instructor as she came out of a shower in the girls' locker room, changes into a conversation between Chiron, the Centaur, and Venus. When Chiron demeans his own birth to console Venus for the bar-barous manner of hers, she resents the apparent condescen-sion and strikes back with the reminder that his mother Philyra asked to be metamorphosed into a linden tree rather than suckle the monster she bore (21). This painful truth turns Chiron's thought to his youthful imaginings of his mother's calm attentions and gestures of love in the move-ments of the linden trees that he examined. Still, despite his attempts at reconciliation with his mother through the linden tree, Chiron felt that "an infantile resentment welled up bit-terly within his mature reconstruction" (23). The depriva-tion of a mother's love has burned within his soul an image of all womankind as shallow and selfish. So, through "the prism he had made of the tale," Chiron could reduce Venus in his own mind or, to bring it back to the world of Olinger, Caldwell could express his sense of estrangement from the women around him (23). This process of reduction, of course, is one function of the Greek myth throughout the novel.

Just as the image of the tree is intimately connected with women in Caldwell's mind, so in Peter's dreams. Where the metaphor expresses Caldwell's sense of estrangement, how-ever, the dream of his girl friend Penny turning into a tree brings a sense of exaltation into Peter's adolescent life. Through his observation of her silent metamorphosis, Peter gains a new insight into the nature of Penny's love for him, a recognition that it is "a sheltered love, young as she was, recent as our touching was, little as I gave her; she would sacrifice for me" (51). While the tree-metaphor contains elements of a Freudian sublimation of repressed sexual desire, it also operates within the context of the dream to bring Peter to a kind of celebration of the mystery of human love. This eventually leads him to admit his love for Penny openly and experience the bittersweet ecstasy of first love (244-246).

One final element of this conceivable earth that takes on the aura of the holy is the land itself, the farm on which the Caldwells live. Like an ancient earth-mother, George's wife Cassie senses the wholeness that comes to a man, the mystical solidarity with Nature that arises from working the soil. This Peter and his father cannot accept. To Cassie, "the country represented purity"; to George, the farm was merely eighty acres of dead, cold, thankless land (59, 198). These attitudes remain unchanged even at the end of the novel. Cassie tries to persuade George to quit teaching and farm the land with her, to find his happiness as a farmer, but he will have none of it: " 'I hate Nature. It reminds me of death. All Nature means to me is garbage and confusion and the stink of skunk——brroo!' " (291). When Cassie is defeated through the remarks of Peter's grandfather, Peter, who overhears the discussion from his room, is glad, for he no more wanted to sink into the soil than did his father. In Updike's own terms, Peter and his father daily flee from the world of feminine earth and matter to a world of masculine mind and spirit. These sexual polarities, running through much of Updike's fiction, come into particular focus in his next novel, *Of the Farm*.

Up to this point, I have been demonstrating how earthly things move in a sacral atmosphere in *The Centaur*. In what follows, I will be discussing the effect that various elements of the inconceivable heaven have upon Caldwell and Peter.

First among these is the sky. Innumerable descriptions present an artful visual image of the various moods in which the sky hovers over Olinger. But the sky also takes on a greater significance: "The sky shows itself to be infinite, transcendent. It is pre-eminently the 'wholly other' than the little represented by man and his environment."[16]

That this transcendence affects Caldwell is apparent in the very first pages. As he walks to Hummel's garage to have the arrow removed from his ankle, "the clear blue of the towering sky seemed forceful and enigmatic," and "in the face of spatial grandeur, his pains seemed abashed" (5-6). Then, before returning to his classroom, Caldwell "gasped fresh air and stared sharply upward, as if in answer to a shout. Beyond the edge of the orange wall the adamantine blue zenith pronounced its unceasing monosyllable: I" (19). In general, Caldwell views the sky as the source of thunder, the abode of Zeus-Zimmerman, a terrible and awesome god. The threat of this god's thunder breaks off his mental seduction by Venus-Vera (30). Likewise, when he catches Mim Herzog leaving the office of Zimmerman with her lipstick smeared, he feels in the sullen sky the oppression of his hastening fate (201). Caldwell is weighed down with a sense of estrangement even from the elements of heaven. It is left to Peter to find in the sky a fascinating reflection of his airy dreams.

When it begins to snow between the basketball games, somehow men are united with the sky. "Snow puts us with Jupiter Pluvius among the clouds" (238). Through the power in the air, Olinger undergoes a kind of incarnation, takes on a new life. As Peter and his father stride through the storm after the games, Peter's observation of the snowflakes' shadows under the city lights leads him to cosmic thoughts: "It fascinates him; he feels the universe in all its plastic and endlessly variable beauty pinned, stretched, crucified like a butterfly upon a frame of unvarying geometrical truth" (256). And he draws an analogy between this phenomenon and the movement of the stars, until his mind boggles at the attempt to envision a universe that both ends and does not end. Through his perception of the snowflakes appearing and disappearing under the lights, Peter becomes sensitive to the relativities and immutabilities of the universe, to finiteness and infinity, to the death that ends earthly existence and to life after death. Like practically all of Updike's characters, Peter feels the dipolar attractions of life. In his mind he moves back and forth over the mysterious boundary called death.

But unlike the youthful Updike, who felt "suspended quite pointlessly in an immense void of indifferent stars and mathematically operating atoms" when he experienced similar thoughts, Peter is filled with hope.[17] Forced to stay in town because their car breaks down, on the second night Peter and his father sleep in Vera Hummel's guest bedroom. The next morning Peter finds the room radiant in the aftermath of the storm. "I thought, *This morning has never occurred before,* and I jubilantly felt myself to be on the prow of a ship cleaving the skyey ocean of time" (271). Peter's notion of time is just as exhilarating as his conception of mind-boggling space.

Certainly, in *The Centaur,* from the first time that George Caldwell recites the proverb "Time and tide for no man wait" to the final *Now* where he accepts his life, time is one of the *invisibilia* which is a major preoccupation for Peter and his father. Bound up with this preoccupation—with the irretrievable loss of the past, the flow of the present, the hope of the future—is another of the *invisibilia* which is probably at the source of all myth, namely, death. Regardless of their formal religious beliefs, Caldwell and Peter must be considered religious men because of their attitude toward time, for their refusal to live in the historical present alone. In the three days that Peter and his father are each other's greatest responsibility, they become vividly aware of time's power over life, of the possibility that "time constitutes man's deepest existential dimension; it is linked to his own life, hence it has a beginning and an end, which is death, the annihilation of his life."[18] But Caldwell and Peter perceive a transhuman quality in time. Through their actions and thoughts, Peter and his father reveal a belief in a reversible and recoverable time, in a sort of eternal mythical present that can be periodically reintegrated by means of rites. Through the reconstruction of his life's events in terms of the Greek gods, Caldwell attempts to reconcile himself to the environment from which he feels so alienated. This reintegration he achieves at the end of the novel. Likewise, through the reactualization of his father's life, Peter attempts to stave off possible disintegration in his own life. Through the conversion of his memories into myth, he sets up a model for his imitation and expresses his nostalgia for immortality. Both act within the realm of sacred time.

The first time George Caldwell brings up the proverb, "Time and tide for no man wait," he does so in a somewhat joking yet serious attempt to grasp its meaning. He rebels against the complacency of the proverb because he believes "that God made man as the last best thing in His Creation. If that's the case, who are this time and tide that are so almighty superior to us?" (63).

The adolescent Peter is even more determined than his father to discover an answer to the tyranny of time and the inevitability of death. Behind his desire to be an artist is the wish to answer in a human way the inconceivable elements of heaven, to stop time and give immortality to the fleeting moment. Art is the ritual by which Peter will achieve the eternal mythical present. This becomes apparent while Peter daydreams over his breakfast and admires a section of one of his paintings on the kitchen wall. "Looking at this streak of black, I relived the very swipe of my pallet knife, one second of my life that in a remarkable way had held firm. It was this firmness, I think, this potential fixing of a few passing seconds, that attracted me, at the age of five, to art.

For it is at about that age, isn't it, that it sinks in upon us that things do, if not die, certainly change, wiggle, slide, retreat, and, like the dabs of sunlight on the bricks under the grape arbor on a breezy June day, shuffle out of all identity?" (62).

In the three days that follow this breakfast, death becomes a reality for Peter in its imminent possibility for his father. What sustains Peter through this ordeal is not only his growing appreciation of his father and his love of Penny, but also the myth of the City and the Future that he has created for himself. Ironically, we are able to perceive the breakdown of this myth in our views of Peter as "an authentic second-rate impressionist painter," in a drab city studio, in a future which he to some extent sees as his past. Nonetheless, despite Peter's later attempts to discover a more meaningful myth in the life of his father, the myth of the City and the ritual of Art were sufficient for his adolescent days. The City means so much to Peter because there he will escape the heaviness of the soil, there he will visit the temples of his religion, there he will become famous as an artist. One time, on an overnight visit with his father to his Aunt Alma in New York, he had almost come to a partial realization of this dream. But his father's blundering had blocked it; they never reached the museums that contained the works of his beloved Vermeer, and Peter was denied the sacramental encounter he so desired. "That these paintings, which I had worshipped in reproduction, had a simple physical existence seemed a profound mystery to me: to come within touching distance of their surfaces would have been for me to enter a Real Presence so ultimate I would not be surprised to die in the encounter" (85).

Despite this frustration, the adolescent Peter continues to hope and plan for the future. On the first night that he and his father are stranded in the city, Peter is left alone in a hotel room while his father returns to lock the car. He looks out the window over Alton, the second city in his life, and imagines that the cars, stoplights, and shadows of people merge "in a visual liquor whose fumes were the future." He becomes excited by the vibrations of the city's neon advertisements on the walls of his room. The end result is an esthetic experience that convinces Peter he will be able to overcome the inconceivable: time and death. "My sense of myself amplified until, lover and loved, seer and seen, I compounded in several accented expansions my ego, the city, and the future, and during these seconds truly clove to the center of the sphere, and outmuscled time and tide. I would triumph. Yet the city shuffled and winked beyond the window unmoved, transparent to my penetration, and her dismissal dwindled me terribly" (165-166).

And, as we have seen, the city dismisses Peter the same way in his adulthood. After the shattering of Peter's semi-transcendent myths of the City and the Future, Peter searches for meaning in the Past. Now the story of his quietly joyful and self-sacrificing father which Peter narrates to his mistress resurrects the Real Presence of the father he had never completely touched. Only now is Peter ready to grasp the full significance of his father's life for his own living.[19]

In the sacralized universe that has been described thus far, what are the consequences for man? Apparently, the actions of Caldwell would be the same in a humanistic atmosphere that makes the postulate of the sacred unnecessary. He is a genuinely funny person who delights his students by his unpredictability.[20] He is a compulsively charitable person who allows others to take advantage of him. He is an effusively grateful person who feels obliged to recognize the least kindnesses shown to him by others, even by a hotel clerk. He is an embarrassingly soulful person who ignores the social proprieties to engage anyone he meets in serious discussion, minister, homosexual, or drunk. He is an essentially abstracted person who neglects his clothing and material needs, so much so that his doctor accuses him of a lack of respect for his body. Most of these blundering ways are an annoy-

ance and frustration to Peter, but in the three days that
father and son must remain in town, the gifts he has received
from his father become apparent to Peter.[21]

Because the relationship that grows between Peter and his
father is so genuine, because Caldwell comes alive as a
memorable character, some of the critics, as I have demonstrated, have deemed the addition of any other elements in
their lives as pointless. Yet, in refusing to grant Updike's
donnée, in desacralizing the universe that he presents, these
same critics ignore Updike's point about man as a creature
who participates in the conceivable and inconceivable. Man
is not merely a victim of his existential situation. Every man
is also a mediator between heaven and earth, a bridge-
builder, a priest. Although Peter speaks of the "classic degeneration" from his grandfather to himself, from the priest
to the teacher to the artist, both he and his father preside
over the rituals that grow out of God's Creation. The religious
function of Art for Peter I have already discussed. The significant ritual sections that remain for discussion are the
teaching experiences of the first and third chapters, the obituary, and the final chapter.

George Caldwell's lecture on the universe replaces the
Greek myth of creation with the modern myth of evolution.
Instead of magical invocations, the mystifying numerical
figures and Latin terms of science are used. The manner in
which Caldwell reduces the entire development of the universe to the equivalent of three days, then of the past twenty
minutes, has the effect of bringing all history into an eternal
present. The chalk that turns into a large wet larva, the paper
airplane that becomes an openfaced white flower, the trilo-
bites that are cast upon the floor and eaten by one of the
girls, the humming of the boys, the calm undressing of Iris
Osgood by Mr. Zimmerman, the intercourse of Deifendorf
and the Davis girl, the smell of the stable: all these elements
of Joycean hallucination create a timeless space in which
Caldwell unwillingly leads the students to the climax of their
Dionysiac rites (34-46).

In itself, this lecture need not be seen as a ritual action, not even as "a material hymn to a material universe." It does take on this added significance because it is obviously paralleled by the episode of Chiron teaching the children of Olympus in chapter III. Here, step by step, the teaching takes on the character of a religious rite. In the preparatory part of the chapter, while Chiron hurries to his class, the sonorous series of names for the herbs and flowers and poisons that Chiron uses create an unearthly quality; the recitation of his druggist's knowledge bears the character of invocation. This naturally leads into the central portion of the chapter, the hymn to Zeus, to the Lord of the Sky, to "the god of existence pure." Concluding their hymn of praise and petition with a request for a sign of his benevolence, the children and the Centaur see a black eagle arrow across the sun. While the class is caught in a moment of awe and communion with their god, even Chiron achieves a qualified harmony through the experience. With this initial invocation completed, Chiron proceeds to his daily lesson, the Greek explanation of the Genesis of All Things, clearly a parallel to Caldwell's previous lecture. Instead of the evolutionary scheme, there is a story of the universe set in motion by love (93-99). The contrast could not be stronger. Here there is pure love; in the first chapter there is unbridled sex. Here there is harmony; in the first chapter there is chaos. Through the juxtaposition both Caldwell's success and his failure, his wholeness and his separateness, gain emphasis. In the movement from early times to the present, the tendency of the world to run toward disorder becomes clear. At the same time, the point is being made that we need intense moments, communion with the transcendent, in the modern world as well as in the Greek.

The chief function of ritual in this novel, however, is to serve as an action against death. Chapter V can be understood in this fashion. With its stock language, its stereotyped phraseology and predictable content, the obituary for George

Caldwell amounts to a hagiography. There is the same type of confusion of the real and the ideal in this obituary as there is in classical hagiography. As an imaginary composition of Peter, the obituary becomes a torment, a wish-fulfillment of everything that he hoped his father would achieve, a document to gain for his father the respectability Peter wanted him to have, and a means to hold his father in life.[22] For Peter, encasement in print operates like Art (171-175).

Finally, the most significant ritual action against death is Caldwell's acceptance of life in the last chapter. With Peter sick in bed, Caldwell walks from his house to the car, to return to the daily routine of teaching. On the way, he struggles with his desire for death and his feel for life, with his sense of estrangement and harmony, with the two moods that were expressed in the first and third chapters. His first view of the snow-covered fields makes him aware of the disharmony between earth and heaven. "White, she was white, death's own color, sum of the spectrum, wherever the centaur's eye searched. He wondered, Had not the castration of Sky worked a terrible sterility upon Gaia, though she herself had cried aloud for rescue?" (294). Because of the poverty in his own life and his sense of failure in providing for Peter, Caldwell feels the same sterility, the same rejection of his pleas. "Sky, emasculate, had flung himself far off raging in pain and left his progeny to parch upon a white waste that stretched its arms from sunrise to sunset" (295).

Yet even in the deathly whiteness of winter, the incipient buds upon the trees and bushes show promise of future life. As the meaning of these signs sinks into Caldwell's mind, a new sense of hope and harmony accompanies it. He recalls an explanation of the world's apparent evil that his priest-father had given to him as a boy: *"All joy belongs to the Lord.* Wherever in the filth and confusion and misery, a soul felt joy, there the Lord came and claimed it as his own. . . . And all the rest, all that was not joy, fell away, precipitated, dross that had never been. He thought of his wife's joy in the land and Pop Kramer's joy in the newspaper and his son's joy in the future and was glad, grateful, that he was able to sustain these for yet a space more" (296). At this moment Caldwell himself experiences a vision of the freedom that has come to him through the gift of himself to others. A mood of religious celebration overwhelms him. Sky and Gaia meet again in his own body. "Only goodness lives. But it does live" (297).

He comes to a turn in the road. With his first view of the black Buick and of the Amishman's silo breaking the line of the field, he is brought back to earthly reality; he sees the land as brutish. He realizes that for these past few days he has been saying goodbye to everything in his life before escaping from its tedium. But he is going nowhere. His life will continue; death is not ready to take him. A great weariness overtakes him as he considers the continued estrangement of the life he must lead, "the prospect of having again to maneuver among . . . all that overbearing unfathomable Olinger gang" (297-298).

Other modern writers have built novels around the same central motifs with which Updike has been concerned in *The Centaur*. Ralph Ellison's *Invisible Man* uses the same informing myth of death and rebirth. In Robert Penn Warren's *All the King's Men*, Anne, like Peter, feels the need of a ritual to express her acceptance of the past when she returns to her childhood home. In contrast, characters like Faulkner's young aristocrats Gavin Stevens and Quentin Compson are obsessed with the suffocating effect of the past. In one form or another, James Joyce's *Ulysses*, James Agee's *A Death in the Family*, James Purdy's *Malcolm* and *Eustace Chisholm and the Works*, and Warren's *All the King's Men* focus upon a young man's search for a spiritual father and for his own identity. Still, none of these novels fictionalize man's yearning for God as *The Centaur* does.

Flannery O'Connor, with her ritual and religious preoccupations in *Wise Blood* and *The Violent Bear It Away*, comes the closest, but there is an important difference. While Peter moves from the innocence of the adolescent's ideal world to the adult's recognition of death's inevitability, Tarwater and Hazel Motes do not lose innocence. They are doomed from the very beginning and become more and more involved in the corruptions of the world until, at the very bottom of the pit, they discover light and achieve redemption through some extreme act.[23] Tarwater's involuntary baptism of the idiot child which he is attempting to drown and Hazel Motes' self-blinding after the failure of his attempts to deny his belief in God are sacramental actions that display the inevitability of salvation despite man's refusals. Where Flannery O'Connor stresses the action of God upon man, Updike stresses the movements of man toward the Transcendent.

Both Updike and O'Connor insist upon the union of the temporal and the eternal in their view of human existence. Updike's characters yearn for this union as an integration into a greater reality; O'Connor's characters on the other hand show a great reluctance to face the divinely transcendent. The significant factor is that behind O'Connor's novels lurks the historical reality of Christ's death on Calvary. As a result, the meeting of the eternal with the temporal causes a wrenching in her character's lives as powerful as the tearing of the soul from the body in death. If any fact of Christianity lurks behind Updike's novels, it is the historical reality of Christ's resurrection.[24] Drawn toward opposite poles of the one reality, Updike creates rituals of harmony and Flannery O'Connor creates rituals of violence.

So then, the ritual actions of *The Centaur* normally bring man into contact with God not in a direct fashion, nor through the mediation of the institutional Church, but through the *visibilia et invisibilia,* the humanly attainable and humanly transcendent which are contained in God's creation. Caldwell and Peter can face the inconceivable because they are sensitive to a sacral universe. Through the re-enactment of his father's life, Peter gains insight for his continued wrestling with the problems of love and existence, time and death. Through recognizing the resonances between the Greek myth of Chiron and his father's life, Peter receives the energy to embrace "the joy of struggle, the satisfaction of compassion, the triumph of courage" (28). In his memories, his father has become a mythic hero like Christ or Chiron, who has offered his life as a sacrifice for others.[25] In return for this sacrifice, Peter understands, his father received a new life and a new freedom. With his present insight, Peter can do the same.

The sacral universe necessary for these actions cannot be realized unless we admit the validity of the mythic consciousness, for the author and his characters; our judgment of *The Centaur* radically depends on the acceptance or rejection of this point. For the mythic consciousness always implies an act of belief. It gives to man the sense of all nature, from its highest to its lowest forms, becoming the one *society of life*, by its "constant and obstinate negation of the phenomenon of death."[26] Through such a consciousness, the *whole man* can feel dreams and aspirations and experiences. By its transformation of a particular situation into a paradigm, myth makes rite dynamic and meaningful. Without such a living myth, ritual is an empty shell.

The rejection of this type of mythic consciousness can easily follow from the kind of naturalistic bias that is insensitive to the Barthian view of heaven and earth. In my opinion, Norman Podhoretz was operating at least partially on that bias when he attacked the use of myth for George Caldwell's story. Since he misread *The Centaur* as the story of a man who commits suicide for the sake of his son, it is quite understandable that he felt some important motivation to be missing. But reading the story too literally, he saw the myth as simply creating "a fake aura of profundity" without recognizing the comic, ironic, and dramatic uses of the myth.[27]

Even granting the validity of fictionalizing the Barthian

view of heaven and earth through myth and ritual, one is still faced with the problem of whether Updike produced a successful fiction. Arthur Mizener objected to "the incoherence between the realistic novel that constitutes the heart of *The Centaur* and the mythology that is attached to it, an incoherence that would exist even if the mythology were successfully represented."[28] My own purpose in this entire chapter has been to demonstrate that such a neat division between realistic and mythic norms will do violence to our experience of this novel. Updike has successfully interwoven the mythic and the naturalistic narratives in *The Centaur,* but it is not always the same pattern that emerges. Sometimes the two narrative strings vibrate in harmony, or echo each other, or work in counterpoint, or merge into each other, as in the final chapter. In an illuminating essay on Updike's novels, Tony Tanner has suggested what may be the real failure of this novel. Updike surely wants to suggest another world which interpenetrates and exists behind this one. He successfully incorporates that world into his narrative. Yet the effect of *The Centaur* is to leave us unconvinced of this other world. The "material clutter" overwhelms the transcendent.[29]

The failure is not a failure of style or art, but a failure of vision. For Karl Barth, the relationship between heaven and earth is a sign of the covenant between God and Man. In *The Centaur,* this sign value of the world is implicit, but God is still a vague, bloodless Being, not much more specified than the Something Beyond after which Rabbit runs. The name of the Lord occurs repeatedly in conversational clichés, spontaneous ejaculations, or brief prayers of petition.[30] On various occasions, Caldwell expresses a basic trust in God's providence.[31] But the God of Caldwell and Peter is at its best not a vividly conceived, personal God. When Peter prays for his father, "the prayer was addressed to all who would listen; in concentric circles it widened, first, into the town, and, beyond, into the hemisphere of sky, and beyond that, into what was beyond" (124). The so-called atheist Peter and his father truly live within a sacral universe but have not made the final leap of faith from the humanly conceivable and humanly transcendent to the Divine. They are almost there but not quite.

Nonetheless, *The Centaur* is a high-water mark in Updike's search for meaningful ways to express religious reality in the twentieth century. It elaborates on man's perplexities and on the contradictions of our time, especially for the dedicated searcher after Truth. With greater conviction and optimism than in the first two novels, *The Centaur* declares the existence of God in our world of spirit and matter. Above all, it declares the significance of man and the possibility of love, even in the face of hardships and absurdity. Caldwell, and now possibly Peter, are willing to go beyond the pleasure-pain principle upon which Harry Angstrom operates to exercise their freedom of choice within its limitations and accept the discipline of its consequences.[32]

In the afterglow of *The Centaur* comes *Of the Farm*, which traces out the new directions to be pursued more intently in *Couples* and *Rabbit Redux*. As these new directions gather force, Updike may produce another mythic novel to express the culmination of his insight before moving still beyond.

5

SHRINE AND SANCTUARY: OF *THE FARM*

American novels in which the land itself becomes a character generally flow out of our experience in the open spaces west of the Mississippi. In the midwestern farm novels of Ole Rölvaag or Willa Cather, the land takes on the role of realistic antagonist or fructifier of life. When Alexandra Bergson of *O Pioneers!* looks to the land "with love and yearning," the land brings forth harvests of human passion and aspiration as well as of grain. Recalling his first experience of Nebraska's warm earth, Jim Burden of *My Antonia* equates happiness with dissolution into its completeness and vastness. In *The Professor's House,* Father Duchene reveals a sense of mystery around man's struggle with Nature when he speaks to Tom Outland about the former hardy residents of the lofty mesa: "Like you, I feel a reverence for this place. Wherever humanity has made that hardest of all starts and lifted itself out of mere brutality, is a sacred spot."[1] Man may be brutalized in his struggle for survival or defeated in his confrontations with the land. But more often than not, he must actively accept the earth to become a complete human person and to transcend the earth's limited yet inspiring force.

The New Mexican novels of Frank Waters and William Eastlake, less ground-tied and more aware of the sky as transcendent being, develop an "out and up" view of salvation. A kind of mysticism grows out of the meeting with the high plains and vistas of the Southwest. William Eastlake, for example, concludes *Portrait of an Artist with 26 Horses* in this manner: "They flew lightly and all together up a gaudy-thrown profusion of raging color and the sharp high scent of Indian Country until they topped out on the end of a day, on a New Mexican sky infinity of burnished and dying gold."[2] Leaving behind the physical world, the low-lying place of trials, they share in the expansiveness which is part of a religious experience.

The eastern land which is the place of action in *Of the Farm* is not the open country of Nebraska or New Mexico. It is the same compact Pennsylvania countryside which is the setting for the Olinger stories. It is not a land from which man must wrest his existence, but a fallow land of no particular use, in danger of being encroached by housing developments for suburban living. Like the Indian country of the Southwest, this Pennsylvania Dutch country is permeated with presences. It emanates a sense of transcendence and wholeness, out of its integration with the Pennsylvania sky, which an older generation could substitute for belief in God, but with which a younger generation can hardly communicate.

Filled with many of the same memories, *Of the Farm* appears to be a sequel to *The Centaur*. Joey Robinson's mother is an aged version of Peter's mother; her tales of how her father lost his money during the depression, of how she had managed the move back to the farm, of how her husband, a school teacher, and her son Joey hated the farm, are reminiscent of elements in *The Centaur*. Likewise the throatclearings, dignified gestures, and love for newspapers of Joey's dead grandfather, and the clowning, restlessness, and frantic activity of his dead father recall Peter's grandfather and father. Like *The Centaur, Of the Farm* presents an action that occurs over a weekend, from Friday through Sunday. Where one of the primary concerns in *The Centaur*

was the investigation of the relationship between the adolescent Peter and his father, a central problem in this novel is
the relationship between Joey, now in early middle age, and
his mother. Where the adult Peter was an artist with a Negro
mistress, Joey is recently divorced and now married to the
woman with whom he had been running a protracted affair.
Where *The Centaur* dealt with man's exercise of freedom in
relation to God and the sky, *Of the Farm* deals with man's
exercise of freedom more in relation to other human beings
and the earth. *Of the Farm* continues the theme of *The
Centaur,* presenting a different solution to the struggle between desiring freedom and giving love than the sacrifice
of Chiron for Prometheus.[3]

At first reading, what ostensibly happens on this particular weekend seems to warrant the accusations of thinness in
plot and evasion of responsibility so often charged against
Updike's fiction. Joey Robinson, with his new wife and her
eleven-year-old son Richard, visits his widowed mother, now
living alone on her Olinger farm. Over the weekend Joey
will mow the field which she is no longer strong enough to
do; meanwhile, his second wife and his mother will get
acquainted. Upon the arrival of Joey's reconstituted family,
Mrs. Robinson feeds them, and the adults talk into the night.
On Saturday, Joey begins to mow the field, in fulfillment of
regulations from the soil bank, but an afternoon rainstorm
forces him to stop prematurely. Richard reads, talks to
Grammy (as Mrs. Robinson tells him to call her), mediates
the minor differences that arise. Peggy prepares breakfast,
does the dishes, sweeps the house, sunbathes, and hoes.
Sunday morning, Joey and his mother go to church. On the
way home, she has one of her mild attacks, probably brought
on by the emotions which she has been experiencing this
weekend. As Mrs. Robinson settles down to rest after the
doctor's visit, Joey and his family, the field partially mowed,
acquaintances set up, bargains made, turn to the city. This
is the stuff of ordinary life colored by the pastoral lyricism
of Joey's first person narration.

Behind this deceptively static situation, however, an extremely subtle inner activity is in motion. Much of the dialogue of the three adults takes on the characteristics of the trout fisherman's technique: the devious and careful approach, the judgment on how much freedom to give, the setting of the hook before exerting full pressure. This applies to Mrs. Robinson in particular; Peggy is more impatient, blunt, and direct; Joey is usually the fish. As Joey's wife and mother catch him and pull him one way or the other, a delicate emotional balance is constantly being threatened, broken, or re-established. On the side of Joey's mother are his associations with the farm and the past; on the side of his wife are the hopes that he has for his freely chosen future life.

What further enriches this struggle over personal freedom and allegiances is its placement into a context of cyclical structures. Through the Friday-to-Sunday time span, with its freedom from the responsibilities of the ordinary work week, the novel has the potential for developing a sense of holiday similar to that which surrounds the annual poorhouse fair. This possibility is aborted, however, by the point in the cycle of the seasons at which Joey makes his return to the farm: early fall, the season of oncoming death, visible on the land and in the growing weakness of his mother. Peggy's menstrual cycle, analogous to those of the moon and earth, in juxtaposition with the notion of womanhood expressed in the Sunday sermon, emphasizes woman's role in the continuous renewal of life and the conquering of death. Finally, the physical mementos, the reminiscences, the associations which present sights and actions arouse, all lead Joey to return to the past, to the values of his former way of life. "Past relationships evoked by the farm influence present ones. Joey's father and first wife, though physically absent, . . . become palpable as sights, sounds and smells trigger Joey's memory. . . . As in James' *The Turn of the Screw,* those absent roam the house exerting pressure, influencing decisions, determining emotional alignments."[4]

While these recurrent patterns underlie the entire novel, they are muted in comparison to their use in the previous two novels. Here, these basic elements of ritual are representative of a way of life irrevocably lost to Joey. Through the use of ritual, Harry Angstrom tried to rebel against the materialistic world around him, and George Caldwell, as well as Peter, found a *modus vivendi* to meet alienation. Joey Robinson, by accepting the values of the modern world, has effectively divorced himself from the world in which his mother lives and has practically made it impossible for himself to achieve any transcendent communion through ritual.

The moment that Joey sets foot on the farm, he finds himself in a world where past and present constantly interact. His first sight of his mother is a shock to him; her movements are so slow in comparison to the young woman who had outraced his father from the barn.[5] The old pink blouse that she is wearing brings back to his mind "childhood Easters" (8). Upon entering the house, he sees the gifts that he had sent his mother over the years. Rather than give him pleasure, they confront him with his present corruption; his expensive gifts have been cheap substitutes for the giving of his love (15). With each of his visits home, Joey has increasingly resented the pictures of himself, the schoolboy gifts and certificates on display: "I was so abundantly memorialized it seemed I must be dead" (15). He cannot shake the impression that "the invisible mementos and objects around me seemed gathered into the intense expectance of the votive implements in a shrine" (42).

One of the most vivid presences in this "shrine" to the past is that of Joey's first wife, Joan. He immediately notices that a formal portrait of her, which had been taken twelve years ago at his mother's request, had been removed from its usual place on the living room wall. But when he puts Richard to bed that evening, Joey discovers the picture above the bed. Attempting to evade Richard's question about the "attractive girl" on the wall, Joey can only shakily explain,

" 'This house is too full of me' " (19). Coming downstairs with the image of Joan still fresh in his mind, he finds himself comparing his mother's inferior position at the sink with Peggy to the dominant position in housework that she insisted upon with Joan (27-28). When his gaze returns to the photograph while he is talking with Richard on the second night, it takes on the character of a religious picture: "She seemed engaged in some vigil, her eyes uplifted, her arm glowing; and it seemed unlikely that her hope, whatever it was, would be rewarded here in this old lonely farmhouse" (126). This saint-like after-presence of his first wife is similar to the remote, inward, and cool beauty suggestive of romantic poetry that attracted him to Joan in the first place (109).

Although there are no photographs of Joey's father, his presence is also very real. Shaving with his father's razor on Saturday morning and nicking the curve of his jawbone just as his father often did, Joey enters into communion with his father in a way that he had never experienced before. He gets into his father's skin, remembers the sheepish smile with which he used to come down the stairs, realizes for the first time that his father's clumsy shaving "was one of the many small self-abuses with which my father placated the specter of poverty" (49-50). The sharpness of the knives in the kitchen, while surprising Joey, also reminds him that his "father had cared about knives and tools, and might have made a good craftsman had he not been expected, like me, to work with intangibles" (108).

Everything about the house leads Joey back to the past. Even something as insignificant as "a rhomboid of sun mottled with the slightly shivering shadows of grape leaves" on the kitchen floor strikes a resonance in him. "This patch of sun had been here, just this shape, twenty years ago, morning after morning" (50). When he is removing his wet clothes upstairs, he feels that he is in "a glade of ghosts" (99). The spot on the floor where his grandmother had last fallen invokes her death. The window through which his grandfather had watched for the mailman gives substance to the old man. But the most powerful reminder of his past life in this house is the type of conversation that will also be significant on this weekend: "Talk in our house was a continuum sensitive at all points of past and present and tirelessly harking back and readjusting itself, as if seeking some state of equilibrium finally free of irritation" (29).

In such an atmosphere, Joey feels himself being pulled into the mythology which his mother has created for the values that have meaning in her life and for the kind of life that she wants Joey himself to remember and continue. He understands the complexities of her thinking: "As primitive worshippers invest the indifferent universe with pointed intentions, so my mother superstitiously read into the animate world, including infants and dogs, a richness of motive that could hardly be there—though like believers everywhere, she had a way of making her environment supply corroboration" (23). He also realizes that Peggy, who shares nothing of their past life, cannot possibly be in sympathy with this thinking: "My mother within the mythology she had made of her life was like a mathematician who, having decreed certain severely limited assumptions, performs feats of warping and circumvention and paradoxical linkage that an outside observer, unrestricted to the plane of their logic, would find irksomely arbitrary. And, with the death of my father and my divorce of Joan, there was no inside observer left but myself—myself, and the adoring dogs" (31).

Joan and his father have been drawn into his mother's platonic esthetic of Nature and Art. As his mother reminisces about the experiences that he and his first wife shared on this farm, however, Joey is startled to discover that his mother is incorporating him in her myth in such a way that it will separate him from his present wife who is very different in character from Joan (25). To avoid this distancing, he attempts to qualify her words and later, after a scene in which his mother deliberately smashes some dishes, he also suggests that she smash all the pictures of himself with which she has filled the house (119). In a sense, his present life with Peggy demands an annihilation of his past.

Central to Mrs. Robinson's mythology is the special attitude which she bears to the farm. The house itself has become a kind of shrine to her dreams for Joey. More significantly, the entire farm is not just a tract of unused land; it is a sanctuary, a sacred place. At his first glimpse of the unused land, young Richard poses the crucial question that has often tempted Joey to have the land sold, "What's the point of a farm nobody farms?" (4). Told to ask Mrs. Robinson that question, Richard receives an unexpectedly pleasant answer. " 'Why,' she said rapidly, 'I guess that's the point, that nobody farms it. Land is like people, it needs a rest. Land is just like a person, except that it never dies, it just gets very tired' " (24). For Mrs. Robinson, as for the mothers in "Pigeon Feathers" and *The Centaur,* the farm has a living quality; man and the soil mutually mirror each other, though man will not live forever. Even more, the farm is her sacrament, her means of communication with God, her handle on human wholeness: " 'If I couldn't see and touch Him here on the farm, if I lived in New York City, I don't know if I'd believe or not. You see, that's why it's so important that the farm be kept. People will forget that there could be anything except stones and glass subways' " (70).

Stimulated by the boy's fascination, Mrs. Robinson even weaves a fantasy in which she and Richard will develop the farm into a "*people* sanctuary" for refugees from the trials of modern existence (71). Still later on Saturday, when Richard speaks of his boredom in the city, Mrs. Robinson expresses the pleasure, tinged with nostalgic sadness, which she experiences in the rhythms of the year on the farm: " 'Well I don't wonder,' my mother said, 'living in that air-conditioned city where the seasons are all the same. Here on my farm every week is different, every day is a surprise' " (110). In fact and fantasy, the farm is "a kind of resonator of the sacred" for Mrs. Robinson.[6] It is a center in the middle of chaos. It is a fixed point in the "formless fluidity of profane space." It makes possible communication between heaven and earth. It gives wholeness and orientation to those who are open to its beauties.[7] This Nature religion, a fusion of Mrs. Robinson's vague notion of God and her dedication to the land, is an inheritance from which Joey has excluded himself through his life choices. He is no longer able to "touch" God.

As the weekend wears on, two confused motives emerge for the clashes that Mrs. Robinson precipitates: the fear of her approaching death and her distaste for Peggy. In her utopian people sanctuary, Richard was to "mark the diseased people for destruction." When Peggy remarks that it sounds more like a concentration camp, Mrs. Robinson reacts with the tearful remark that " 'people must be told when they're no longer fit to live, they mustn't be left to guess at it, because it's something nobody can tell herself' " (71-72). Coupled with the fear of her physical death is Mrs. Robinson's frustration over the death of her dreams for Joey. She wanted him to leave Olinger, to become a poet, to stay married to the esthetic Joan. In the parrying between Mrs. Robinson and Peggy, Joey's mother "swept forward with a fabulous counter-system of which I was the center, the only child, the obscurely chosen, the poet, raped, ignorantly, from my ideally immaterial and unresisting wife and hurled into the shidepoke sin of adultery and the eternal damnation of my children's fatherlessness" (135). Mrs. Robinson is convinced that Peggy will bring about her death in the next twelve months as well as the destruction of her son Joey. In his eagerness to mirror and answer his mother's fright at her coming death, Joey finds himself agreeing with her: *"Ruin.* It pleased me to feel myself sinking, smothered, lost, forgotten, obliterated in the depths of the mistake which my mother, as if enrolling my fall in her mythology, enunciated: 'You've taken a vulgar woman to be your wife' " (140-141).

Just as Mrs. Robinson has created her own mythology, through which she incorporates her son into her own private demesne, so Peggy also has her own mythology. She appropriates Joey through her sexuality. Her opposition to the life-style of Mrs. Robinson becomes clear when Peggy asks Joey's mother what she gave her husband in return for the farm that he self-sacrificingly gave her. Peggy is angered by Mrs. Robinson's answer that she gave her husband his "freedom" because she considers this a failure to possess Joey's father; "it had touched the sore point within her around which revolved her own mythology, of women giving themselves to men, of men in return giving women a reason to live" (31). As Howard Morrall Harper, Jr., has pointed out, Peggy's mythology is akin to D. H. Lawrence's idea of sexual polarity.[8] Her gift to Joey has been "to let him be a man." Finally, in the climactic contest of words between the two women on Saturday evening, all the points of Peggy's dissatisfaction with Mrs. Robinson as a woman, wife and mother, merge in one massive complaint: "My mother had undervalued and destroyed my father, had been inadequately a 'woman' to him, had brought him to a farm which was in fact her giant lover, and had thus warped the sense of the masculine within me, her son" (134).

Peggy's belief that women are to give themselves to their men and that men are to possess their women finds concrete expression in her marital relationship with Joey. While Joey always felt as if he were smothering in sexual intercourse with Joan, with Peggy he feels a sense of "pelvic amplitude," of sky, space, and freedom (8, 47). Peggy is truly his possession; her largeness is a sign of his weath. Joey takes pride in his ownership, and Peggy apparently discovers a renewed purpose for life in the way he takes her (33, 62-63). During their adulterous affair, she had already explained to him how he succeeds where her husband McCabe failed to make her feel like a woman. *"You act as though you own me. It's wonderful. It's not something a man can do deliberately.*

You just do it" (82). So then, both Peggy and Joey interpret sexual possession as a freeing agent. The platonic ideals
of Joan and McCabe are smothering in the bedroom.

These clashing mythologies, the sacrality of the land and
sexual polarity, underlie the resentments which Mrs. Robinson and Peggy feel toward each other and which occasionally burst into verbal differences. Much of the tension, however, simply grows out of misunderstandings and misinter-
pretations, innocent enough, even foreseeable to Joey. When
Mrs. Robinson speaks of her own father as "a pretty ugly
customer," Peggy feels obliged to remark how fond Richard
is of his father. Her failure to see Mrs. Robinson's use of the
word *ugly* as a term of endearment irritates Joey (22). The
ideological differences come through more clearly in conversations such as the one about Joey's father. Peggy cannot
accept "the frame of assumptions and tolerances in which my
mother's description of my father's anguished restlessness as
'his freedom' was beautifully congruous" (31). Puzzled, she
can only ask a further question, "Can you give a person
freedom?"

Under Peggy's frontal attacks, Mrs. Robinson's barbs have
to give way to more direct statement. When Joey's mother
attempts to get Peggy's permission for Richard to drive the
tractor with the gently sardonic question, " 'How can Richard
manage my people sanctuary if he can't drive a tractor?' ",
Peggy cuts in with a gratuitously ruthless reflex, " 'He's not
going to manage anything for you. He's not going to be
another Joey.' " With her subtlety crushed, Mrs. Robinson is
reduced to the weak reply, " 'Dear Peggy, one Joey is enough
for me' " (92). Even when Mrs. Robinson speaks of Joey's
three children by his previous marriage, whom she is convinced she will never see again, Peggy accuses her of trying
to needle Joey and herself (104-105).

Mrs. Robinson does have her moments of ascendancy,
however. When she feels that Peggy is jealous of the relationship that is growing between herself and Richard, she boldly

states her grievances about Peggy: "She takes my grandchildren from me, she turns my son into a gray-haired namby-
pamby, and now she won't let me show this poor disturbed
child a little affection, which he badly needs!" (112). Although Peggy strives to maintain the upper hand by a remark
about Mrs. Robinson's treatment of her husband, Joey's
mother manages to sink Peggy into tears with the counterthrust: " 'Poor Joan had ideas as to how I should do my
wash, but at least she never offered to revise my marriage
for me' " (112-113). At this point, Joey, who normally
remains a passive observer of the conflict, comes to his wife's
aid: " 'You ask for advice, for pity. You carry yourself as
if you've made a terrible mistake. You pretend you emascu-
lated Daddy and when some innocent soul offers to agree
with you you're hurt' " (113).

So the tensions emerge, grow, break forth, and subside.
They reach a kind of climax on Saturday evening when Mrs.
Robinson deliberately breaks some dishes in the kitchen
because she hears Richard whispering in the living room.
No longer attempting any subtleties, Mrs. Robinson speaks
out of her frustration: " 'I'm tired of being hated. I've lost
everything but this child's respect and I don't want him whispering' " (117). Peggy, just as tired of what she terms "so
much neuroticism," decides to return to the city that very
evening. Within an hour's time, however, Richard convinces
his wife to stay and, between eight-thirty and ten, the two
women engage in the kind of conversation that was the purpose of the visit, even though its tone restlessly moves from
disagreement to peaceful reminiscence. The dialogue, as Joey
the non-participant (reading a book) perceives it, is a quest
into the past for the identities of himself and his father: "Two
exasperatingly clumsy spirits were passing, searching for, and
repassing one another; deeper and deeper their voices dived
into the darkness that was each to the other, in pursuit of
shadows that I supposed were my father and myself" (134).
In this clash of personalities and mythologies, each is testing

her own freedom, attempting to curtail the freedom of the other, being forced to recognize the other's freedom in the end.

While Joey seems to be the subject rather than an agent of the conflict, it is through his sensibility that we experience the entire weekend. Through his narration we become aware of his own conflicting emotions as well as of the rivalry over him. He is convinced that his mother had ruined his first marriage, and he wants her to be polite to Peggy on this visit (43). In bed with Peggy on the first night, he blurts out the resentment which he feels against his mother: " 'I'm thirty-five and I've been through hell and I don't see why that old lady has to have such a hold over me. It's ridiculous. It's degrading' " (45). He is still not free of his mother; neither is he totally secure in his wife. One of his fears, re-newed after he learns that Peggy had intercourse with McCabe after their divorce, is that he had been tricked into marrying someone that McCabe was glad to discard (94). He also senses a certain lack of accommodation toward his mother's foibles on Peggy's part. In the "collision of dark-nesses" of which the Saturday evening conversation is com-posed, he feels that his "mother's darkness was nurturing whereas Peggy's was cold, dense, and metallic. Surely in be-coming my wife she had undertaken, with me, the burden of mothering my mother, of accommodating herself to the warps of that enclosing spirit" (135).

He sees the farm as a trap and a menace to this marriage. But he also comes to appreciate the farm as a symbol of his mother's freedom, of the freedom she thinks that she has given him, and of their common heritage.[9] On this weekend, Joey responds to his participation in nature with the breath-lessness of a primitive man, despite his avowed dislike for the farm. At an outside pump, he enters into mysteries beyond Olinger: "I drank from the tin measuring cup that my mother had carelessly left on the bench one day and that under the consecration of time had become a fixture here. Its calibrated

sides became at my lips the walls of a cave where my breath
rustled and cold well water swayed. Against my shut lids the
blue sky pressed as red; I would gladly have drowned" (66).
Here Joey evokes a symbolism often noticed in modern times.
Louis Bouyer has remarked that "modern psychologists have
rightly insisted upon the relationship of this sacredness of
grotto and spring with a longing for the Maternal Womb, for
Mother Earth and the maternal waters."[10] A similar sense
of enchantment, with sexual overtones, overcomes Joey when
the rain begins to fall upon him in the field (96). Everything
speaks to him a language beyond the material: "Moving in
air, I feel even dust, which makes me sneeze, as the sofa's
angel, and pollen as immanent flowers" (99).

The central episode of the novel, in which Joey early
combines the two mythologies, is the mowing of the meadow,
a simple physical act which is also "a complex symbol of filial
piety, the sexual act, the fulfillment of seasonal rhythms and
the foreshadowing of the death of the mother."[11] On the
night before the mowing, Joey reflects upon his wife in terms
of possession of earth and sky. Peggy, "surveyed from above,
gives an impression of terrain, of a wealth whose ownership
imposes upon my own body a sweet strain of extension;
entered, she yields a variety of landscapes. . . . Over all, like
a sky, withdrawn and cool, hangs—hovers, stands, *is*—is the
sense of her consciousness, of her composure, of a non-
committal witnessing that preserves me from claustrophobia
through any descent however deep" (46-47). Joey then floats
into a dream that used to recur while he was considering
divorce from Joan. In the dream Peggy, "so in love with the
farm and so eager to redeem, with the sun of her presence,
the years of dismal hours I had spent here," brings joy to
his existence on the farm (48). In dream and reflection,
redemption and wholeness are his through Peggy.

These thoughts influence Joey's reaction to the actual mowing. The manner in which he attacks the job amounts to a
rite of war, of taking possession of the land. His mother

imitated the motions of love when she mowed the field, tracing its borders in an embrace and ending with a small central triangle of grass. Joey slices up the middle "in one ecstatic straight thrust" and then whittles away at each side with various maneuvers. He becomes so completely and intimately absorbed in his rhythmic movements that his communion with nature is transformed into communion with his wife:

Black-eyed susans, daisy fleabane, toadflax, goldenrod, butter-and-eggs each flower of which was like a tiny dancer leaping, legs together, scudded past the tractor wheels. Stretched scatterings of flowers moved in a piece, like the heavens, constellated by my wheels' revolution, on my right; and lay as drying fodder on my left. Midges existed in stationary clouds that, though agitated by my interruption, did not follow me, but resumed their self-encircling conversation. Crickets sprang crackling away from the wheels; butterflies loped through their tumbling universe and bobbed above the flattened grass as the hands of a mute concubine would examine, flutteringly, the corpse of her giant lover. The sun grew higher. The metal hood acquired a nimbus of heat waves that visually warped each stalk. The tractor body was flecked with foam and I, rocked back and forth on the iron seat shaped like a woman's hips, alone in nature, as hidden under the glaring sky as at midnight, excited by destruction, weightless, discovered in myself a swelling which I idly permitted to stand, thinking of Peggy. My wife is a field (58-59).

Although Joey does not touch God, the sexual transcendence that he feels comes very close to a union with the cosmos. This experience makes it possible for Joey to attempt a harmonization of the farm with his marriage later in the novel.

Joey attends the Sunday service with his mother for much the same reasons that Harry Angstrom or David Kern in "Churchgoing" attends liturgical services: to regather himself and to renew old ceremonies (148-149). The youngish minister, reminiscent of Reverend Eccles, preaches a sermon that offers Joey the possibility of touching God through Peggy as his mother touches Him through her farm. With Genesis 2:18 as his text, the minister presents an exegesis of the creation of Eve, in the course of which he makes several

points about the nature of women: that Man and Woman
were put upon earth, "not, as some sentimental theologies
would have it, to love one another, but to *work* together"
(150); that Woman, taken *out of* Man, is less than equal to
man; that Woman, made *after* Man, is the finer and more
efficient creation; that Woman is the life-principle for death-
oriented Man:

A rib is rounded. Man, with Woman's creation, became confused
as to where to turn. With one half of his being he turns toward her,
his rib, as if into himself, into the visceral and nostalgic warmth
wherein his tensions find *r*esolution in *dis*solution. With his other
half he gazes outward, toward God, along the straight line of
infinity. He seeks to *solve* the riddle of his death. Eve does not.
In a sense she does not know death. Her very name, *Hava,* means
'living.' Her motherhood answers concretely what men would answer abstractly. But as Christians we know there is no abstract
answer, there is no answer whatsoever apart from the concrete
reality of Christ (162).

What the minister further suggests is a recognition of
differences, of a necessary partnership in the performing of
God's work on earth. Woman in her very existence reminds
man of his responsibility to be kind as well as to be strong
and to believe. Adam, in naming Eve, accepted this responsibility and tied himself ethically to the earth. In identifying
Peggy with "a field," Joey has staked out his property, he
has tied himself to the earth. Whether he has accepted the
concomitant ethical responsibility is questionable. When his
mother interprets the sermon as an excuse for some woman's
pain, he changes the subject.

As mowing the field stirred in Joey the desire to own it
instead of selling it, so the possibility of lingering on to care
for his sick mother after her attack excites him. He sees the
farm as numinous. When Peggy disrupts this vision with the
practical suggestion that his mother will probably need a
trained nurse, he suddenly and angrily realizes that in reality
he will be unable to harmonize his newly found love for the
farm with his love for Peggy: "I knew it was by accident that
she had come between me and my momentary vision of the

farm, the farm as mine, in the fall, the warmth of its leaves and the retreat of its fields and the kind of infinity of its twigs. . . . But my failure to be able to see both her and the farm at once seemed somehow a failure of hers, a rigidity that I lived with resentfully, in virtual silence, until at two-thirty promptly the doctor came, smelling of antiseptic soap and sauer-kraut" (170).

In the end, even at the bedside of his mother, Joey's thoughts irresistibly turn to New York, the city of his escape. The weekend was marred by quarrels and now, his mother's attack. The mowing remains unfinished. In his last words, using their old allusive and teasing language, Joey speaks to his mother of *our* farm. Non-committal about what he will do with the farm after her death, Joey pretends the weekend has changed nothing of the past. An equilibrium is set. But he knows that he cannot contain both Peggy and the farm, so he is simply evading his true feeling and the decision he has already implicitly made.

The loss of things from his past life haunts Joey throughout the novel. When he notices the geraniums on the window sill of his mother's bedroom, he realizes that their existence depends on his mother's care, and he feels "a thousand such details of nurture about to sink into the earth with her" (167). This sense of loss had already permeated his dream on Saturday night. While mowing in the dream, Joey nicks something that he fears is a nest of pheasant eggs. Upon investigation, he discovers it to be his son Charlie from whom he is separated. But he does not become aware of this at once and sees only "a stunted human being, a hunched homunculus, its head sunk on its chest as if shying from a blow" (146). When he finally recognizes his son, he vows never to be parted from him. Yet in real life he is.

In this sense of losses, *Of The Farm* is a sad and tragic story. Kenneth Hamilton has expressed it well:

It is not merely that Mary Robinson, who is "of the farm" and of the rich, natural life that it represents, is left alone to die, deprived

of grandchildren who might inherit the land she loves. The tragedy
is Joey's, who has by his own decision lost his past and given away
his children. He recognizes that he cannot "see" both Peggy and
the farm at once, so he gives up the farm. Change and death are
inevitable on a farm; but there is continuity there, and mutual
support between the generations. Joey has lost the right to say
"our" of anything. He cannot say to Peggy that Richard is "our"
child. He cannot share a common past with her—he does not
even know the circumstances that led to Peggy's divorce. . . . The
links that tie us to nature and to one another have all been broken, and the faith that alone supports human values has been
made impossible. Joey, the frog who seeks a treasure, has, all un-
knowingly, sold it cheap.[12]

The drive for power, the pride of possession, has replaced
the drive for love and sacrificial sharing in Joey Robinson.
"As he has been possessed by a doting mother, he wishes to
possess, to own others, not for the sake of loving but for the
sake of having. There is nothing in his experience which
demands giving."[13] In his progress toward freedom, he discards one thing after the other. For all practical purposes,
he has discarded any sacred commitment to God. By divorce,
he has discarded his personal commitments to his first wife
and children, though he still has bad dreams about them.
He discards the shackles of the past with which his mother
tries to bind him. He discards an ideal, transcendental view
of life for an earthy sexual view.

In theory, then, this is a novel about freedom. Peggy is
the way of escape for Joey from his past, from the world of
the farm and from his first wife. But one captivity is simply
exchanged for another. Peggy does not offer any real alternative to his mother, as this weekend makes clear.[14] Both women
are struggling to gain dominance over Joey, the one through
the myth of the sacred past, of Art and Nature, the other
through the myth of male ownership. Peggy, through the
denigration of her own personhood in this myth of male
sexual dominance, controls by submission. The openness and
freedom which she gives Joey is a temporary illusion.

Joey and Peggy are members of the self-indulgent new

generation. They are affluent, selfish, sensuous people who easily confuse sexual attractions with a need for freedom, who disregard the needs of others to do what they please. They *exist,* and Updike presents them for what they are. They are not seekers after truth like Harry Angstrom, with whom they otherwise closely identify. They are not too concerned with the meaning of life like George and Peter Caldwell. They cannot truly love, because they do not give unselfishly. "The search which in the earlier novels gives leading characters purpose and direction and keeps them afloat above a hell of hopelessness is not present here."[15] Joey does not understand that *freedom from* is an illusion unless it includes *freedom for.* He is a new kind of leading character for Updike's novels.

Rachael Burchard has considered the characterization of Joey a flawed production in which two distinct voices emerge: the voice of John Updike the narrator in Joey's poetic insights and sensitivity to nature, and the voice of Joey the actor in his banal dialogue and insensitivity to human emotions and need. As a consequence, she finds the characterization incredible but suggests that the problem could have been solved if Updike had employed an omniscient point of view instead of first person narration.[16] For me, the disparity between Joey's thoughts and actions is quite acceptable for the simple reason that a sensitivity to beauty in Nature by no means leads automatically to a sensitivity for human beings. A sensitivity to others demands a willingness to care, to sacrifice, to give. Joey responds to beauty only so long as it makes no demands on him. He is not as emancipated from his mother's platonic idealism as he thinks he is. Neither is he as loving as the wife with whom he is sexually infatuated leads him to believe.

Finally, then, the significance of ritual is less obtrusive and more subtle in *Of the Farm* than in any of the previous novels. In the cyclical rhythms of nature with which Mrs. Robinson is in harmony, the total pattern of the universe is presented to us. Her mythology as well as Peggy's, with their opposing views of giving and receiving, is clear enough. What is missing, however, is the sense of celebration that Harry Angstrom craves and through which George Caldwell is able to face life with joy and strength. Although Joey's ritual taking possession of the farm approaches this sense of celebration, there is never any question of his communion with any ultimate reality. "The ceremonial gesture of cutting the weeds is only an evasion of his duty to accept the responsibilities of love."[17] He has freely chosen a way of life in harmony with the contemporary world. As a consequence, he refuses to accept any responsibility for his past or for his family, and the refusal kills any ceremonial connection between himself and tradition. The question remains—and it will be given full attention in *Couples*—can belief in heaven persist at all once man has rejected the right order in creation?[18]

6

THE CHURCH OF CHAOS: *COUPLES*

While *Couples* is probably the most widely read Updike novel to date, it has also received the harshest treatment from the critics. Among the failures for which the book has been attacked are a shallow concern for the human predicament, a "falsification of American life," flat characterization, and most of all, a capitulation to a shoddy, pastel-colored pornography.[1] In 1968, my own reaction to the novel was one of confusion and disappointment. I could sense that *Couples* was in harmony with the vision of America in the Pennsylvania novels, but were all these orgasms necessary? I was willing enough to enter into the dull experience of these very jaded affluent people for the sake of insight, but wondered if Updike hadn't betrayed his artistic integrity for the easy rewards of pornography.

Without much gusto, I nevertheless concluded that there was a valid point to the apparent pornography and that Updike was successful in depicting one of the moral dead-ends modern America was choosing to enter. With that I consigned the book to collect dust. In the context of 1972, however, *Couples* holds up remarkably well. After the radical shifts in our abortion laws, after triple-X movies and the voluminous literature about female orgasm, the sexual elements of *Couples* seem quite muted. With this perspective, the characters move into center-stage, credible in their sadness or tempered happiness. Despite their childishness, perhaps because of it, these Americans gain our concern. Foxy's anguish over her decision to have an abortion is poignant, just as Angela's pain when she discovers the full truth about her husband's affair with Foxy. Situations which seemed contrived at first reading seem less so on further reading, once the experience of the novel has penetrated. The gray tones of the novel are not flaws in Updike's art but necessary for the scene which he is presenting: "The reason for suburban life is isolation from the poverty, misery, and noisomeness of the human race; its aim is security, placidity, likemindedness. The end is flatness. . . . It is not Updike's failure but his achievement that the couples are flat, and yet even in their flatness human beings."[2]

Ritual plays a significant role in the lives of these couples, but with quite different outcome than in the earlier novels. As a lead-in for this discussion, a consideration of "The Music School" will be helpful, since I believe that the view of the world which underlies *Couples* is a subtle extension of the more direct statement made in this short story.

The locale of the short story is the basement of a Baptist church where Alfred Schweigen is waiting for his daughter to complete her weekly music lesson. Meanwhile, he reflects upon some apparently insignificant happenings of the past twenty-four hours, upon the musical and religious experience of his past life, and upon the present direction of his life. At a friendly gathering the evening before, a young guitar-strumming priest had explained the rationale behind the production of thicker Eucharistic wafers; this morning Alfred had read a newspaper account of a former acquaintance's senseless murder in his home. The priest's explanation had hinged upon a return to the literal meaning of Christ's words, *Take and eat:* "The word is *eat,* and to dissolve the word is to dilute the transubstantiated metaphor of physical nourishment. This demiquaver of theology crystallizes with a beautiful simplicity in the material world; the bakeries supplying the Mass have been instructed to unlearn the science of a dough translucent to the tongue and to prepare a thicker, tougher wafer—a host, in fact, so substantial it *must* be chewed to be swallowed."[3] By reflecting upon this bit of information in relationship to the newspaper item about the man shot at his dinner table, Alfred begins to sense a connection: "I perceive in the two incidents a common element of nourishment, of eating transfigured by a strange irruption, and there is a parallel movement, a flight immaculately direct and elegant, from an immaterial phenomenon (an exegetical nicety, a maniac hatred) to a material one (a bulky wafer, a bullet in the temple)."[4]

While this theme is struck in variations at key points of the story, for the moment Alfred turns his attention to the sights and sounds around him—"hints of another world." Thinking of his own difficulties in attempting to master an instrument in relation to the ease with which the priest had played and to the hopefulness with which his eight-year-old daughter approaches her lessons, Alfred views the process as a cycle: "How great looms the gap between the first gropings of vision and the first stammerings of percussion! Vision, timidly, becomes percussion, percussion becomes music, music becomes emotion, emotion becomes—vision. Few of us have the heart to follow this circle to its end."[5] His daughter, only beginning this cycle, usually returns to him with a feeling of satisfaction, "as if the lesson itself has been a meal." He loves driving her home "through the mystery of darkness," a task which is his because his wife has a regular appointment with her psychiatrist at this time, because of his infidelity to her. As before, Alfred must say: "I do not understand the connection, but there seems to be one."[6] The music of his life is off-key.

Having reached an impasse with these thoughts, Alfred drifts into reflections on his own psychiatrist's comment that he needs to humiliate himself, something that Alfred connects with the confessions that were part of the Lutheran communion services of his adolescence. He relives the ritual: the sounds, the reception of *"the true body of our Lord and Saviour Jesus Christ,* given unto death for your sins," the strained look that he saw upon the faces of the other participants in this mystery while he held the wafer in his mouth. "And it distinctly seems, in the reaches of this memory so vivid it makes my saliva flow, that it was necessary, if not to chew, at least to touch, to embrace and tentatively shape, the wafer with the teeth."[7] In his own earlier experience, as in the priest's theologizing, the nourishment, the refreshment, the victory over sin and death that comes from sharing in the life of Christ, demands some active participation and commitment from the suppliant.

Recalled to the present, Alfred knows that he is neither musical nor religious. The irruptions of the immaterial into his life have struck no chords, caused no transubstantiation. In this failure, he has a bond with his contemporaries: "My friends are like me. We are all pilgrims, faltering toward divorce. Some get no further than mutual confession, which becomes an addiction, and exhausts them. Some move on, into violent quarrels and physical blows; and succumb to sexual excitement. A few make it to the psychiatrists. A very few get as far as the lawyers."[8] From his recollection of one such woman, who entered last night, saw the priest, took two steps backward, regained her composure, then moved forward, Alfred gains the coda for the fugue that he has been composing, just as his refreshed daughter emerges from her lesson: "the world is the host; it must be chewed." To conquer death day by day, life must be accepted actively and hopefully, not allowed to melt in the mouth.

From this full-bodied use of Christian ritual to lead Alfred Schweigen to an active acceptance of life, one comes to the peculiar use of ritual to underline the completely secular outlook of the ten couples whose life together is related in

Couples. The common element between the novel and the story is still nourishment and refreshment. Sex, the meal of sharing each other, is the Eucharist of this group. More than ever, the world is the host to be chewed. Here the movement from an immaterial phenomenon to a material one goes from the search for love or the fear of death to sexual intercourse. The description of Alfred's acquaintances as pilgrims moving toward divorce is a fair description of these ten couples, too. Infidelity and consequent psychiatric sessions form part of the pattern for the pilgrimages of both groups.

On the dustjacket of *Couples* we are told that "the circle of acquaintance is felt as a magic circle, with ritual games, religious substitutions, a priest (Freddy Thorne), and a scapegoat (Piet Hanema)." At the very outset of the action, Angela repeats to her husband Freddy Thorne's opinion about the couples: " 'He thinks we're a circle. A magic circle of heads to keep the night out. He told me he gets frightened if he doesn't see us over a weekend. He thinks we've made a church of each other.' "[9] Updike's original intention had been to write a short story about a group of couples operating like a volvox, like an organism which creates behavior and makes demands upon the individuals within it. To work out the configurations necessary for such a complex organism, he had to expand the story into this novel. And here is the way in which he conceived the evolution of such social organism: "The ménages in the book are meant to be seen within the large ménage, of people who know each other, who are asked to know each other *really,* to accept and forgive each other in an almost psychoanalytical way. Friendship edges into group therapy. Group therapy hardens into institutions, miniature churches or cells."[10]

One of the bonds among the couples is a "conspiracy of mutual comprehension" which the Hanemas betray at the end (431). In its beginnings the liaison between Frank Appleby and Marcia Little-Smith appears to be "a conspiracy to praise the absent" (113). At a party, Foxy ministers with words to

the worried Ben Saltz (231). This new church, grounded in
pretexts and evasions, depends upon psychical and physical
interpenetration for its rites. Necessarily introspective and
inner-directed, such a group looks to itself for its ideals or
myth to live by. "Duty and work yielded as ideals to truth
and fun. Virtue was no longer sought in temple or market
place but in the home—one's own home, and then the home
of one's friends" (106). Choosing to close themselves off
from the larger world around them, these couples improvise
an easy companionship and substitute "a circle of friends and
participation in a cycle of parties and games" for the forms
of the country club, for the "rigid marriages and formalized
evasions" of their parents.

An indication of how completely these couples have become disattached from the outside world is their attitude
toward the news items which they learn from television or
Time or the daily newspapers. Matters like the sinking of
the *Thresher,* the downfall of Diem, the presence of Pope
Paul in Jerusalem, the initiation of a peace conference over
Vietnam are no more integrated into the narrative than they
are into the lives of these ten couples. They might chit-chat
about these items at a cocktail party, but really don't care to
become actively involved with large social or political issues.
There is only one liberal activist among them, Irene Saltz.
Even the death of President Kennedy cannot put a halt to their
weekly party; only Piet feels the need for "some ceremony of
acknowledgment to gallant dead Kennedy" (203). Outside
happenings deflect off the pleasure-seeking lives of these couples. They exemplify the epigraph from Paul Tillich: "There
is a tendency in the average citizen, even if he has a high
standing in his profession, to consider the decisions relating to
the life of the society to which he belongs as a matter of fate
on which he has no influence—like the Roman subjects all
over the world in the period of the Roman empire, a mood
favorable for the resurgence of religion but unfavorable for the
preservation of a living democracy."

In a sense, by taking us from Palm Sunday of 1963 through the next Spring, Updike gives us the liturgical cycle of this church. The ritual following of the seasons through basketball, tennis, touch football, and skiing serves as "an inexhaustible excuse for gathering: a calendrical wheel of unions to anticipate and remember, of excuses for unplanned parties" (108). At the parties, games of sport naturally evolve into word games like "Ghosts" or "Truth" or "Impressions" or "Wonderful," whose greatest danger and interest is the exposure of the individual (240). Like Professor Dalrymple in Robert Penn Warren's "The Unvexed Isles," who made a hollow ritual out of his Sunday afternoon parties, these couples come together to escape responsibility and evade the unpleasant.[11] Through these fun-gatherings, they develop a feeling of community; a rhythm is set up by which each is available to the other. But such demands, based on connections of play and divorced from the work life, cannot be maintained for long without being destructive.[12]

Most of the men work in highly specialized fields like biochemistry or miniaturization for space programs, professions which are difficult to explain to others or guarded by secrecy. Generally, these men view their work as a pact with the meaningless world, something which must be done to support their fleeting pleasures (139). Their leisure does not grow out of their work as part of the rhythm of a full life, and so it turns into license. Piet, an old-fashioned man, voices nostalgia for an earlier America, in which his Dutch-speaking parents found satisfaction in their work and lived simple lives. In this town of play, the oldtime craftsmen Adams and Comeau, and Piet himself, are "foiled by mass-production techniques and dehumanizing mechanization."[13] Foxy herself

was to experience this sadness many times, this chronic sadness of late Sunday afternoon, when the couples had exhausted their game, basketball or beachgoing or tennis or touch football, and saw an evening weighing upon them, an evening without a game, an evening spent among flickering lamps and cranky children and leftover food and the nagging half-read newspaper with its weary portents and atrocities, an evening when marriages closed in upon themselves like flowers from which the sun is withdrawn, an evening giving like a smeared window on Monday and the long week when they must perform again their impersonations of working men, of stockbrokers and dentists and engineers, of mothers and housekeepers, of adults who are not the world's guests but its hosts (73-74).

Fun and play, divorced from meaningful adult work as it is for these couples in Tarbox, produce only absurdity and ennui and malaise. With such shallow rituals, which only temporarily satisfy needs, the group is doomed to death, to destroy itself, from its very beginnings. In the same way, the game of baseball and life itself lose meaning in Malamud's *The Natural* when Roy sells out, when he ceases to relate the game to suffering and love, and the team falls apart.

More than anything else, *Couples* is a book about the game of sex. Foxy remembers her first affair, with the Jewish Peter, as a game where she enjoyed being used and abused as his toy (262). In focussing upon the transitoriness of his affair with Foxy when he desires to terminate it, Piet considers that "they had been let into God's playroom," and now "the time had come to return the toys to their boxes" (323). Piet Hanema the builder has affairs with Georgene Thorne, Bea Guerin, Carol Constantine, and the pregnant Foxy Whitman. Freddy Thorne demands a night with Angela Hanema for arranging Foxy's abortion. The sexual games of the Applesmiths and Saltines gain major prominence in chapters two and three. Practically every affair ends in dust and several marriages are destroyed, but Piet's final marriage to Foxy is still a "happily ever after" ending.

This game of sex, more than the other elements of play within *Couples,* participates of the nature of ritual not only because of its patterned repetitions but also because of its mystic and lyrical qualities. The language itself in which this

sexual behavior is presented is not clinical but lyrical, rhythmic, and ritualistic. Given the amoral quality of life in
Tarbox and its focus on pleasure, the sacralization of sexual
activity per se is a natural consequence. Oral sex in particular becomes a fumbling attempt to solve the painful problem
of dualism. "Mouths, it came to Piet, are noble. They move
in the brain's court. We set our genitals mating down below
like peasants, but when the mouth condescends, mind and
body marry. To eat another is sacred" (435). If knowledge,
which is articulated by the mouth and tongue, is the key to
salvation, then fellatio and cunnilingus become serious attempts "to join symbolically the flesh to the spiritual vehicle
of salvation."[14] The prevalence of such actions should not
be viewed as esthetic embarrassments, but rather as indica-
tions of a strong American drive toward a healthy paganism:
"to regain unity with our bodies, our sexuality, our passions."[15] They are an attempt to heal the fragmentation
brought about by our Manicheism. They may be a travesty,
but not a parody, of the eucharistic sacrament by which the
Word made flesh enters into communion with man.

Rudderless because they have found their parents' concept
of God inadequate for their needs, these people decide that
there is no God. Only two persons, Piet and Foxy, are prac-
ticing Christians, but by the end Piet feels that he has lost
faith and Foxy defiantly declares herself "a Christian living
in a state of sin" (434). Freddy Thorne cannot believe in
the Christian Church, one of the comic things of the Western
world (146). Much of Christ's sermons is looked upon as
terrible advice (140). Nobody, not even Piet, believes the
tired old tales of the Bible (346).

With no divinely transcendent reality available to them,
these people must at least "humanize" themselves. People is
all they have. "Instinctively in the loneliness which results,
they seek comfort from one another. Their longing for the
assurance of a faith in *something* creeps into their games and
their conversations until they establish rituals which roughly

parallel religious worship."[16] At one of the earlier parties, Freddy Thorne articulates the myth underlying these rituals: "I love you, all of you, men, women, neurotic children, crippled dogs, mangy cats, cockroaches. People are the only thing people have left since God packed up. By people I mean sex. Fucking. Hip, hip, hooray" (145).

What these couples seek is an absolute and undemanding love. The search for God is reduced to the search for sexual fulfillment and, in the case of Piet, for an ultimate comfort. Passion becomes a substitution for the Incarnation, to reconcile spirit and flesh, good and evil. Since these people make no distinctions between "sex" and "love," the Christian concepts of morality with which they were raised become distorted. "God is love" is transmuted into "sex is god." "Love your neighbor" becomes "lay your neighbor" (140). Concern for others is narrowed to an avoidance of inflicting pain or hurt (418). Believers like Piet and Foxy, who search without knowing what they seek, accept the behavioral patterns of the nonbelievers and follow the secular code of action. "They search for an ultimate which will comfort and accommodate them, one which will remove burdens of guilt and responsibility, one which will require little or nothing in return. They want a god who is entirely permissive, who loves but does not punish, who provides but does not require tribute."[17] They expect the same kind of permissiveness from their friends, a relationship in which there is only a narcissistic sharing of comforts and toys. They shun genuine love like tooth decay, because it threatens, it smells and it hurts (145).

The sexual rites of these couples are doomed to fail because they celebrate sentimentality, not a genuine human encounter with transcendent love. Piet's notion of sacrament reveals how shallow and amorphous his religious feeling is. To him a sacrament would be "Angela and another man screwing and me standing above them sprinkling rose petals on his back. . . . Sprinkling blessings on his hairy back" (220). Such a rite cannot incarnate the divine, cannot unite mind and body except as inefficacious sign. The nourishment of such a sacrament comes not from Christ, or the host, or the world, but from candy. When Piet wants to celebrate his happiness over Foxy's delivery, he gobbles a handful of his children's candy corn (288).

The one serious opinion which Piet claims to hold pictures America's relationship to God through this same image: *"I think America now is like an unloved child smothered in candy. Like a middle-aged wife whose husband brings home a present after every trip because he's been unfaithful to her. When they were newly married he never had to give presents"* (200). When Foxy asks who the husband is, he answers: *"God. Obviously. God doesn't love us any more. He loves Russia. He loves Uganda. We're fat and full of pimples and always whining for more candy. We've fallen from grace."* The condom and the candy wrapper are the discarded wrappings of this society's futile sacraments.

What these people are attempting to create is a clandestine sexual utopia, the post-pill paradise. *Couples* is cousin to Hawthorne's *The Blithedale Romance.* Coverdale and Priscilla and Hollingsworth and Zenobia and Westervelt are in love with each other in varying degrees, just as the couples in Tarbox are. A description of Blithedale applies just as accurately to Tarbox: "Their perpetual masquerade hides their true identities from one another." Blithedale is dedicated to work, Tarbox to play; both novels question the idealism behind the communal effort. Both novelists deal with eroticism; Hawthorne by innuendo, Updike overtly. In both cases the utopian experiment eventually founders on sexual intrigue.[18]

In the utopia of *Couples,* where all sexual activity receives celebratory treatment, regardless of its moral content, how does one differentiate the genuinely ludicrous from the esthetically awful? Where religion's integration of love of God with love of others is replaced by a solemn ritual of humanistic sex, how does one differentiate sex as love from

sex as lust? What makes one coupling more authentic than
another when every coupling is an act of participation in a
sacred universe? Some critics have placed the novel's weakness in its blur of these distinctions.[19] But if the following
two perspectives are maintained in reading *Couples,* the blur
comes into focus. On the one hand, the lyrical celebrations
of "good" sex, regardless of the techniques used, are an
almost Ginsburgian affirmation of the holiness of the body,
of the need to recognize the wholeness of the body with the
human spirit. On the other hand, sex is merely a sterile
game, meant to be judged negatively, whenever these people
have divorced it from the maintenance of personal integrity,
social responsibility, and a relationship to transcendent
meaning.[20]

In an excellent critique of *Couples,* Robert Detweiler has
kept this double perspective in mind. Moreover, he has noted
the plurality of perspectives achieved in the novel through
the use of various points of view (such as editorializing
omniscient author, third person reflector, interior monologue,
dramatic dialogue) and the different perspectives assumed by
the characters themselves. "Perspective in *Couples* suggests
as its basis the atomic motions and electromagnetic force
fields of the Einsteinian universe rather than the more simply
ordered time and space of an older world picture."[21] Granting
the validity of the novel's pluralism, he also reads *Couples*
from its many different angles of plotting: the plot of fortune,
the plot of characterization, the plot of thought. According
to traditional morality, the characters steadily degenerate.
They suffer a string of losses that force them to choose without freedom new modes of living, spiritual, physical, or voca-
tional. These more or less sympathetic characters suffer because they do not see the values of marriage in a secular
world. A disillusionment grows out of their adulteries and
leads to the precarious survival of their marriages. But at
least Piet and Foxy are educated to a new kind of wholeness
or satisfaction. "Only they had ceased flirting with life and

had permitted themselves to be brought, through biology, to this intensity of definition" (342).

Piet's carpentry, Ken Whitman's biochemistry, a general concern with matter (is it chaotic or systematic?): all reveal a preoccupation with structure throughout the book. Man might make a mess of his own life's particular patterning on the social and domestic levels, but he still participates in a vaster eternal pattern, with starfish, cells, and stars, from which he cannot deviate. Intuitively, these people sometimes sense a reality beyond their comprehension and control, as Carol admits in explaining her choice of "baby's fingernails" for the game of Wonderful: " 'What a lot of work, somehow, ingenuity, *love* even, goes in making each one of us, no matter what a lousy job we make of it afterwards' " (238). In their cruel, jaded, clumsy, heartless sexual games, these couples act out a pattern rooted in the biochemical sources of life. This Updike conveys under the surface of apparent randomness in the lives of these people.[22]

Biochemistry, a manmade pattern to build a path across the chaos and unlock the pattern that underlies the universe, holds the secret of life. The irony of Ken Whitman's situation lies in the fact that he has lost his human connection with his wife while researching the various chemical bonds which hold life together (399). Nevertheless, it is in the areas of science that modern man faces the interpenetration of answered and unanswered questions. It is in these areas, where men like Ken probe the metabolism of starfish and "chlorophyll's transformation of visible light into chemical energy" to reverse decomposition and death, that modern religion could articulate a meaningful myth for today (95). " 'If a clever theologian ever got hold of how complex it is, he'd make us all believe in God again' " (33).

Unable to bridge the gap between their answered and unanswered questions for lack of any such myth, these people search outside themselves for a solution to the problem of dualism which can be solved only within themselves:

Because there is no understanding of the essential coupling of flesh and spirit in each individual, in our contemporary Western society lonely halves of couples go around seeking to find the other half that shall make a complete self, as in the myth expounded by Aristophanes in Plato's *Symposium.* The perverse and desperate sexuality of Tarbox is the result of the illusion that man is embarked on the quest to discover an original sexual wholeness lost by the fall into the flesh. From such a perspective life is a pit of sadness out of which there can be no escape except through death, though people try to recover their lost innocence either by pretending that they can enter post-pill paradise or by traveling to the Virgin Islands.[23]

On these islands, Foxy remembers past *"lovemaking as an exploration of a sadness so deep people must go in pairs, one cannot go alone"* (451). This inability to walk alone, which Foxy transcends at the end of the novel, is the basic mistake of these modern Americans, the core of their loss of nerve.

Before moving into a discussion of how this loss of nerve is concretized in the guilts of Piet, it can be noted that *Couples* joins other modern novels like D. H. Lawrence's *The Rainbow* or *Lady Chatterley's Lover* and Hemingway's *For Whom the Bell Tolls* in its pagan celebration of ritualistic sex. After rejecting Skrebensky in *The Rainbow,* Ursula Brangwen discovers a transcendence of modern industrialism, a union with the cosmos and a renewal of life in her marriage to Birkin. In *Lady Chatterley's Lover,* Connie, who was caught in a marriage with a living dead man, is brought back "in touch" with life through the tender sexual ministrations of the crude gamekeeper, Mellors. For Robert Jordan in *For Whom the Bell Tolls,* sex brings a cleansing, an answer to *nada,* an ecstasy, a union with the cosmos. When Maria thanks him for helping her enter *la gloria,* he realizes that she is talking of the kind of mystic joy found in El Greco or St. John of the Cross. Intangible, it is nevertheless as real as the earth's revolutions around the sun (380).

Piet and Foxy stand comparison to Mellors and Connie. Piet the hired man helps Foxy escape from a husband who is just as dead as Clifford because he has compartmentalized his emotions for the sake of science. And Foxy helps Piet face death in a way that Ursula helped Birkin. But the earlier novels seem strangely naive and innocent in their celebration of sex when placed against *Couples*. Here sex does not produce the joy and ecstasy found in Lawrence's and Hemingway's novels. The optimism about discovering human wholeness through sexual activity is now seriously questioned. Sex itself is reduced to a mechanical act of minimal pleasure in a dehumanized society, as Philip Roth has also portrayed it in *Portnoy's Complaint*. Such activity does not serve as a quest for the transcendent, as it did in *Rabbit, Run*, but rather as an antidote for boredom and emptiness.

With no belief in God and consequently in an afterlife, sex becomes a defiant worship of Death itself. With the kind of fearful, superstitious belief in a wrathful God which Piet harbors, sex becomes a quest for an answer to death. Virile Piet spends all his energy in negating death, while impotent Freddy accepts Death as the only God that exists (370). By actively propagating his nihilistic belief and presiding over its rites, Freddy Thorne becomes the "king of chaos" for these people, the "local gamesmaster," the priest of this Church of Death. Like the old man and the old waiter in Hemingway's "A Clean, Well-lighted Place," he is a celebrant of *nada*.

One of the ways the couples evolve a common identity is through their rejection or tolerance of Freddy (32). They loathe him for his crude remarks but are also fascinated. They delight in the word games which he organizes at their parties. He takes the fate of them all to be "suspended in this one of those dark ages that visit mankind between millennia, between the death and rebirth of gods, when there is nothing to steer by but sex and stoicism and the stars" (372). Dressed in "sacerdotal white," he prods his dental patients to confess, to get their guilt off their minds, since it is "good for the soul" (358). But Freddy's "antiseptic truth" is sometimes frightening to these people. They would rather suffer the pain of toothache than face the possibility of losing the tooth (241).

When Freddy arranges the abortion for Foxy, Piet mush-mindedly interprets his action as "probably the most Christian thing" he ever did, as an act of love for his friends (398). But Freddy has his price: one night in bed with Piet's wife Angela. When he cannot get aroused by Angela, who to his disappointment is just as fleshly as any other woman, he spends the night talking to her about his god, "Big Man Death," whom he smells every day between people's teeth. Death literally gives him orgiastic delight; " 'death is being screwed by God' " (370).

In opposition to Freddy's excitement over rotting enamel and his drilling at people's vulnerabilities, in opposition to Angela's cool appreciation of Freud's notion that we all "carry our deaths in us," Piet is unwilling to adjust to the fact of irreversible decline. He seeks a footing in the sliding. One night he has a dream of a plane crash which fills him with dread for days: "Piet thought, *The waste*. Such ingenious fragility utterly betrayed. The cost. The plane streamed straight down. . . . He knew there could be no pulling from this dive and awoke in darkness, convinced of his death" (256). Insomniac after this nightmare, he is overwhelmed by a fearful vision of death, evocative of the chorus's lines in Eliot's *Murder in the Cathedral*. As remedies for his fear, he turns to erotic images, to prayer, to the thought of Foxy's healing touch. Her belief in him, her adoration of him, is the only thing that carries him through his terror. Later on, reflecting upon the starlight which pierces the darkness for aeons, he feels that his gaze, then his death, will move outward in a similar eternal straight line. He experiences a gigantic slipping, a sinking upwards, that makes him grip the earth and Foxy more firmly (272).

Piet's promiscuity results in both the strengthening of his fear of death and the allaying of it: "He loved any woman he lay with, that was his strength, his appeal; but with each woman his heart was more intimidated by the counterthrust of time. Now, with Bea, he had made a ledge of guilt and hurled himself secure into the tranquil pool of her body and bed. . . . Death no longer seemed dreadful" (336). Searching for life in his sexual encounters, Piet only manages to produce death. When he makes Foxy pregnant, he calls upon his fierce God to kill the fetus: "In Foxy's silken salty loins he had planted seed that bore his face and now he wished to be small and crawl through her slippery corridors and, a murderer, strike. God forgive. No: God do. God who kills so often, with so lordly a lightness, from diatoms to whales, kill once more, obliterate from above, a whip's flick, a finger down her throat, erase this monstrous growth. For Thine is the kingdom" (346). But the abortion is only a convenience, an attempt to hide the truth. The closest Piet comes to any genuine acceptance of death is the truth that he recognizes in the drug-dilated eyes of John Ong, dying of cancer, of "how plausible it was to die, how death, far from invading earth like a meteor, occurs on the same plane as birth and marriage and the arrival of the daily mail" (428).

In all the general decay and waste at least two human activities can hold out temporarily against inevitable dissolution—building and love.[24] Building, giving form to space and enclosing it with fine workmanship like that of Adams and Comeau, is a way to fend off the void. But the ultimate defense against entropy is in the act of love. In man's desire to take up the mirror position with woman, life continues and is renewed. "She was double everywhere but in her mouths. All things double. Without duality, entropy. The universe God's mirror" (52). Such images of couples or pairs, of narcissistic mirrors, of symmetry and repeated patterns, permeate the novel to produce an effect of double vision, of two worlds or of a person turning in on self.[25]

Piet is also double-minded, another ambivalent Updikean character, and in that lies the source of his obsessive guilt. His belief in God does not rest on any commitment to Him; his willingness to procure Foxy's abortion and his Don Juanian movement from woman to woman reveal that. His actions clearly proclaim him a hedonist. Rather, his belief is really a twitch emanating from his fears. He cannot quite face the truth that he no longer lives by a belief in God, and yet he still clings to an unresolved emotional residue that includes fear and punishment, a sense of implication in evil, and an uneasiness about his own dishonesty.

One of the realities which Piet has never been able to accept has been the death of his parents on an icy Michigan road; he clings to their memory by punishing himself: if he had been with them, the combination of events would have been different and they would be alive (318). Ever since then, Piet feels the struggle to live as an effort to maintain balance on a slippery road or to keep from falling through thin ice.[26] He never feels fully at home in the cozy "why not?" atmosphere of the post-pill paradise (91). He feels his life as a "crusty knot in his chest where betrayal had compounded betrayal" (353). One of the reasons for his chronic insomnia is guilt over the web of duplicities which he has woven to conceal his affairs: "He itched to thump Angela awake: the desire to confess, to confess his misery, his fornication with Foxy, rose burning in his throat like the premonition of vomit" (273). The WASH ME sign marked in the dust on the tailgate of his pickup truck is an ironic confession of his need for cleansing from guilt, a plea to a silent universe (80).

Even stronger than the sense of personal guilt is the vague guilt which expects punishment regardless of the individual's action. By our birth we are already implicated in evil, as Harold tells Janet at the beginning of their affair: " 'We'll all be punished no matter how it goes. That's a rule of life, people are punished. They're punished for being good, they're punished for being bad. . . . People are even punished for doing nothing. Nuns get cancer of the uterus because they don't screw' " (136).

We all share in the original sin of Adam and Eve. Janet Appleby justifies her adultery with Harold as a pattern of vengeance for the affair between Frank and Marcia. She thinks to undo the wicked apple with a kiss, but in the end their liaisons degenerate into a cynical *ménage à quatre* of convenience, and their morality into a concern about being caught by the others (154, 157). Piet too shares this fear of being caught. He also views Foxy as the Eve who introduced him to sin: "She had demanded that he know. Straight string of his life, knotted. The knot surely was sin. Piet prayed for it to be undone" (376). In an ironic reversal of values, the myth of Eden is being replayed in Tarbox. Piet and Foxy are by no means innocent in the same sense as Adam and Eve. They live in Sodom, an illusory paradise, not in Eden. The immediate cause of their banishment from Tarbox is a disregard for its unspoken rules. Ironically, their expulsion is a salvation. They recognize the deceptions and hypocrisies of Tarbox, the lack of warmth and honest communication. Piet becomes released from a morality of neurotic guilt. On the ground of honesty with each other, they can begin a new life tempered but not paralyzed by the past.

Tristan-like, Piet had thought to allay his fear of death and longing for the infinite by marrying Angela, an ideal woman who would embody his nostalgia for the unchangeable part of himself "which is in Heaven, forever removed from change and corruption." But Angela, this Tristan's Iseult, is an "unattainable woman who vanishes at the instant she is possessed.[27] Life with Angela became an attempt to tolerate the intolerable, to deny what cannot be denied—the passing of time and inevitable death.[28] Piet's accumulation of unresolved responsibilities and painful emotions translated itself into a diffuse sense of guilt. Guilt fed on his illusory attempt to reconcile Christian belief with hedonistic amorality. In one of the love letters that Foxy sent him, she analyzed his malaise in this fashion: *"Sometimes I think you underestimate God—which is to say, you despise the faith your fear of death thrusts upon you. You have struck a bad bargain and keep whittling away at your half"* (265-266). Only when he is convinced that God has withdrawn from him, only when he is forced by circum-

stances and Foxy's honesty, does Piet become freed from the
chains of guilt. At the end, married to Foxy, it is possible for
him to live with a degree of happiness because he is no longer
paralyzed by guilt.

Piet is a man who does strange things to hurt himself
(199). He recognizes himself as a scapegoat type who wants
to be laughed at (318). He is a passive man who does not
take control of his life but just lets things happen (412). With
these qualities added to his sense of guilt, Piet becomes a
natural victim for the other couples who purge themselves in
his own suffering. Even before his fall, Tarbox had a way of
feeding off the misfortunes of anyone who could not play the
game without getting caught. When Ben Saltz lost his job and
the rectangular arrangement between the Saltzes and Con-
stantines broke down, nasty gossip about them linked couple
to couple. Piet expected Ben to be destroyed by this expulsion
from the group, but was shocked to discover Ben acting like
"a man who deserves a holiday like any other, who had done
something necessary and was now busy surviving, who—Piet's
impression was—had touched bottom and found himself at
rest, safe" (255). One could fall into the pit and come out
alive.

After the exposure of Piet's affair with Foxy and his expulsion from his own home, he lives in fear but is at least re-
deemed from Freddy Thorne's spell. Freddy is no longer a
threatening priest of atheism; he is simply a dentist in a material world (407). Without forcing the comparison to a
sacrificial victim, Piet's downfall can be seen to have a sober-
ing effect upon the couples. Although they avoid him for fear
of contamination by his failure, they are still awakened to the
consequences of the games with which they have been tinker-
ing. They return to their children, and they reject their sexual
and psyche-probing rites for a more neutral sort of gathering:
"One night, when once Freddy would have organized a
deliciously cutting psychological word game, to 'humanize'
them, they drew up two tables and began to play bridge"
(456).

For Piet and Foxy, the three days of intense sex which they share at the end of the novel are a purgation from the suffering that their former passion and guilt have caused and a destruction of their narcissism, of the hold of the Tristan and Don Juan myths over them. No longer in love with love itself, they celebrate the reality of their inescapable love for each other. No rite of reconciliation with the divine or of union with a cosmos secularized by technology, their sexual encounter nevertheless ritualizes the newfound honesty toward which they have been directed through their affair. Although Piet and Foxy had both been dishonest with their first mates, there is the chance that they will be more authentic in their living with each other. "The new vision suggests that freedom of choice is more basic to such authenticity than the institution of marriage."[29]

Honeyhaired Foxy had been caught in a marriage that was not really of her own choosing; after her break-up with her Jewish lover as a young girl, everyone, especially her mother and father, felt that Ken was just the man for her. She finally faces her mother with her dissatisfaction just before her baby is born: " 'You ask me about Ken. I think what's wrong with him is that I didn't choose him. You chose him. Daddy chose him. Radcliffe and Harvard chose him. All the world agreed he was right for me, and that's why he's not. Nobody *knew* me. Nobody *cared*. I was just something to be bundled up and got out of the way so you and Daddy could have your wonderful divorce' " (281).

In her affair with Piet, Foxy feels that she is asserting her own identity for the first time. She has at last exercised her *"right of choice*—free of habit or command or compulsion" (262). She faces her own decisions, painful though they might be, her decision to abort Piet's baby and her decision to leave Ken. She is her own arbiter, she accepts no morality outside herself and is willing to accept the consequences (360). She also understands the tension with which she must struggle between subjugating Piet and keeping him free to act as his own person. From the Virgin Islands, where she has gone to obtain her divorce from Ken, she writes to Piet: *"You married Angela because your instinct told you she would not possess you. I would. To be mastered by your body I would tame you with my mind. Yet the subconscious spark in me that loves the race wants instead to give you freedom, freedom to rape and flee and to waste yourself, now that the art of building belongs entirely to accountants."* After a few hours, she adds to this letter, *"What I wrote this afternoon please read understanding that its confusions are groping toward truth. I am unafraid to seek the truth about us. With Ken I was always afraid. Of coming to the final coldness we shared"* (450).

Piet is less clear-headed and straightforward about what he is doing. When Angela first asks his approval to go to a psychiatrist, he panics because her better health would give him less excuse to leave her. It would be another way for her to hold onto him. He does not really want that, for "to him she was exhausted, a stale labyrinth whose turnings must be negotiated to reach fresh air and Foxy" (211). He feels "time sliding, houses, trees, lifetimes dumped like rubble, chances lost, nebulae turning," and he screams out, "Let me go!" But the scream remains locked within his heart.

When Angela makes the first move toward divorce, after several sessions with her psychiatrist and the exposure of the truth about Piet, she gives all the reasons why she wants him to leave: he adores her to escape loving her, he enjoys making her feel frigid so that he will be free to do what he pleases, she is tired of being bullied. In silence, Piet looks upon her as a messenger (angel) of the Calvinist God who "lifts us up and casts us down in utter freedom, without recourse to our prayers or consultation with our wills" (414-415). He struggles against her decision only to intensify it; that is what he really wants, someone else to choose for him. Let it be Angela. Let it be God. Not to decide is to decide. Like Joey Robinson, he temporizes until things happen.

Finally, after Piet has suffered most of the reversals that flow from his exposed adultery, the Congregational Church is struck by lightning; the fire blazes despite a heavy downpour, "as if a conflict in God's heart had been bared for them to witness." The crowd who come to gape have in the glow of storm and fire an ashen look; Sodom receives its punishment. Out of a pile of books retrieved from the Church, Piet picks up a soaked pamphlet, a sermon dated 1795, which becomes an ironic commentary on the spoiled America in which he lives: *It is the indispensable duty of all the nations of the earth, to know that the LORD he is God, and to offer unto him sincere and devout thanksgiving and praise. But if there is any nation under heaven, which hath more peculiar and forcible reasons than others, for joining with one heart and voice in offering up to him these grateful sacrifices, the United States of America are that nation* (443). Looking over the crowd, Piet watches "his wife walk away, turn once, white, to look back, and walk on, leading their virgin girls" (444). She is the wife of Lot, a pillar of salt, dead to Piet. That evening the smells of destruction permeate Tarbox. When Piet takes Carol to bed, "the bedroom, like many rooms in Tarbox that night, smelled of wet char and acidulous smoke" (446).

Several reviewers have complained that this burning of the Church is too contrived, too artificially portentous, an unconvincing resolution to the furious sinning of the previous pages. But if one keeps in mind the kind of character that Piet is, the fire does not seem overdrawn at all. It is a simple act of God, an act of Nature, which to Piet is a sign of the withdrawal he wants to see. Piet lets things happen, discovers direction in circumstance. In Angela's ouster, he reads a sign from God of his freedom from his first wife. But during the period when he lives in the garret apartment, he is still shackled by his neurotic fear-based morality. Waiting for his fierce God to remove the burden, Piet interprets the burning of the Church as a punishment, an irrevocable destruction of the past, a declaration of abandonment by God, a sign for him to move into a new way of life. The burning of the Church demands "an acceptance of fate where everyone is 'beyond all blaming'." This is a tremendous relief to Piet; he is released from his oppressive paralysis of guilt into a kind of freedom where he can choose Foxy without any qualms.[30]

The final ceremony of the novel is the removal of the weathercock from the ruined Church. The schoolchildren cheer—it sounds like "jubilant jeering" to Piet—and form a spontaneous parade before encircling the elders gathered for a photograph with the rooster, but the empty sky contains only two parallel jet trails, no sign of God's presence. While Piet is touched by this scene of joy, he also senses that the removal is a sign of a death within himself. He has died to his old style of life—his work with Gallagher, his wife and girls, his fearful strivings. The loss of Angela is a real loss, but even before he fully admitted it, Piet had wanted Foxy the most.[31]

Now he gets what he wants, and he is satisfied. But in getting what he wants, he is reduced as a significant person within a social group. He loses some of his selfhood in his gain, just as he suffers the possibility of stagnation in the relaxation of his search. Tony Tanner has put it this way:

More than any religious implications, it is this feeling which the book communicates most strongly—that to allow the self to be absorbed into the compromised environment is tantamount to losing one's selfhood (a deeply American feeling); at the same time life *in* that environment, with a well-loved wife and a well-built house, is the best antidote to that great cosmic dread and sense of universal waste which besets Updike's characters.[32]

Through an unthinking cyclical pattern of activities, these couples have attempted to fill the void in their shallow lives. Viewing the transcendent as non-existent or irrelevant to their lives, they only succeeded in communicating to each other a boredom and a lack of joy that makes this a sad book about a sad time. But there is some hope for a new world, perhaps

7

THE RITES OF DEATH: *RABBIT REDUX*

If there is any one word to encapsulate *Rabbit Redux,* it must be "O.K." Used over fifty-five times throughout the novel, "O.K." is a significant part of the dialogue between astronauts Aldrin and Armstrong which serves as epigraph to the final chapter, and it is the very last word in the novel: "He. She. Sleeps. O.K.?"[1] A word which takes on the color of its context, "O.K." generally expresses a cautious acceptance, a noncommittal *yes,* a qualified *yes* that looks with yearning to *no.* It can be an assurance or an evasion, especially of disagreement and anger, or a sign of capitulation, of a willingness to settle for less than the truth. It is a term that expresses concern as well as a laissez-faire attitude. Sometimes, it is a signal that an attack is about to begin or a signal that a conversation is to be concluded. It even gains the force of decision in some instances. As a question, it wheedles permission or approval.[2] Above all, it is a term of ambiguity. When Jill tries to conclude a quarrel with an "O.K.?", Rabbit "hesitates among the many alternatives she seems to be presenting. Laughter, anger, battle, surrender" (200).

A perfect gloss for the heavy use of this ritual word is Harry's remark: " 'Halfway isn't all the way but it's better than no way' " (131). He is a man caught between *why?*

and *why not?* When a policeman interrogates him after the fire about Skeeter's presence in his house, he tries to explain: "Why did he permit Skeeter to move in on him? Well, the question was more, Why not? He tries, 'Well, when my wife walked out on me, I kind of lost my bearings. It didn't seem to matter, and anyway he would have taken Jill with him, if I'd kicked him out. I got so I didn't mind him' " (327). Harry is a passive and self-righteous American who does not take his life into his own hands but lets it happen. He often seems an exhausted being because his energy is directed into a pessimism and a boredom produced by his refusal to make choices. This has led some of the critics to characterize him as "too passive and inarticulate to count," "too often a mere pincushion receiving the thrusts of others."[3] That is exactly the point. It is not necessarily a lack of moral focus if we are asked to care for a man whose life is a mess, a man sometimes very perceptive and sensitive and warm, at other times selfish and callous and unthinking. See this man in the middle, where we ourselves often choose to live. *Rabbit Redux* says something right about our own age.

One critic has suggested that the title of this novel is a deliberate irony, placing Everyman Rabbit against *Astraea Redux,* the return of the star, written by John Dryden to commemorate the ascension of England's Charles II.[4] Others have referred to the medical meaning of the term, "bringing one back to health," to argue for a cautious hopefulness as the basic tone of this novel. But it is just as possible that the title simply reflects Updike's desire to write a sequel to *Rabbit, Run,* further to chart the course of Rabbit's life in present-day America. Like Anthony Trollope in his two novels of political life, *Phineas Finn* and *Phineas Redux,* Updike concentrates on the social milieu in which his characters move, with merely an indication of the actual policies of national government. Both authors deal with ordinary characters and the failing of the old ways.

Ten years after he had run down that street in Brewer,

Rabbit is back with his wife Janice in a new middle-class housing development called Penn Villas, on the outskirts of Brewer and Mt. Judge. He works with his father as a linotype operator for the Verity Press in Brewer. His mother is slowly moving toward death through the involuntary shakings and hesitations of speech that accompany Parkinson's disease. The rumor that his wife is having an affair with Charlie Stavros, a Greek-American salesman with whom she works at her father's Toyota agency, proves true when Janice leaves Harry and thirteen-year-old Nelson for Stavros. In the ten years since Rabbit ran in search of the Something Beyond, he has settled into the System.

While *Rabbit, Run* was a spring book, set in the time of resurrection, *Rabbit Redux* is an autumn book. It begins in late July and ends in October, a time when the fruits of summer are collected and things begin to die. But this is also 1969, and the initial chapter is synchronous with man's first landing on the moon, July 16 to 20. As an organizing image of the novel, this event works in counterpoint to events on earth. While man takes his giant step on the moon, things are falling apart for Rabbit and America. Men watch the liftoff at the bar where Harry and his father meet each evening after work, but "they have not been lifted, they are left here" (7). In the six o'clock news that evening, all about space, Rabbit perceives nothing but emptiness, a reflection of his own life: "They keep mentioning Columbus but as far as Rabbit can see it's the exact opposite: Columbus flew blind and hit something, these guys see exactly where they're aiming and it's a big round nothing" (22).

The America which sends men to the moon is also a country of riots in the streets and war in Vietnam. Television brings the turmoil of the summer into the living room—riots and demonstrations, the on-again-off-again skirmishes in Vietnam, the Arab-Israeli conflict, the trial of the Chicago 8. Images from the public experience of America even impinge on the love-making of Rabbit and Janice after the confession of her affair:

Janice turns on the television set without sound, and by the bluish flicker of module models pantomiming flight, or riot troops standing before smashed supermarkets, of a rowboat landing in Florida having crossed the Atlantic, of situation comedies and western melodramas, of great gray momentary faces unstable as quicksilver, they make love again, her body a stretch of powdery sand, her mouth a loose black hole, her eyes holes with sparks in them, his own body a barren landscape lit by bombardment, silently exploding images no gentler than Janice's playful ghostly touches, that pass through him and do him no harm (69-70).

National rage and guilt fuse with Janice's own guilt and love and rage; national fears and dreams merge with Rabbit's own inadequacy to satisfy her appetite.

This America has replaced the Something Beyond as Rabbit's hope. By the flag decal on his Falcon and by his rabid defense of the war, Rabbit expresses his trust that America is the crown of the nations, that America will continue to shower her blessings and comforts upon the "little men" like himself who do their share to make the country great (11, 18). America is a mother who promises goodies to her children if they behave; she feeds her citizens on candy and ice cream (392). This America fills her homes and cities with plastics and neon and packaged goods, the mass-produced hamburgers of Burger Bliss. Even the narrative mirrors the fragmentation of this showy multi-media world: headlines flash through Harry's mind about his own life, news items that Harry is setting in newstype interrupt the flow of action, asterisks separate the paragraphs of discontinuous thought and action when Harry smokes marijuana.

But the American Dream is too frothy. A steady diet of sweets leads to early rot and death. Educated to want things, the young who are protesting against the war are more likely demanding "their daddy's share of the pie" right *now* (274). They share in the kind of materialism with which Updike has characterized the young in a review of Hemingway's *Islands in the Stream:* "The new generations, my impression is, want to abolish both war and love, not love as a physical act but love as a religion, a creed to help us suffer better. The sacred necessity of suffering no longer seems sacred or necessary."[5]

Mim, Rabbit's sister who is now a call girl on the West Coast, believes that the American dream of material comforts is turning the country into a desert, from the west toward the east. The rules for living in the desert are not rules for a vulnerability that makes love possible, but rules for survival. The young are preparing to live in the desert. They are trying to kill the softness of sex and love and personal property, even if they kill themselves in the process: " 'They're burning it out with dope. They're going to make themselves hard clean through. Like, oh, cockroaches. That's the way to live in the desert. Be a cockroach. It's too late for you, and a little late for me, but once these kids get it together, they'll be no killing them. They'll live on poison' " (361).

What are the rites which make life meaningful in this public and private world running down toward chaos and selfish survival? It seems that there are none. All is a dry husk. Harry has given up the search for the Something Beyond through sex; it is now at best a temporary relief of pressure. He returned to Janice to settle into the routine expectations of domestic life in America, he has taken on the role of a "responsible citizen," but in 1969 America's values are changing at a rate Harry cannot assimilate. Janice explains to Stavros that Harry " 'put his life into rules he feels melting away now. I mean, I know he thinks he's missing something, he's always reading the paper and watching the news' " (53). He has gone "pale and sour," gaining a "weakness verging on anonymity" (4).

Janice and Harry have become locked rooms to each other, and certainly one of the reasons for this breakdown in communication and love has been the terror stirred in Harry by the death of Rebecca June. That killed the possibility of reaching transcendence through sex for him. When he fled after the baby's death, the "womb and the grave, sex and death" had all seemed like a pit to him and in his return, he refused to have another baby: "sex with her had become too dark, too *serious,* too kindred to death, to trust anything that might come out of it" (36). Both Harry and Janice have vaguely connected the baby's death with the activity of God (37, 54). Harry's fear has produced boredom with his marriage for himself and a repressed anger in Janice. Part of her anger is a response to watching "a beautiful brainless guy" go dead from day to day (74). She justifies her affair because she cannot comprehend the terror which has driven him to cling to her, only feels its oppressiveness (34). Moreover, she feels renewed by her affair because Stavros loves life, makes her feel that sex is holy where Rabbit has come to hate sex, and treats her like a worthwhile person instead of the "dull dumb broad" that Harry continually calls her (63, 73).

When Rabbit first hears the rumor of Janice's affair, he is actually filled with hope. Maybe this new set of facts will break open his life, will destroy his "stale peace" with Janice (6). The ecstasy, the freedom from the nets of life, the light shining through the holes punched in reality by basketball or the stained glass window or sex have all been shut off. He needs a new rite to lead him out of the darkness of his existence but he does not search for it, only waits for it to happen.

If anything can stir Harry out of his lethargy, it is the topic of Vietnam. In the Greek restaurant on the family's night out, he enters into a rabid argument with Stavros that embarrasses Nelson. What especially infuriates him is the treachery and ingratitude of liberals like Stavros and young revolutionaries who do nothing but complain about America instead of recognizing America's attempts to bring happiness to the whole world (45). At this point in history, he sees no other alternatives but war. Little wars are better than big ones; halfway is better than no way. The religious fervor which is at the heart of his patriotism will make him quite susceptible to Skeeter later on: "America is beyond power, it acts as in a dream, as a face of God. Wherever America is, there is freedom, and wherever America is not, madness rules with chains, darkness strangles millions. Beneath her patient bombings, paradise is possible" (47). With nothing else to believe in, Harry needs to hang onto this myth.

The verbal violence which Harry demonstrates here explodes into a physical violence when he learns the truth about Janice on Saturday morning. For just a moment, when he hits Janice, a hole is punched in the darkness of his passivity. Through this action of knocking her open, he may achieve an ecstasy, the intense moment he had sought so avidly in sex ten years ago: "Harry feels a flash of pleasure: sunlight in a tunnel. He hits her three, four, five times, unable to stop, boring his way to that sunlight, not as hard as he can hit, but hard enough for her to whimper" (64). When Janice doubles over to protect herself, he is surprised by the beauty her face gains in abasement. She lets out a shriek, spits at him and screams the truth of her sleeping with Stavros.

As she shouts, Harry returns to his passivity. The light recedes in the tunnel; he silently mourns the passing of the ecstasy with the subdued violence. But he does not really care enough to fight for his wife, even when she tries to rouse his anger further. The best he can muster is a nasty remark which reveals that self-protection is his top priority: " 'No, see him if you want to. Just as long as *I* don't have to see the bastard' " (78). By refusing to face the situation between him and Janice, he gives her the final impetus to leave him.

In this week of the moon landing, there is no other ritual available to Rabbit to achieve any experience of his wholeness than this moment of aborted violence. That the America in which he lives has no remaining ceremonies to draw men together in joy is further highlighted by the marvelous set piece about the baseball game to which Harry and Mr.

Springer take Nelson that same Saturday afternoon. Even this
once meaningful American ritual has gone sour:

> The ball game is boring. The spaced dance of the men in white
> fails to enchant, the code beneath the staccato spurts of distant
> motion refuses to yield its meaning. Though basketball was his
> sport, Rabbit remembers the grandeur of all that grass, the excited
> perilous feeling when a high fly was hoisted your way, the homing-
> in on the expanding dot, the leathery smack of the catch, the
> formalized nonchalance of the heads-down trot in toward the
> bench, the ritual flips and shrugs and the nervous courtesies of the
> batter's box. There was a beauty here bigger than the hurtling
> beauty of basketball, a beauty refined from country pastures, a
> game of solitariness, . . . a game whose very taste, of spit and dust
> and grass and sweat and leather and sun, was America. . . . Rabbit
> waits for this beauty to rise to him, through the cheers and the
> rhythm of innings, the traditional national magic, tasting of his
> youth; but something is wrong (83).

The crowd is sparse, loud, coarse and unkind and murderous
in its epithets, a gathering of drunks, delinquents, bookies,
cripples, the senile. The players do their job listlessly, "spe-
cialists like any other, not men playing a game because all
men are boys time is trying to outsmart." The game does not
fill the "scared hollow" that Janice's confession has created.

The chapter ends with a birthday party for Harry's mother,
during which the truncated family gathers around the television set to watch earthman take his first step on the moon.
At that very moment, Rabbit's mother touches him in such
a way that she communicates her knowledge of his trouble.
His reply enfolds both experiences: " 'I know it's happened,
but I don't feel anything yet' " (100). Passivity numbs pain.
In the following chapters, space travel recedes into the
background but continues to serve as informing metaphor
for Rabbit's response to the bleakness of modern America.
In *Rabbit, Run,* especially in Rabbit's dream of lovely life
eclipsed by lovely death, the moon had been a source of
beauty and mysticism for him. Now space exploration has
demythologized the moon. Harry remains grounded on earth,
his "inner light trip" of ten years ago defused, and it is up

to Jill, the eighteen-year-old runaway whom Harry brings home from Jimbo's Lounge, to search for meaning and to stir the ashes of Harry's yearning for God.

Most of the sexual activity between Harry and Jill is mechanistic, empty pleasure which expresses anger or fear or frustration rather than love. One evening, Harry refuses the oral sex which Jill usually offers him. Instead, he takes her so forcefully that she gains an insight into the violence which is seething within him (163). On a Saturday afternoon in late summer, they link in a position of sixty-nine for love-less friction under a planetary television screen. "By the time she trembles and comes they are crying over secrets far at their backs, in opposite directions, moonchild and earthman. 'I love you,' he says, and the fact that he doesn't makes it true. She is sitting on him, still working like some angry mechanic who, having made a difficult fit, keeps testing it" (202). In the spirit that characterizes so many of their sexual meetings, Jill had wanted Harry to cleanse her, to "fuck all the shit out of me" (201). Such angry sex, where the other becomes a battlefield, can no longer serve the search for the transcendent. Through this mechanistic exercise, they unlock the despair deep within them and both break into tears. Jill pleads that there must be a better world than the one in which they live. Instead of the affirmation he would have given ten years ago, Rabbit simply answers, *why not?* Today he sees less chance to escape the loneliness and empti-ness of America.

As becomes more apparent during Jill's stay with him, Harry's passivity is really a cover for his fear or anger. "He had never been a fighter but now there is enough death in him so that in a way he wants to kill" (127). Under prod-ding, the cover slips away. When he thinks he is being chased across a bridge by two blacks, his fear crystallizes into cour-age; his body braces to meet the threat and he finds an exhilarating readiness to kill within him (138). When he feels defensive before Jill's disparaging remarks about his

house, he commands her to strip so he is not alone in his
fear (142). When Stavros tries to bargain with him about
Janice, he attempts to divert the discussion into an argument about Vietnam as a safe enough release for his resentments (181). When he learns that Jill has taught Nelson how
to hustle for a guitar, maybe just as disturbed to see his son
easy in underpants before her, he slaps Jill, squeezes her wrist,
verbally assaults her, wants to bomb that terrain. He hopes
to experience the flash of ecstatic light that was almost his
when he attacked Janice, but he only experiences cold fury
when she defiantly tries to get away from him and a blankness when she hisses the truth that he hurt her for his own
pleasure, not out of concern for her or Nelson or the Law
(169).

In the quiet moments between sexual encounters and emotional outbursts, Jill speaks to Nelson and Harry of her past
life: her vision of God, her hell on drugs. On the very first
night, Jill tells Harry how her former boyfriend kept her on
drugs so he could find God through her visions. In the end
he had no interest in anything at all except his next fix (145).
Harry becomes interested, questions her on the appearance
of God. But Jill will only say that once God was like the
glossy chute of a monstrous lily, before she pounces upon
him in furious oral sex (146). The idea is planted; when
Skeeter enters the picture, Harry will be ready for his rites.

In the evenings Jill speaks to Nelson of God and beauty
and meaning. When Nelson does not understand her view
that man transforms matter and spirit into their opposites,
she explains that behind the transformation is the desire to
return all of creation to its original wholeness, to a full
awareness called ecstasy: " 'Anything that is good is in ecstasy.
The world is what God made and it doesn't stink of money,
it's never tired, too much or too little, it's always exactly
full. The second after an earthquake, the stones are calm.
Everywhere is *play*, even in thunder or an avalanche' " (159).
Her vision will be repeated in Skeeter's view that a great calm

will follow the chaos of revolution. Dirt and death and distortion enter the universe through human ego, human consciousness. God's consciousness is the only untainted one; non-human things act without self-consciousness. Human matter mars spirit, distorts and refracts the divine which is faithfully mirrored in Nature. Her vision of the universe is another variation on the Allegory of the Cave.

While he listens with fascination, Rabbit considers Jill's view futile, mainly because he himself has tried that route without success. The search for the light of God only led him to chaos and the neglect of responsibility: " 'I once took that inner light trip and all I did was bruise my surroundings. Revolution, or whatever, is just a way of saying a mess is fun. Well, it *is* fun, for a while, as long as somebody else has laid in the supplies. A mess is a luxury, is all I mean' " (172). Later on, Rabbit responds in a similar fashion to his mother's advice that he leave Brewer and his wife behind, that he take care of himself and pray for his own rebirth. Rabbit can no longer slough off his responsibilities that completely. Beneath his passivity there is some genuine feeling and love for his wife and son. He feels that his mother is asking him to kill Janice, to kill Nelson, and he silently resists: "Freedom means murder. Rebirth means death" (198).

One evening, Jill recites the full story of her bout with drugs in language that rhymes, strumming her guitar for background. The presentation is so smooth that Rabbit wonders if it has been rehearsed or performed often, like a ceremony of introduction. Her nostalgic ritual, through which Jill mourns the mundane love she wanted from her lover Freddy instead of the God of death which he offered, creates an artistic elation in her. She carries the mood to bed, where she demands a kind of worship from Harry; esthetic and sexual emotions fuse to form a pattern that leads nowhere (175).

With the sudden intrusion of Skeeter, who is in hiding from the police, the situation is ready for Harry's entry into the sacramental rites of drugs and dialogue. Skeeter brings a perverse kind of life to these two whites, middle-aged Harry and rich young Jill, who have both come to the end of the road in their search for meaning, who are both dried out. The rites which Skeeter performs and into which he drags first Jill, then Harry, celebrate a mixture of love and hate, rage and liberation, death to slavery and resurrection to a new life, an ecstasy over a vision that leads to chaos. Skeeter, the anti-Christ who mixes black history with religious nihilism, is probably the most vibrant and credible black in literature written by a white man.[6] In this well-programmed novel of good sustained writing, with some of the most taut and authentic dialogue Updike has ever written, the characterization of Skeeter is a real achievement, a bold experiment which is successfully realized. He far surpasses the silent black who victimizes Mr. Sammler in Bellow's *Mr. Sammler's Planet,* another novel which attempts to "analyze the chaos of the present."[7] Malamud comes closest to Updike's success with his creation of Willie, the black man who insinuates himself into the life of Harry Lesser in *The Tenants.*[8]

For an introduction, Skeeter assaults Harry with an ecstatic ritual dance in which he hails himself as the incarnate black Jesus and mocks Harry's beliefs and racial or sexual inhibitions with taunting blasphemies and obscenities. He immediately stirs in Harry "a pit of scummed stench impossible to see to the bottom of" (208). The fear soon changes into anger; Harry has to fight his way up from the pit. Skeeter's obscene dance creates another opening in the tunnel, makes it possible for Harry to punch his way to the ecstasy he felt when he hit Janice. As Jordan found a ritualistic release for violence in the unthinking activity of killing in *For Whom the Bell Tolls,* Harry tries to discover a similar release in battering the people around him: "He is packed so solid with anger and fear he is seeing with his pores. He wades toward the boy deliciously and feels his fists vanish, one in the region of the belly, the other below the throat. . . . He wants to pry this creature open because there is a soft spot where he can be split and killed; the curved back is too tough, though knuckles slammed at the hole of the ear do produce a garbled whimper" (210-211). This whimper of submission is important to Harry; he experienced no ecstasy when Jill responded with defiance.

Guilt follows anger, the calm after the violent moment. Soon after Harry lets Skeeter slip into his life, Jill organizes the meetings of the new brotherhood—nightly sessions of structured discussions and readings to educate Harry in the new America, or more accurately, in the failings of the old America. This is necessary, Jill explains in the name of the nebulous "we," because Harry has never had the chance to reflect upon his life. He has had to work on instinct alone, since the System forced him into mindless action. As a result, with time to think only on techniques that exploited his usefulness, like basketball and printing, he has accumulated an irrelevant God and an angry patriotism and an old wife. " 'You accept these things as sacred not out of love or faith but fear; your thought is frozen because the first moment when your instincts failed, you raced to the conclusion that everything is nothing, that zero is the real answer. That is what we Americans think, it's win or lose, all or nothing, kill or die, because we've never created the leisure in which to take thought. But now, you see, we must, because action is no longer enough, action without thought is violence. As we see in Vietnam' " (228-229). So Harry will be given a chance to re-direct his life. Characteristically, he raises no great objections.

In the evening homilies that follow, Skeeter instructs Harry with his views on slavery and revolution. Fear controls relations between blacks and whites, even between the four of them, says Skeeter, a fear based on the religion of the pilgrims, which produced "the meanest most de-balled Jesus the good Lord ever let run around scaring people," and on the white man's greedy need to keep control of the

capitalistic dog-eat-dog system which he divinized after the
Civil War (242). In Skeeter's opinion, the inevitable revolution which must rock America will come not from blacks
responding to injustice, but from the children of the rich who
impatiently want the power of their fathers. In the great calm
that must follow the chaos, the new black Jesus, Skeeter or
someone like him, must use this open space to restore those
aspects of our human nature smothered by the power struggles of technology.

Rabbit receives the haranguing docilely enough, only occasionally responding to Skeeter with a cliché born of his
prejudice. Some of his docility stems from his ambivalence
toward blacks. With blacks he is physically uncomfortable
yet fascinated; prejudiced yet open to their suffering and
humanity. Before Skeeter moved into his household, Harry's
knowledge of them came only from superficial contacts at
work or television images of riot. He is willing to listen.
Now, with Skeeter in the house, even a skit from *Laugh-In*
where Arte Johnson and Sammy Davis Jr. both play the
dirty old man, staring at each other "like one man looking
into a crazy mirror," creates a moment of communion (247).
The four of them laugh together at the reflection of America,
at the reflection of their own actions in this bluish shadow,
this image twice removed from reality.

Talk heals. The readings from Skeeter's books become a
regular ritual, a structured way to open Harry's mind. But
brotherhood and communion come through marijuana. After
his first clumsy attempts at Jimbo's Lounge, and after an
initial fear of how Nelson will interpret the action, Harry
readily joins Jill and Skeeter in their nightly sacrament. Jill
holds the reefer "reverently as food" as they pass it from
person to person (231). Aside from being too passive to
resist this new element in his household's routine, Harry
latches onto this rite as a way to see Jill's God, possibly to
reach the light which has opened at the end of the tunnel
through his moments of violence. Although Harry has claimed

that the "inner trip" is over for him, his readiness to try again reveals the unresolved yearning buried deep beneath his stolidity.

As the marijuana begins to clutch at his body during the day, with a hangover worse than liquor, he vows, "Never again. Let Jesus come at him some other way" (253). Still, in the evening the smoke continues to fuse with his veins to produce a universal well-feeling toward Jill and Skeeter and Nelson, a confusion of his identity with theirs interpreted as union and love. As these smoke-and-talk sessions proceed, Jill's original orderly structuring begins to crumble. The destructive nature of the new black Jesus becomes clear, the rites turn orgiastic.

On one occasion, Skeeter feels pentecostal tongues, God's fire of cleansing and inspiration, descend upon him. In his vision, the blank ceiling vibrates, then white on white, one white hole pours out of a hole in the other. The holes are the nothingness created by an expanding universe; what comes through them is a constant renewing force of life upon the earth, God's rain. Vietnam is one of these holes, a white pustulating sore where God reveals himself to us. Vietnam is the end, the bottom of the well, and the beginning, says Skeeter: " 'It is where God is pushing through. He's coming, Chuck, and Babychuck, and Ladychuck, let Him in. Pull down, shoot to kill, Chaos is His holy face' " (261). Nelson screams to stop the vision. He wants God to stay where he is; he wants to grow up average and ordinary like his father. In answer to Nelson's cry for life, Skeeter tells him that even his father is learning, slowly, how to die, to let go. The gospel that Skeeter preaches is not a gospel of power or common sense or love, but a gospel of death, of confusion and sameness and salvation only through acceptance of himself.

Harry and Skeeter do agree on one point: one dislikes America if he dislikes Vietnam. Both see Vietnam as a face of God, as a holy place, as a death-dealing way for God to make his terrible revelation to the world. A demonic coalition rises between the two men that frightens Jill and Nelson, makes them feel as outsiders (264). In truth, Vietnam is the answer for both men's need to do violence, just as Robert Jordan discovered a myth to cover his psychological need for violence in the clichés of the Spanish Civil War. The new Jesus in which Harry is about to express his belief is a purging and liberating Jesus, the Jesus who brings the sword and releases from paralysis: " 'He will be a living flame of love. Chaos is God's body. Order is the Devil's chains' " (275). When Skeeter proclaims himself " 'the Christ of the new Dark Age,' " Harry, filled with the sacrament of sweet smoke, professes his faith: " 'I believe.' Rabbit drags on his own joint, and feels his world expand to admit new truths as a woman spreads her legs, as a flower unfolds, as the stars flee one another. 'I do believe' " (277).

Like Freddy Thorne, Skeeter is a priest of Death. He binds Harry to his church through his vision of Vietnam and Jill through drugs. Skeeter begins Jill's captivity by procuring some mescaline so that she can tell him about God. But the only God Skeeter wants to see is a mirror image of himself. When he tries to extort this vision from her in the early stages, she still does not see Jesus in him, even though she is drugged. All she sees is " 'a black crab. A chrysalis of mud' " (257). However, as she becomes increasingly dependent on Skeeter, she also becomes a "believer." She will say anything, that Skeeter is the Lord Jesus, her Savior, the one she loves more than herself, just so he will shoot the jism of heroin into her veins. Once he has drawn this perverse credo from Jill, Skeeter proceeds to prepare the needle for her rite of temporary salvation (300).

In the beginning, Rabbit makes no attempt to stop Skeeter because the possibility of Jill's visions excites him. When she calls upon him for help, to keep her free of Skeeter's clutches, his only answer is "What can I do?" He "feels paralyzed, by the rain, the thunder, by his curiosity, by his hope for a break in the combination, for catastrophe and deliverance" (252).

Catastrophe does come, in the form of heroin addiction and the fire. By the time Rabbit is ready to show his love for Jill even by some small action, it is too late. She is by then under the power of another mystic lover (301).

Only the child Nelson, with his unwillingness to see anyone get hurt, with his innocence of evil's inevitability, holds out against Skeeter. During Jill's deterioration, he calls upon his father to do something about it. Rabbit responds that people cannot be controlled in what they want to do; they have their own free wills. But Nelson cannot accept his father's laissez-faire attitude; if his father cared at all, the destruction of Jill could be controlled (292). A pattern of blame begins to grow in Nelson's mind which will break into full fury when Jill dies. A situation that might lead a believer to blaspheme turns Nelson against his father, since he has been raised to believe in nothing higher than his father's head: "Blame stops for him in the human world, it has nowhere else to go" (325).

One of the significant scenes in the downward progression of these salvific rites into orgy centers on a reading from Frederick Douglass. As Rabbit reads aloud how the young Frederick witnessed a slaveholder beating the slavegirl Esther, Skeeter tears off his shirt in a "brittle dance" and begins a violent dance of rape with Jill. She covertly enjoys the violence of their wrestling until she sees that Harry recognizes her enjoyment, then she runs upstairs. While Harry continues to read, Skeeter strips naked and stretches on the sofa to hear the words with his pores. " '*It was a resurrection from the dark and pestiferous tomb of slavery, to the heaven of comparative freedom. I was no longer a servile coward, trembling under the frown of a brother worm of the dust, but my long-cowed spirit was roused to an attitude of independence. I had reached a point at which I was not afraid to die*' " (282-283). Stirred by the ecstasy which the boy felt in pommelling the slavekeeper, Skeeter affirms his own excitement with frenzied *yeses* and masturbation.

Harry flees the room deeply aroused both by what he has

read and by what he has seen, filled with guilt, fear, and attraction. Upstairs, while Jill shivers under her growing need for drugs, Harry cannot break through the terror of the pit which his reading has opened up: "a vision of bottom-less squalor, of dead generations, of buried tortures and lost reasons. Rising, working, there is no reason any more, no reason for anything, no reason why not, nothing to breathe but a sour gas bottled in empty churches, nothing to rise by; he lives in a tight well whose dank sides squeeze and paralyze him" (284). For both Jill and Harry, everything is crashing down into the pit which Skeeter has opened.

Finally, in the interracial fellation that Skeeter sets up as a psychodrama, all the possibilities of hate and love between the races, of sexual fascination and terror at the darkness of the pit, come into focus in a most intimate form. For Jill, this is the price she will pay to get her fix from Skeeter. With Skeeter playing the white man and Jill the oppressed black woman, the fellation becomes a ritual to humiliate the white and to atone for white racism. Harry is forced to witness this atonement, enjoys playing the voyeur but cannot bring him-self to participate when invited. He is fearful of being sucked into the darkness which he felt pulling on him when Skeeter masturbated on the sofa. Significantly, the rite re-mains unconsummated, interrupted by another voyeur at the window (297-299).

These rites of rage and death, which lead Jill and Harry deeper and deeper into chaos, are reflected in the disjointed sequence of events through this entire section. Like Vietnam, this private war proceeds through holes punched in staleness. Finally, inevitably, the catastrophe which Harry expects to deliver him from the pit happens. The combination cracks open. When vindictive neighbors set his house on fire, the drugged Jill dies in the holocaust. The God of Chaos strikes again; "death is in heat" (324). Given a central viewing position among the spectators, Harry still feels "peripheral, removed, nostalgic, numb" (319). One thing becomes clear:

a love and rapport has grown between him and Nelson during these past months of waste and mess. After raging at his father, Nelson still accepts his father's silent ministrations of care while he vomits. Harry quietly holds his son from drowning; he himself would drown at this moment if he did not reach out in love (323).

After Jill's body is removed and the firemen leave, Rabbit enters his house, with smoke and mist rising. Like the smell of failure in his life, the smell of smoke will cling tenaciously for a long time, but Harry is somehow cleansed by the fire. A demon leaves him. The burning of his house has been purgative rather than punitive: not the fire hailed down upon Sodom, but the fire of Pentecost: "Flame sinks back, then bursts out again, through roof or window, in tongues: dragon's taunts" (319). Following the season of violence which engulfed Harry's hopes for a break in his life's growing sameness, the fire operates like the ritual cleansing which Anselmo, Jordan's trusty old assistant in *For Whom the Bell Tolls,* feels necessary after the bloodshed of the revolution: "If we no longer have religion after the war then I think there must be some form of civic penance organized that all may be cleansed from the killing or else we will never have a true and human basis for living. The killing is necessary, I know, but still the doing of it is very bad for a man and I think that, after all this is over and we have won the war there must be a penance of some kind for the cleansing of us all."[9]

To some extent, the fire also operates like the fires in Flannery O'Connor's *The Violent Bear It Away.* There the fire indicates "a burning clean of impure ways of seeing. Tarwater's development consists of various painful illuminations: he sees his role as prophet in the burning of the shack where his great-uncle died, he sees it in the burning lights of Memphis, and he sees it in the burning trees at the end of the novel."[10] In *Rabbit Redux,* the fire indicates a burning clean of accumulated waste, of deterioration, of impure ways of *doing* rather than of *seeing.* God acts in terrible ways in

both novels, but not with the same effect. At the end of
The Violent Bear It Away, Tarwater is ready to witness
to God's mercy in the city, after being confirmed by the
pentecostal fire of the Spirit. But Rabbit receives no great
illumination; for him the fire has simply burned a hole in
staleness, has created an open space, a great calm, in which
further life is possible.

With the burning of the house, rites that seek to allay the
deadness and staleness of life come to a halt. Harry is laid
off because the Verity Press is shifting to modern offset
processes, Mim returns for a visit from the west coast, Harry
and Janice return to each other like two lunar capsules cau-
tiously linking in space. The action winds down to a kind
of resolution.

When Mim first speaks to Harry, she understands at once
that her bumbling, warm, sentimental brother has been terribly hurt in a way that he is unwilling to share with those
who could love him. He has transferred his pain into "reserves
of resentful energy" which erupt in verbal attack or sarcasm
(360). Part of his reticence covers the anger stirred by his
caring, for his country or for his wife. A larger part of his
reticence stems from his fastidiousness, his reluctance to
reveal an inner confusion. Mim was never fastidious like her
brother, never minded things getting messed up. She has
fallen and accepts the fact that all things must fall.

During her short stay, Mim tries to get her brother to see
himself as he really is. She relays Stavros' theory to him that
" 'you like any disaster that might spring you free. You liked
it when Janice left, you liked it when your house burned
down' " (366). She tries to stir him out of the new passivity
into which he has fallen: " 'Everybody else has a life they
try to fence in with some rules. You just do what you feel
like and then when it blows up or runs down you sit there
and pout' " (370). Even going to work day after day for ten
years he did simply because it was the line of least resistance,
says Mim. For a short time, Mim's words give Harry pause,

but he soon returns to his old habit of transferring blame:
" 'Any decent kind of world, you wouldn't need all these
rules' " (373).

Meanwhile, Janice's affair with Stavros is coming to its
conclusion. Although Janice feels like "mud made radiant"
with Stavros, she is unable to elicit any permanent commitment from him. After one of their quarrels, he has an attack.
By giving all her energy to her lover during this attack, by
filling the hole made by his pain with all her emotion and
will and body, she pulls him through. She herself is healed by
her giving: "The mark upon her as a giver of death has been
erased. As in fucking, she has been rendered transparent,
then filled solid with peace" (387). But she also realizes that
her presence in Stavros' apartment creates a lack of order
that disturbs, might even destroy him. Filled with love and
peace, she understands that it is time to leave: "Spirits are
insatiable but bodies get enough. She has had enough, he has
had enough; more might be too much. She might begin to
kill" (388).

The Harry to whom Janice has decided to return is strug-
ling with an uneasy sense of responsibility for the death of
Jill. While the fire has cleared much of the detritus out of
his life, her death was the price of the cleansing. Harry did
what felt right, he acted like "a fucking Good Samaritan,"
but now shifts between guilt and justification. What had he
wanted to explain to Jill's mother after her death? "That it
was not his fault. Yet Nelson thought it was. For taking her
in? But she was unsheltered. For fucking her? But it is all
life, sex, fire, breathing, all combination with oxygen, we
shimmer at all moments on the verge of conflagration, as
the madhouse windows tell us" (346).

Part of his guilt is certainly his pain over the way in which
he failed Jill. When he sleeps late after losing his job, Jill
comes to his bed in fantasy. Her attentiveness and pensive-
ness, "her daughterly blind grass-green looking to him for
more than shelter" stirs him to tears (381). He had shut

himself off from the pain and possibility of giving her genuine human warmth. "Why? He had retreated into deadness and did not wish her to call him out. He was not ready, he had been hurt" (380). Protecting his own vulnerability, he had hardened himself against love because he was still smarting from the failures which had accumulated in his life. Too late, as with his decision to have another child, he regrets his action. A sense of sin, a sense of the burden of free will, of being allowed by God to do evil, to turn away from Him, to mess up: all fill Rabbit with a free-floating guilt still unattached to any specific responsibilities. Like so many of Updike's characters, Rabbit is a "man in the middle." Not only between heaven and earth, but also between life and death, between knowing he is criminal and never being caught, between the remorse of guilt for what cannot be undone and the fear of facing present or future responsibilities (330).

So it is a chastened Rabbit to whom Janice returns. He is not converted from his bigotry, but his picture of America is tempered because he has lived with an experience of America utterly alien to his own. On Moratorium Day he is mildly amused at his father's passion against the anti-war demonstrators instead of sharing his anger (350). He is beginning to realize that we all have a hand in the evil of the world. But he still tends to shift his own responsibilities. Even in the cautious re-linking with his wife, he tries to blame Jill's death on Janice's desertion. His wife, however, will not accept responsibility for anything he did after she left. She will live with her own responsibilities but insists that he bear his own. In this new attitude of Janice lies one reason for hope that the two of them can begin a renewed life together (395).

Another reason for hope lies in Rabbit's final confession to his wife that he feels guilty about everything. If he can localize this vague guilt, if he will face the mess which he himself has actually made and then move beyond the fear of repeating the mistake, Rabbit will begin to accept his own humanity—a mixture of good and evil, of order and chaos. He will then no longer consider himself Nobody but Somebody (404). One critic has suggested that Rabbit gets by with paying only a small price here, quite possibly because Updike wants to show that we do get off without paying immediately, that poetic justice is a fiction which we may as well do without in the twentieth century.[11] The price he pays is the price that we all must pay: the necessity of living for the rest of our lives with what cannot be undone.

Harry has learned a few lessons during the past ten years. Running gets one nowhere but back to the starting point. Freedom inevitably involves responsibility. The search for the transcendent, for the wholeness of ecstasy, does not find its answer in nature: everything wastes and rots (310). Neither is the answer in sex: " 'But all this fucking, everybody fucking, I don't know, it just makes me too sad. . . . There must be something else' " (398). But the answers are not all in yet. Rabbit has not yet discovered that God forgives us for the evil we do, that He does not demand perfect order while we live on earth, that He saves by genuine love as well as by catastrophe. Maybe he never will. For now Rabbit reintegrates. Or like a bunny nestles back into the burrow. Again. Until 1979?

8

FLESH/SPIRIT/DIVINITY

In several ways, John Updike is the Anthony Trollope of twentieth century America. Even his working habits resemble Trollope's—systematic writing in the morning, the rest of the day for other pursuits. If he maintains the pace which he has set during the past fifteen years, he will produce as prolific a canon. Both men have the ability to immerse themselves in a given sphere of life and portray it credibly. Trollope depicted the great middle class as it was in mid-Victorian times: the small gray worlds of clerics and politicians and lawyers in provincial England. Updike depicts the lower- and upper-middle classes as they live in mid-twentieth century: the circumscribed worlds of salesmen and schoolteachers and biochemists and linotypists and housewives in suburban America. As the best of Trollope's novels have considerable value for sociological insights into a mellow and tranquil age now forever past, so the best of Updike's novels may serve the same function for our restless and chaotic age.

Updike has received the same praise which Henry James bestowed upon Trollope, that "his great, his inestimable merit was a complete appreciation of the usual." Like Andrew Wyeth, to whom he has also been compared, he delights in the accumulation of details, in the momentary arrest of the

minutest things of ordinary existence which sometimes produces a sense of wonder and sometimes an impression of
brilliant surfaces over a void.[1] Beyond the surfaces of Wyeth
or the pleasant tales of Trollope, however, Updike has more
deeply scrutinized the conscience of America.

In doing so, he has written many-layered novels that cannot be judged by the standards of a rigidly naturalistic tradition. He suggested his own bent away from realism when he
reviewed Harry Levin's *The Gates of Horn:* "Prose narrative
needs to refresh itself at the springs of myth and dream. Is
this to be deplored? The contemporary attempts to shake
off the heavy spell of realism, however seemingly formless
and irresponsible, are a worthy phase of man's attempt to
educate himself through Literature."[2] In the words which he
put into the mouth of Henry Bech in "The Bulgarian Poetess,"
Updike has most likely expressed his opinion of the successes
and failures of his own technique:

> He told them, told them shamelessly, in a voice that surprised him
> with its steadiness, its limpid urgency, how once he had written,
> how in *Travel Light* he had sought to show people skimming the
> surface of things with their lives, taking tints from things the way
> that objects in a still life color one another, and how later he had
> attempted to place beneath the melody of plot a countermelody
> of imagery, interlocking images which had risen to the top and
> drowned his story, and how in *The Chosen* he had sought to make
> of this confusion, the theme itself, an epic theme, by showing
> a population of characters whose actions were all determined, at
> the deepest level, by nostalgia, by a desire to get back, to dive,
> each, into the springs of their private imagery.[3]

Many critics have criticized the countermelody of imagery
which Updike has placed beneath the melody of his plots as
too pretentious and complicated because they have artificially
severed his imagery from his plots. One reason his plots often
look thin is that he chooses to portray quiet dramatic situations of everyday suburban America, where the conflict is
often enclosed in the trivial and apparently insignificant, as
in the weekend visit in *Of the Farm,* the games and cocktail

parties of *Couples,* or the predictable daily routine of Harry
Angstrom in *Rabbit Redux.* Updike's imagery usually reveals
the small conflicts and inner workings of his characters' minds
as they act within these subdued plots. The dreams and night-
mares and daytime fantasies of his characters, as the inner
springs of their action, are perhaps even more significant
than what they do. Their inner imaginative lives are often
much more vivid than the external reality of the society in
which they live and move. In his attempts to place the strivings of the inner self in opposition to the gray outer world,
Updike is truer to life as most of us live it than those critics
who demand showiness in plot construction rather than imagery. There is even a streak of dishonesty in their criticism if
they are unhappy with Updike because he does not portray a
kind of realism which refuses to accept any kind of spiritual
reality beyond Man.

The manner in which Updike tempers his lyrical idealism
with irony and realistic detail puts him in a camp with
Nathaniel Hawthorne. Both men are self-conscious stylists
who rely on ambivalent symbolism at key points in their
narratives. The critics of both accept the short stories more
readily than the novels. Both are deeply concerned with the
residues of Puritanism in America, with the sins and guilts
of their own age.[4] Updike's vision of a world moving toward
entropy, a vision of waste that becomes most explicit in his
last novel, prevents his prose from falling into a sentimentality that Hawthorne did not always escape. Because Updike
has increasingly focussed upon the sulphur which drifts up
from the Void when we exclude the sacral from our experience, he has even been called "our chief Dante."[5]

What is unique in Updike's fiction is his continuous integration of the process, the function, and the *spirit* of ritual
to express spiritual yearning in an apparently materialistic
universe. Unlike most writers who introduce ritual into their
works, he does not take over the ready-made rites of the
established churches to provide himself with borrowed rhythms

or structures, except for occasional stories like "The Music School" and for various metaphors scattered throughout his work. Rather, he investigates the profound emotional significance of ordinary situations and actions which are inherently recurrent. Then he attempts to indicate the ceremonies, the beginnings of a new liturgy, which America is developing to perpetuate the emotional significance and make it meaningful.

No doubt at all, Updike is out to characterize his country, to map the backroads and windings by which America is choosing to evade or fumble toward the truth of life. Like Fitzgerald, he explores "what shapes and setups in the soul have bred this activity, what failures, withdrawals, lapses of nerve, fits of impatience, attacks of impotence lie there."[6] The chaos which has moved toward centerstage in Updike's work is a reflection of the chaos and tiredness and emptiness in American life. Very few of his characters "have experienced the capacity to love" and as a consequence, all the activity which they pursue seems "miserably meaningless," filled with a "central hollowness."[7] His characters will be able to love each other truly only when they get beyond sex as mechanical pleasure, beyond fear or anger as the impulse for coupling. The suggestion is there that characters like Piet, Foxy, and Harry Angstrom are learning that lesson in spite of themselves, as slowly and painfully as we modern Americans are.

The emotion which Updike has attempted to ceremonialize is simply the desire for life, usually expressed as a hope of a resurrection, of heaven, of immortality, as an anguish over the passing of time, as a craving for the divinely or humanly transcendent. The belief in God, the hope of heaven, the insistence on something spiritual beyond our crass daily existence is at the heart of Hook's and Elizabeth Heineman's actions in *The Poorhouse Fair* and of Harry Angstrom's in *Rabbit, Run*. From *The Centaur* on, however, the divine transcendent gives way more and more to the human. While George Caldwell believes in a God, his son Peter

does not and consequently searches for the courage to live
in a re-enactment of his own past, for immortality in an
attempt to combat the erosions of time. The union of the
temporal with the eternal is still seen as necessary for the
complete humanization of man. What Peter attempts to
achieve through his narration of his mythic past with his
father is "to pack the past and the future, indeed the whole
of scattered being, into the present moment—thus to possess
all things in a single instant and to demolish the narrow
gates of both space and time."[8] In his desire to freeze into
permanence an instant of illumination, Peter, while still subject to the inevitable movement of time, is trying to share in
that quality of eternity or of immortality which is best described as stasis. In terms of traditional theology, his impulse
"represents a disease of the feelings and a collapse of the true
metaphysical mind: it is a fraudulent aping of religion and
Christianity, and of that final religious idea of eternity as the
one eternal now, without sequel, and without insecurity, or
the loss of any good thing."[9]

What Peter accomplishes is a ritual relation of himself to
a finite reality instead of to an ultimate reality. In his atheism,
he still depends on what Joachim Wach calls a "pseudo-
religion."[10] Thus he joins the ranks of Conner, for whom
welfare-statism serves the same end, and Joey Robinson, his
wife Peggy, and all the couples of Tarbox, Massachusetts, for
whom "the cult of life as such or of the sexual drive," a type
of Lawrentian biologism, substitutes for any divine religion.

While this shift in the beliefs of Updike's major characters
suggests an acceptance of the death of God and the necessity
of a purely human solution to the desire for life, the mythical
dimensions of the fictional universe in which these characters
move make it clear that Updike considers their "brave new
world" empty, sterile, and inhuman. This he states explicitly
through the debate of Hook and Conner in *The Poorhouse
Fair*. He also castigates the smugness and materialism of the
middle-class society in which Harry (in *Rabbit, Run*) and

George Caldwell live through their alienation from it, their rejection of its values, their insistence on transcendent values. In *The Centaur,* however, there is again a turning-point in Updike's approach. Peter Caldwell as well as the protagonists of the next three novels, *Of the Farm* and *Couples* and *Rabbit Redux,* accept the values of the society in which they live. Yet this solution to the problem of life is also seen as unsatisfying, as leading to unhappiness and futility. Diana Trilling has remarked on this moralistic tendency in *Couples:* "Although it is a morally ambiguous book Mr. Updike has written, its first moral premise is clear enough: SEX, if not sinful in itself, is the readiest attribute or resource of life bereft of spiritual guidance and purpose. The sexuality through which corrupted or diminished spirit announces itself diminishes and corrupts the spirit yet further."[11] More and more, Updike is presenting us with images that depict a generation's loss of soul.

If the thrust for the rituals of Updike's characters stems from the desire for life, it can just as truly be traced to the fear of death. Tony Tanner has remarked that perhaps the most convincing element in Updike's fiction is "the continual presence of fear—that fear engendered by the realization that everything decays, erodes, deteriorates and dies."[12] Updike shares with other American authors like Ralph Ellison "that nightmare of formlessness, of the progressive fading of all identities."[13] The question which he poses for us, especially in his most waste-filled works, is this: Does a blind universe run down into death, or does a living God will life for it?[14]

Death raises another question. Although Conner, Hook, Harry Angstrom, George and Peter Caldwell, Joey Robinson, Piet Hanema, Freddy Thorne, Foxy Whitman, Jill and Skeeter find radically different solutions to the problem of life, all of them are attempting to answer a variation of the basic question, "If I must some day die, what can I do to satisfy my desire to live?" John Dunne, in *The City of the Gods,* has summarized the most significant answers to that question through the centuries; John Updike has clearly explored some of those same solutions in his novels:

What man may hope is not that he may escape death but that he may, notwithstanding death, satisfy his desire for life. He may hope by sharing the experience of life and death to consort with the gods or he may hope that his own experience of life will be relived by posterity, or, if he despairs of mortals consorting with immortals and of the dead consorting with the living, he may at least hope to make the most of his own life and death. He may hope by his deeds to leave an immortal past to those who live after him, he may hope to live the equivalent of everywhere and always, he may hope to survive death in his public person, he may hope for everything within the scope of an autonomous life and an autonomous death. Seeing that life is subject to disease, decay, and death, and is lived in ignorance of its meaning, it is true, he may hope to escape from life and to enjoy instead the immortality of the spirit. If he relies not upon his own knowledge and power, though, but upon that of the God to whom the dead are alive, the God who reveals himself in the risen Christ, he may hope rather to lay down his life subject as it is to evil and to take it up again released from all evil, to do what Christ spoke of when he said 'I lay down my life to take it up again' (John 10:17).[15]

People like the couples of Tarbox or Harry Angstrom and Jill and Skeeter fail dismally in their attempts to create a sacramental universe because they refuse to face the pains and sufferings of real material existence. They search for a heaven on earth, an experience of the transcendent which refuses to integrate the messy aspects of human living into the experience of the holy. The pseudo-religions of sex and drugs and revolution and messianism do not answer their craving, only lead to entropy and catastrophe. Through the inevitable movement of all things earthly toward entropy, God reminds these characters of a fact which they are unwilling to face: that in the last analysis they are not independent of Him. He is a primitive God, a fierce and terrible God, the God of thunder in *The Centaur,* the God of rainstorms and fire in *Couples* and *Rabbit Redux.* The passion for life which fills most of these characters is a sign that life continues beyond all earthly entropy, but it is a sign which only a few characters like David Kern recognize and respond to with joy. Most of these people have withdrawn from God and interpret their lovelessness as His lack.

Modern man often rejects ritual as superstition, but in all of his novels, John Updike reveals that even in twentieth century America man instinctively returns to rituals to answer his fear of death and his need for ecstasy and wholeness. Updike demythologizes our creed that man need not look beyond the human and the material. He points the way to a transcendent belief, but a belief that cannot be reached too quickly, too readily, by denying the material existence which is ours. Quick paths to transcendence tend to pseudo-religions. So he demonstrates through the Church of Freddy Thorne and the Church of Skeeter.

The holy is not an evasion of the painful, but an acceptance of pain and death which leads to fuller involvement in life *here and now:*

The world of the sacraments, the world into which the liturgy introduces us, is not a world in its own right, standing aloof from the world of ordinary living. It is rather the meetingpoint of the world of the resurrection with this very world of ours in which we must live, suffer and die. And this very fact implies that liturgical life, far from taking us out of real life, far from making us indifferent to or uninterested in real life, on the contrary positively sends us back into it in order to carry out fully in it the Mystery which has come to us through the sacraments.[16]

Instinctive rituals will usually lead to chaos and death, to tangential approaches to the divinity, if we expect them to replace the efforts of mind and will. Such rituals bring our flesh and spirit into union with the divine only if grounded in a constant search for truth and in a willingness to commit ourselves, in faith and love, to other men and women and to the divine, "with no holds barred." Once, that ground was spuriously supplied by our culture. Today, in the fragmented America in which we live, the shaping of the foundations for our rituals and for our living is the responsibility of each person's choices more than ever before. Even in the face of entropy, we can continue to love.

NOTES

Chapter 1

1. Stanley Edgar Hyman, "Chiron at Olinger High," review of *The Centaur,* by John Updike, in the *New Leader,* February 4, 1963, p. 21.

2. *The American Short Story: Front Line in the National Defense of Literature* (Boston: Houghton Mifflin, 1964), p. 70.

3. *Ibid.*

4. See, for example, "Prometheus Unsound," *Time,* February 8, 1963, p. 87; Harold C. Gardiner, "Some Early Spring Novels," *America,* March 9, 1963, p. 341; Roderick Nordell, "An Updike Mythology," *Christian Science Monitor,* February 7, 1963, p. 7; George Steiner, "Half Man, Half Beast," *Reporter,* March 14, 1963, p. 52.

5. "Norman Mailer vs. Nine Writers," *Esquire,* July, 1963, p. 67.

6. "The Myth in Action," review of *The Centaur* and *Pigeon Feathers,* by John Updike, in the *Spectator,* September 27, 1663, p. 389.

7. "The Youth of an Author," review of *The Centaur,* by John Updike, in the *New Republic,* April 13, 1963, p. 25.

8. "A Has-been, 10 Years Later," review of *Rabbit Redux,* by John Updike, in *Chicago Tribune Book World,* November 14, 1971, pp. 3, 10.

9. "Other New Novels," *New Statesman,* March 28, 1959, p. 453.

10. Donald Barr, "Ah, buddy: Salinger," in *The Creative Present: Notes on Contemporary American Fiction,* ed. Nona Balakian and Charles Simmons (Garden City, New York: Doubleday and

Co., 1963), pp. 37, 38. This presents a fuller account of the stereotype of the *New Yorker* story.

11. *New World Writing 17,* ed. Stewart Richardson and Corlies M. Smith (Philadelphia: J. B. Lippincott and Co., 1960) p. 59; John Updike, *Museums and Women and Other Stories* (New York: Alfred A. Knopf, 1972), p. 164.

12. *Conversation with John Updike,* ed. Frank Gado (Schenectady: Union College, 1971), p. 16.

13. "The Art of Fiction XLIII: John Updike," interview by Charles T. Samuels, in *Paris Review,* XII (Winter, 1968), p. 116.

14. *Midpoint and Other Poems* (New York: Alfred A. Knopf, 1969), pp. 3-44.

15. Michael Novak, "Son of the Group," review of *Couples,* by John Updike, *Critic,* XXVI (June-July, 1968), p. 72.

16. "A Comment," *Times Literary Supplement,* June 4, 1964, p. 473.

17. "The Dogwood Tree: A Boyhood," in *Assorted Prose* (New York: Alfred A. Knopf, 1965), p. 182.

18. John Updike, "More Love in the Western World," review of *Love Declared,* by Denis de Rougemont, in *Assorted Prose,* p. 299.

19. *Ibid.,* p. 287.

20. In *Pigeon Feathers and Other Stories* (New York: Alfred A. Knopf, 1962), p. 186.

21. Wesley Kort, "The Shriven Self: Christianity As a Problem in Three Recent Fictions" (unpublished Ph.D. dissertation, University of Chicago, 1965), p. 147. Also see Howard Morall Harper, Jr., *Desperate Faith—A Study of Bellow, Salinger, Mailer, Baldwin, and Updike* (Chapel Hill: The University of North Carolina Press, 1967), p. 187.

22. Kort, "The Shriven Self," p. 146, and *Pigeon Feathers,* pp. 3-11.

23. Northrop Frye, *Anatomy of Criticism* (New York: Atheneum, 1966), p. 119.

24. "The Dogwood Tree: A Boyhood," in *Assorted Prose,* p. 182.

25. (Vintage Books; New York: Random House, 1964), p. viii.

26. "The Dogwood Tree: A Boyhood," in *Assorted Prose,* p. 186.

27. In *Pigeon Feathers,* p. 245.

28. "Three Documents," in *Assorted Prose,* p. 113.

29. "Flannery O'Connor's Sacred Objects," in *The Vision Ob-*

scured: Perceptions of Some Twentieth-Century Catholic Novelists, ed. Melvin J. Friedman (New York: Fordham University Press, 1970), pp. 70-73.

30. "The Dogwood Tree: A Boyhood," in *Assorted Prose,* pp. 181-182.

31. See, for example, his "Foreword" in *Assorted Prose,* p. ix.

32. "Faith in Search of Understanding," in *Assorted Prose,* pp. 281-282.

33. Kort, "The Shriven Self," p. 147.

34. James E. Miller, Jr., *Quests Surd and Absurd* (Chicago: University of Chicago Press, 1967), p. 17.

35. In *Pigeon Feathers,* pp. 128-137.

36. *Ibid.,* p. 140.

37. *Ibid.,* p. 150.

38. *Ibid.,* pp. 213-214.

39. *Ibid.,* p. 219.

40. *Ibid.,* p. 224.

41. Frye, *Anatomy of Criticism,* p. 105.

42. Northrop Frye, *The Well-Tempered Critic* (Bloomington: Indiana University Press, 1963), pp. 71, 80.

43. In *Assorted Prose,* pp. 51-53.

44. David Darryl Galloway, *The Absurd Hero in American Fiction: Updike, Styron, Bellow, Salinger* (Austin: University of Texas Press, 1966), p. 38.

45. William Van O'Connor, *Sense and Sensibility in Modern Poetry* (New York: Barnes and Noble, 1963), pp. 16-17.

46. *Aspects of the Novel* (London: Edward Arnold, 1963), p. 148.

47. Alice and Kenneth Hamilton, *The Elements of John Updike* (Grand Rapids, Michigan: William B. Eerdmans, 1970), pp. 39, 42, 104.

48. Bryant N. Wyatt, "John Updike: The Psychological Novel in Search of Structure," *Twentieth Century Literature,* XIII (July, 1967), p. 96.

49. *Aspects of the Novel,* p. 150.

50. Richard Chase, "Myth as Literature," in *Myth and Method: Modern Theories of Fiction,* ed. James E. Miller, Jr. (A Bison Book; Lincoln: University of Nebraska Press, 1960), pp. 129, 134-135.

51. Karl Barth, *Dogmatics in Outline,* trans. G. T. Thomson (London: SCM Press, 1949), p. 51; Mircea Eliade, *The Sacred and The Profane: The Nature of Religion,* trans. Willard R. Trask (New York: Harper and Row, 1961), p. 95.

52. Frye, *Anatomy of Criticism,* pp. 106-107.

53. See Chase, "Myth as Literature," in *Myth and Method,* p. 143.

54. See Eliade, *The Sacred and The Profane,* p. 130, and Ernst Cassirer, *An Essay on Man: An Introduction to a Philosophy of Human Culture* (New Haven: Yale University Press, 1966), pp. 95, 154.

55. Kort, "The Shriven Self," pp. 143-144.

56. In *Pigeon Feathers,* p. 228.

57. *Ibid.,* p. 229.

58. *Ibid.,* p. 232.

59. *Ibid.,* pp. 236-237.

60. *Ibid.,* p. 245.

61. *Ibid.,* p. 246, and Michael Novak, "Updike's Quest for Liturgy," *Commonweal,* May 10, 1963, p. 193.

62. *Pigeon Feathers,* pp. 248-249.

63. *Ibid.,* pp. 249-253.

64. Novak, *Commonweal,* p. 194.

65. *Pigeon Feathers,* p. 256.

66. *Ibid.,* pp. 260-261.

67. *Ibid.,* p. 263.

68. *Ibid.,* p. 266.

69. *Ibid.,* pp. 274-276.

70. *Ibid.,* pp. 277-278.

71. *Ibid.,* p. 278-279.

72. *Ibid.,* p. 279.

73. (Coral Gables, Florida: University of Miami Press, 1970), p. 54.

74. Samuels, "The Art of Fiction," p. 100.

Chapter 2

1. (New York: Alfred A. Knopf, 1959), p. 223. Also see the discussion of Updike's own grandparents in the autobiographical sketch, "The Dogwood Tree: A Boyhood," in *Assorted Prose* (New York: Alfred A. Knopf, 1965), pp. 151-155.

2. John Updike, *The Poorhouse Fair* (New York: Alfred A. Knopf, 1959), p. 5. For the rest of this chapter, further reference to this book will be included in the text.

3. Whitney Balliett, "Writer's Writer," review of *The Poorhouse Fair,* by John Updike, in *The New Yorker,* February 7, 1959, p. 139.

4. J. A. Ward, "John Updike's Fiction," *Critique: Studies in Modern Fiction,* V, No. 1 (Spring-Summer, 1962), p. 30.

5. For the notions of time used in this paragraph, see Louis Bouyer, *Rite and Man: Natural Sacredness and Christian Liturgy* (Notre Dame, Indiana: University of Notre Dame Press, 1963), pp. 189-190; Mircea Eliade, *Cosmos and History: The Myth of the Eternal Return,* trans. Willard R. Trask (Harper Torchbooks; New York: Harper and Row, 1959), p. 21; Northrop Frye, *Anatomy of Criticism* (New York: Atheneum, 1966), p. 345.

6. Tony Tanner, "The American Novelist As Entropologist," *London Magazine,* X (October, 1970), p. 16.

7. *Ibid.,* p. 12.

8. *Ibid.,* pp. 11-12.

9. See William F. Lynch, S.J., *Christ and Apollo: The Dimension of the Literary Imagination* (New York: Sheed and Ward, 1960), p. 38.

10. *John Updike: A Critical Essay* (Grand Rapids, Michigan: William B. Eerdmans, 1967), p. 16.

11. *Ibid.,* p. 21. Also see pp. 19 and 22 for the preceding discussion.

12. See James E. Miller, Jr., *Quests Surd and Absurd* (Chicago: University of Chicago Press, 1967), pp. 67-75.

13. "The Art of Fiction XLIII: John Updike," interview by Charles T. Samuels, *Paris Review,* XII (Winter, 1968), p. 112.

14. (New York: Macmillan, 1966), pp. 112-121.

15. Charles T. Samuels, *John Updike: University of Minnesota Pamphlets on American Writers, No. 79,* (Minneapolis: University of Minnesota Press, 1969), p. 34.

16. Tanner, *London Magazine,* X (October, 1970), pp. 5-10.

17. Eliade, *Cosmos and History,* p. 76. For the following discussion of time, also see pp. 85 and 91.

18. "A Comment," *Times Literary Supplement,* June 4, 1964, p. 473.

19. (London: The Hogarth Press, 1948), p. 210.

Chapter 3

1. Olivia Manning, "Faces of Violence," review of *Rabbit, Run,* by John Updike, in the *Spectator,* September 15, 1961, p. 361.

2. "John Updike: Of Rabbits and Centaurs," *Critic,* XXII (February-March, 1964), p. 45.

3. Gerry Brenner, "Rabbit, Run: John Updike's Criticism of the Return to Nature," *Twentieth Century Literature,* XII (April, 1966), pp. 3-14; Larry E. Taylor, *Pastoral and Anti-Pastoral Patterns in John Updike's Fiction* (Carbondale: Southern Illinois University Press, 1971), pp. 71-84.

4. "Four Spiritual Crises in Mid-Century American Fiction," *University of Florida Monographs, No. 14* (Gainesville, Fla., Fall, 1963), pp. 20-24.

5. *The Absurd Hero in American Fiction: Updike, Styron, Bellow, Salinger* (Austin: University of Texas Press, 1966), pp. 27-40.

6. *Ibid.,* pp. 34, 37.

7. "John Updike's Fiction," *Critique: Studies in Modern Fiction,* V, No. 1 (Spring-Summer, 1962), p. 36.

8. *"Rabbit, Run,"* review in the *New York Herald Tribune,* November 3, 1960, p. 25.

9. Alice and Kenneth Hamilton, *The Elements of John Updike* (Grand Rapids, Michigan: William B. Eerdmans, 1970), pp. 142, 145.

10. Fred L. Standley, *"Rabbit, Run:* An Image of Life," *Midwest Quarterly,* VIII (July, 1967), p. 375.

11. Joseph J. Waldmeir, "Only an Occasional Rutabaga: American Fiction Since 1945," *Modern Fiction Studies,* XV (Winter, 1969-1970), p. 476.

12. *Ibid.,* pp. 476-477.

13. See Phyllis R. Klotman, "The Running Man as Metaphor in

Ellison's *Invisible Man,*" *CLA Journal,* XIII (March, 1970), pp. 277-288.

14. Walter J. Ong, "Preface," in Hugo Rahner, *Man at Play* (New York: Herder and Herder, 1967), p. xi.

15. John Updike, *Rabbit, Run* (New York: Alfred A. Knopf, 1960), pp. 5-6. For the rest of this chapter, further references to this book will be included in the text.

16. *Ibid.,* p. 135. Compare the lyricism and solemnity of this opening to a ritual passage in *The Centaur* like chapter III.

17. See pp. 106, 248, 303.

18. *Four Crises,* p. 16.

19. Howard M. Harper, Jr., *Desperate Faith: A Study of Bellow, Salinger, Mailer, Baldwin, and Updike* (Chapel Hill: The University of North Carolina Press, 1967), p. 167. For an extended treatment of this point, see pp. 167-173 of this same book.

20. Andrew Sinclair, "See How He Runs," *Time and Tide,* September 21, 1961, p. 1571.

21. Tony Tanner, *City of Words: American Fiction 1950-1970* (New York: Harper and Row, 1971), p. 280.

22. *The Word of God and the Word of Man,* trans. Douglas Horton (New York: Harper and Row, 1957), pp. 290-291.

23. *Rabbit, Run,* p. 31. A slight variation on this theme is the way in which Rabbit sees his life spreading before him as a wide and straight road during the period that he is attempting reconciliation with Janice. See pp. 205, 209, 218, 248, 284.

24. *The Sacred and the Profane: The Nature of Religion,* trans. Willard R. Trask (New York: Harper and Row, 1961), p. 176.

25. *Ibid.,* p. 178.

26. Dean Doner's "Rabbit Angstrom's Unseen World" is an excellent study of *Rabbit, Run* as an indictment of Humanism. *New World Writing 20,* ed. Stewart Richardson and Corlies M. Smith (Philadelphia: J. B. Lippincott and Co., 1962), pp. 58-75.

27. *The Word of God and the Word of Man,* pp. 287-288.

28. Tanner, *City of Words,* p. 284.

29. (New York: Charles Scribner's Sons, 1940), pp. 159, 236, 379.

30. See Elmer F. Suderman, "The Right Way and the Good Way in *Rabbit, Run,*" *University Review,* XXXVI (Kansas City, Missouri, October, 1969), pp. 13-21.

31. Rachael C. Burchard, *John Updike: Yea Sayings* (Carbondale: Southern Illinois University Press, 1971), p. 50.

Chapter 4

1. The *Dial*, LXXV (November, 1923), pp. 480, 483.

2. Robert Taubman, "God Is Delicate," review of *The Centaur*, by John Updike, in the *New Statesman*, September 27, 1963, p. 406. See also Stanley Edgar Hyman, "Chiron at Olinger High," review of *The Centaur*, by John Updike, in *The New Leader*, February 4, 1963, p. 20.

3. "Half Man, Half Beast," review of *The Centaur*, by John Updike, in the *Reporter*, March 14, 1963, p. 53. For a similar comparison, see Norman Podhoretz, "A Dissent on Updike," review of *The Centaur*, by John Updike, in *Show*, April, 1963, p. 49, reprinted in *Doings and Undoings: The Fifties and After in American Writing* (New York: Farrar, Straus, and Co.), 1964, p. 257.

4. "Pennsylvania Pantheon," review of *The Centaur*, by John Updike, in the *Saturday Review*, February 2, 1963, p. 27. Similar points of view are expressed in Phoebe Adams, "Potpourri," review of *The Centaur*, by John Updike, in *The Atlantic*, February, 1963, pp. 134-135; Eleanor Cook, "Mythical Beasts," review of *The Centaur*, by John Updike, in *The Canadian Forum*, August, 1963, p. 114; Harold C. Gardiner, "Some Early Spring Novels," review of *The Centaur*, by John Updike, in *America*, March 9, 1963, p. 340.

5. "John Updike: *The Centaur*," *Critique: Studies in Modern Fiction*, VI, No. 2 (1963), pp. 110-111.

6. Peter Buitenhuis, "Pennsylvania Pantheon," review of *The Centaur*, by John Updike in *The New York Times Book Review*, April 7, 1963, p. 26. This is remarkably close to John Updike's own view of his role as creative writer, expressed in "The Sea's Green Sameness," in *New World Writing 17*, ed. Stewart Richardson and Corlies M. Smith (Philadelphia: J. B. Lippincott and Co., 1960). Also see Thomas Curley, "Between Heaven and Earth," review of *The Centaur*, by John Updike, in *Commonweal*, March 29, 1963, p. 27.

7. Letter from John Updike, December 7, 1967. Also see "The Art of Fiction XLIII: John Updike," interview by Charles T. Samuels, *Paris Review*, XII (Winter, 1968), p. 103.

8. "Conversation with John Updike," ed. Frank Gado (Schenectady: Union College, 1971), p. 29.

9. John Updike, *The Centaur* (New York: Alfred A. Knopf, 1963), p. 17. For the rest of this chapter, further references to this book will be included in the text.

10. *Pastoral and Anti-Pastoral Patterns in John Updike's Fiction* (Carbondale: Southern Illinois University Press, 1971), pp. 88-90.

11. Jack De Bellis, "The Group and John Updike," review of *The Centaur*, in *Sewanee Review*, LXXII (Summer, 1964), 535.

12. *Dogmatics in Outline,* trans. G. T. Thomson (London: SCM Press, 1949), pp. 60-61.

13. *Ibid.,* pp. 62-63.

14. *Ibid.,* p. 64.

15. *The Centaur, p. 215.* For a similar experience in the dentist's chair, see "Dentistry and Doubt," in John Updike, *The Same Door* (New York: Alfred A. Knopf, 1959), pp. 41-50.

16. Mircea Eliade, *The Sacred and the Profane: The Nature of Religion,* trans. Willard R. Trask (New York: Harper and Row, 1961), p. 118.

17. "Conversation with John Updike," p. 13.

18. Eliade, *The Sacred and the Profane,* p. 71. For the ideas on time that are expressed in this paragraph, I am indebted to Eliade's discussion on pp. 68-113 of this same book.

19. Wesley A. Kort, *Shriven Selves* (Philadelphia: Fortress Press, 1972), p. 73.

20. For an appreciative interpretation of the comic values in *The Centaur,* see Hazel Sample Guyol, "The Lord Loves a Cheerful Corpse," *English Journal,* LV (October, 1966), pp. 863-866.

21. See pp. 92-93, 189-190.

22. In a letter of December 7, 1967, John Updike has said that the obituary is imagined.

23. Jonathan Baumbach, "The Acid of God's Grace: The Fiction of Flannery O'Connor," *The Georgia Review,* XVII (1963), p. 334.

24. See "Seven Stanzas at Easter," *Verse* (Greenwich, Conn.: Fawcett Publications, 1965), pp. 164-165.

25. Norris W. Yates, "The Doubt and Faith of John Updike," *College English,* XXVI (March, 1965), p. 473.

26. Ernst Cassirer, *An Essay on Man: An Introduction to a*

Philosophy of Human Culture (New Haven: Yale University Press, 1966), p. 84. For the description of mythic consciousness in this paragraph, I have depended on the discussion in pp. 75-84 of this same book.

27. *Doings and Undoings,* p. 256.

28. "The American Hero as High School Boy: Peter Caldwell," *The Sense of Life in the Modern Novel* (Boston: Houghton Mifflin, 1964), p. 265.

29. *City of Words: American Fiction 1950-1970* (New York: Harper and Row, 1971), pp. 286, 288.

30. See pp. 15, 71, 81, 120-121, 166, 168, 181-182, 194, 262.

31. See pp. 63, 106, 190, 204, 206, 288, 292.

32. Rachael C. Burchard, *John Updike: Yea Sayings* (Carbondale: Southern Illinois University Press, 1971), pp. 53, 61; Alice and Kenneth Hamilton, *The Elements of John Updike* (Grand Rapids, Michigan: William B. Eerdmans, 1970), p. 159.

Chapter 5

1. (New York: Grosset and Dunlap, 1925), p. 221. Also see Sister Lucy Schneider, C.S.J., "Artistry and Intuition: Willa Cather's 'Land-Philosophy'," *South Dakota Review,* VI (Winter, 1968-1969), pp. 56-63.

2. (New York: Simon and Schuster, 1963). Also see John R. Milton, "The Land as Form in Frank Waters and William Eastlake," *Kansas Quarterly,* II (Spring, 1970), pp. 106-109.

3. Larry E. Taylor, *Pastoral and Anti-Pastoral Patterns in John Updike's Fiction* (Carbondale: Southern Illinois University Press, 1971), p. 104.

4. James R. Lindroth, "Of the Farm," review in *America,* November 27, 1965, p. 692.

5. John Updike, *Of the Farm* (New York: Alfred A. Knopf, 1965), p. 7. For the rest of this chapter, further references to this book will be included in the text.

6. For this notion, see Louis Bouyer, *Rite and Man: Natural Sacredness and Christian Liturgy,* trans. M. Joseph Costelloe, S.J. (Notre Dame, Indiana: University of Notre Dame Press, 1963), p. 156.

7. Rachael C. Burchard, *John Updike: Yea Sayings* (Carbon-

dale: Southern Illinois University Press, 1971), p. 75; Mircea
Eliade, *The Sacred and the Profane: The Nature of Religion,*
trans. Willard R. Trask (New York: Harper and Row, 1961),
pp. 63-64.

8. *Desperate Faith—A Study of Bellow, Salinger, Mailer, Baldwin, and Updike* (Chapel Hill: The University of North Carolina Press, 1967), p. 185.

9. *Ibid.,* p. 183.

10. *Rite and Man,* p. 153.

11. Peter Buitenhuis, "The Mowing of a Meadow," review of
Of the Farm, by John Updike, in *The New York Times Book
Review,* November 14, 1965, p. 4.

12. *John Updike: A Critical Essay* (Grand Rapids, Michigan:
William B. Eerdmans, 1967), p. 45.

13. Burchard, *Yea Sayings,* p. 77.

14. Robert Taubman, "Updike," review of *Of The Farm,* in the
New Statesman, August 12, 1966, p. 233.

15. Burchard, *Yea Sayings,* p. 71.

16. *Ibid.,* p. 86.

17. Richard H. Rupp, *Celebration in Postwar American Fiction
1945-1967* (Coral Gables, Florida: Universtiy of Miami Press,
1970), p. 54.

18. Alice and Kenneth Hamilton, *The Elements of John Updike*
(Grand Rapids, Michigan: William B. Eerdmans, 1970), p. 198.

Chapter 6

1. See the following reviews of *Couples:* Van Allen Bradley,
"Mr. Updike's Fakery," *Chicago Daily News Panorama,* March
30, 1968, p. 10; Melvin Maddocks, "John Updike's Uptown
Peyton Place," *Life,* April 5, 1968, p. 8; Josh Greenfield, "A
Romping Set in a Square New England Town," *Commonweal,*
LXXX (April 26, 1968), p. 186; Raymond A. Sokolov, "Musical
Beds," *Newsweek,* April 8, 1968, pp. 125-126; Diana Trilling,
"Updike's Yankee Traders," *The Atlantic,* CCXXI (April, 1968),
p. 131; Michele Murray, "*Couples* All Surface: 'Updike Has
Narrowed His Vision to the Bed'," *National Catholic Reporter,* IV
(May 1, 1968), p. 11; José Yglesias, "Coupling and Uncoupling,"
Nation, CCVI (May 13, 1968), p. 637. Also see L. E. Sissman,

"John Updike: Midpoint and After," *The Atlantic,* CCXXVI (August, 1970), p. 102; Richard Locke, "Rabbit Redux," *The New York Times Book Review,* November 14, 1971, p. 12.

2. Michael Novak, "Son of the Group," *Critic,* XXVI (June-July, 1968), p. 73.

3. John Updike, *The Music School: Short Stories* (New York: Alfred A. Knopf, 1966), pp. 183-184.

4. *Ibid.,* p. 185.

5. *Ibid.,* pp. 186-187.

6. *Ibid.,* p. 187.

7. *Ibid.,* p. 189.

8. *Ibid.,* p. 190.

9. John Updike, *Couples* (New York: Alfred A. Knopf, 1968), p. 7. For the rest of this chapter, further references to this book will be included in the text.

10. Lewis Nichols, "Talk with John Updike," *The New York Times Book Review,* LXXIII (April 7, 1968), p. 34.

11. L. Hugh Moore, Jr., "Robert Penn Warren and History: 'The Big Myth We Live'," *Studies in American Literature 21* (The Hague: Mouton, 1970), pp. 138-139.

12. "View from the Catacombs," *Time,* XCI (April 26, 1968), p. 75.

13. Larry E. Taylor, *Pastoral and Anti-Pastoral Patterns in John Updike's Fiction* (Carbondale: Southern Illinois University Press, 1971), p. 66.

14. Robert Detweiler, "Updike's *Couples:* Eros Demythologized," *Twentieth Century Literature,* XVII (October, 1971), p. 243.

15. Novak, "Son of the Group," p. 73.

16. Rachael C. Burchard, *John Updike: Yea Sayings* (Carbondale: Southern Illinois University Press, 1971), p. 130.

17. *Ibid.*

18. David Lodge, "Post-Pill Paradise Lost: John Updike's *Couples,*" *New Blackfriars,* LI (November, 1970), p. 515.

19. John Ditsky, "Roth, Updike, and the High Expense of Spirit," *University of Windsor Review,* V (Fall, 1969), p. 113; Tony Tanner, *City of Words: American Fiction 1950-1970* (New York: Harper and Row, 1971), p. 291.

20. Alice and Kenneth Hamilton, *The Elements of John Updike* (Grand Rapids, Michigan: William B. Eerdmans, 1970), p. 53.

21. Lodge, "Post-Pill Paradise," p. 236.

22. Tanner, *City of Words,* p. 291.

23. Hamilton, *The Elements of John Updike,* p. 242.

24. Tanner, *City of Words,* p. 289.

25. See pp. 112, 143, 192, 302, 330, 451.

26. See pp. 19, 60, 259, 338, 430.

27. "View from the Catacombs," p. 68.

28. Detweiler, "Eros Demythologized," p. 241.

29. *Ibid.,* p. 244.

30. "The Art of Fiction XLIII: John Updike," interview by Charles T. Samuels, *Paris Review,* XII (Winter, 1968), p. 101.

31. *Ibid.;* Nichols, "Talk with John Updike," pp. 34-35.

32. Tanner, *City of Words,* pp. 292-293.

Chapter 7

1. John Updike, *Rabbit Redux* (New York: Alfred A. Knopf, 1971), p. 407. For the rest of this chapter, further references to this book will be included in the text.

2. For instances of these usages, see the following pages: assurance—pp. 234, 293; evasion—pp. 58, 73, 166, 219, 293, 303, 347; capitulation—pp. 21, 157, 315, 390; concern—pp. 251, 304; laissez faire—pp. 168, 254, 311; attack—pp. 192, 273, 292; conclusion—pp. 138, 308, 387, 391; decision—pp. 13, 73; approval—pp. 150, 407.

3. Paul Theroux, "A Has-been, 10 Years Later," review of *Rabbit Redux,* by John Updike, *Chicago Tribune Book World,* November 14, 1971, p. 3; Bernard Oldsey, "Rabbit Run to Earth," *Nation,* CCXIV (January 10, 1972), p. 55.

4. Oldsey, "Rabbit Run to Earth," p. 54.

5. "Papa's Sad Testament," *New Statesman,* LXXX (October 16, 1970), p. 489.

6. Richard Locke, "Rabbit Redux," *The New York Times Book Review,* November 14, 1971, p. 22.

7. Charles T. Samuels, "Updike on the Present," *New Republic,* CLXV (November 20, 1971), p. 29.

8. Robert Alter, "Updike, Malamud, and the Fire This Time," *Commentary,* LIV (October, 1972), p. 70.

9. (New York: Charles Scribner's Sons, 1940), p. 196.

10. Richard H. Rupp, *Celebration in Postwar American Fiction 1945-1967* (Coral Gables, Florida: University of Miami Press, 1970), p. 86.

11. Christopher Ricks, "Flopsy Bunny," *The New York Review of Books,* XVII (December 16, 1971), p. 8.

Chapter 8

1. Tony Tanner, *City of Words: American Fiction 1950-1970* (New York: Harper and Row, 1971), pp. 274-275.

2. *Assorted Prose* (New York: Alfred A. Knopf, 1966), p. 228.

3. *Bech: A Book* (New York: Alfred A. Knopf, 1970), p. 67.

4. David Lodge, "Post-Pill Paradise Lost: John Updike's *Couples,*" *New Blackfriars,* LI (November, 1970), p. 516.

5. Cynthia Ozick, "Ethnic Joke," review of *Bech: A Book,* by John Updike, in *Commentary,* L (November, 1970), p. 113.

6. Michael Wood, "Great American Fragments," review of *Museums and Women,* by John Updike, in *The New York Review of Books,* XIX, (December 14, 1972), p. 16.

7. Tony Tanner, "Museums and Women," *The New York Times Book Review,* October 22, 1972, p. 5.

8. William F. Lynch, S.J., *Christ and Apollo: The Dimensions of the Literary Imagination* (New York: Sheed and Ward, 1960), p. 34.

9. *Ibid.,* p. 44.

10. *The Comparative Study of Religions* (New York: Columbia University Press, 1963), p. 37.

11. "Updike's Yankee Traders," review of *Couples,* by John Updike, in *The Atlantic,* CCXXI (April, 1968), p. 129.

12. Tanner, "Museums and Women," pp. 5, 24.

13. Tanner, *City of Words,* p. 276.

14. Alice and Kenneth Hamilton, *The Elements of John Updike* (Grand Rapids, Michigan: William B. Eerdmans, 1970), p. 249.

15. John S. Dunne, C.S.C., *The City of the Gods: A Study in Myth and Mortality* (New York: Macmillan, 1963), pp. 229-230. Also see pp. v-ix, 217-231.

16. Louis Bouyer, *Liturgical Piety* (Notre Dame, Indiana: University of Notre Dame Press, 1954), pp. 266-267.

BIBLIOGRAPHY

Works by John Updike

NOVELS

The Centaur.   New York: Alfred A. Knopf, 1963.
Couples.   New York: Alfred A. Knopf, 1968.
Of the Farm.   New York: Alfred A. Knopf, 1965.
The Poorhouse Fair.   New York: Alfred A. Knopf, 1959.
Rabbit Redux.   New York: Alfred A. Knopf, 1971.
Rabbit, Run.   New York: Alfred A. Knopf, 1960.

SHORT STORIES

Bech: A Book.   New York: Alfred A. Knopf, 1970.
Museums and Women and Other Stories.   New York: Alfred A. Knopf, 1972.
The Music School: Short Stories.   New York: Alfred A. Knopf, 1966.
Olinger Stories: A Selection.   Vintage Books. New York: Random House, 1964.
Pigeon Feathers and Other Stories.   New York: Alfred A. Knopf, 1962.
The Same Door: Short Stories.   New York: Alfred A. Knopf, 1959.

ESSAYS

Assorted Prose.   New York: Alfred A. Knopf, 1965.
Poetry
The Carpentered Hen, and Other Tame Creatures: Poems.
New York: Harper and Brothers, 1958.
Midpoint and Other Poems.   New York: Alfred A. Knopf,
1969.
Telephone Poles and Other Poems.   New York: Alfred A.
Knopf, 1963.
Verse: The Carpentered Hen and Other Tame Creatures
(and) *Telephone Poles and Other Poems.*   A Crest
Book. Greenwich, Conn.: Fawcett Publications, 1965.

FOR CHILDREN

*Bottom's Dream: Adapted from William Shakespeare's A Mid-
summer Night's Dream.*   New York: Alfred A. Knopf,
1969.
A Child's Calendar.   New York: Alfred A. Knopf, 1965.
(Adaptor.) *The Magic Flute, by Wolfgang Amadeus Mozart.*
New York: Alfred A. Knopf, 1962.
(Adaptor.) *The Ring, by Richard Wagner.*   New York:
Alfred A. Knopf, 1964.

UNCOLLECTED SHORT STORIES

"After the Storm."   *Esquire,* January, 1963, pp. 81, 83-84,
123-126.
"Amor Vincit Omnia Ad Nauseam."   *The New Yorker,*
April 5, 1969, p. 33.
"And Whose Little Generation are You? or, Astrology Re-
fined."   *The New Yorker,* October 5, 1957, pp. 38-39.
"Believers."   *Harper's Magazine,* July, 1972, pp. 86-87.
"Commercial."   *The New Yorker,* June 10, 1972, pp. 30-32.
"Correction."   *New Republic,* March 26, 1966, p. 40.
"The First Lunar Invitational."   *The New Yorker,* February
27, 1971, pp. 35-36.
"The Gun Shop."   *The New Yorker,* November 25, 1972,
pp. 42-47.

"How to Love America and Leave It at the Same Time."
The New Yorker, August 19, 1972, pp. 25-27.

"Love: First Lessons." *The New Yorker,* November 6, 1971,
pp. 46-47.

"Ride." *The New Yorker,* December 2, 1972, p. 51.

"The Tarbox Police." *Esquire,* March, 1972, pp. 85-86.

"Unstuck." *The New Yorker,* February 3, 1962, pp. 24-27.

"Vergil Moss." *The New Yorker,* April 11, 1959, pp. 99-
102.

"The Wait." *The New Yorker,* February 17, 1968, pp. 34-
96.

UNCOLLECTED ESSAYS

"An Arion Questionnaire." *Arion,* III (Winter, 1964), p. 4.

"A Comment." *The Times Literary Supplement,* June 4,
1964, p. 473.

"Books." *The New Yorker,* October 2, 1965, pp. 216ff;
October 30, 1965, pp. 223-224ff; February 26, 1966,
pp. 115-118ff; January 7, 1967, pp. 91-94; September
23, 1967, pp. 169-170ff; November 4, 1967, pp. 223-
238; December 2, 1967, pp. 223-232; April 6, 1968,
pp. 167-174; November 2, 1968, pp. 197-201; August 2,
1969, pp. 67-75; April 25, 1970, pp. 133-136; May 13,
1972, pp. 135-144; September 9, 1972, pp. 115-124;
October 21, 1972, pp. 157-167; November 18, 1972,
pp. 242-245.

"Books, Briefly Noted." *The New Yorker,* February 1,
1964, pp. 96-100. Fourteen very brief reviews of current books, including a review of Paul Tillich's *Morality
and Beyond* which is collected in *Assorted Prose.*

"The Dawn of the Possible Dream." *Sports Illustrated,*
February 21, 1972, pp. 38-45.

"Henry Bech Redux." *The New York Times Book Review,*
November 14, 1971, p. 3.

"Letter from Anguilla." *The New Yorker,* June 22, 1968,
pp. 70-80.

"The Mastery of Miss Warner." Review of *Swans on an*

Autumn River, by Sylvia Townsend Warner. *New Republic,* March 5, 1966, pp. 23-25.

"Nabokov's Look Back: A National Loss." *Life,* January 13, 1967, pp. 9ff.

"Outing." *The New Yorker,* June 14, 1958, pp. 28-29.

"Papa's Sad Testament." Review of *Islands in the Stream,* by Ernest Hemingway. *New Statesman,* October 16, 1970, p. 489.

"Writers I Have Met." *The New York Times Book Review,* August 11, 1968, pp. 2, 23.

UNCOLLECTED POEMS

"A l'Ecole Berlitz." *New Republic,* September 6-13, 1969, p. 33.

"Bath after Sailing." Monroe, Connecticut: Pendulum Press, 1968.

"A Bicycle Chain." *The New Yorker,* April 15, 1972, p. 48.

"Bitter Life." *The New Yorker,* January 7, 1956, p. 26.

"Bilked." *The New Yorker,* June 21, 1958, p. 90.

"Business Acquaintances." *New Republic,* October 4, 1969, p. 28.

"Caligula's Dream." *Commonweal,* June 27, 1958, p. 327.

"Capacity." *The New Yorker,* January 5, 1957, p. 29.

"The Cars in Caracas." *The New Yorker,* December 30, 1972, p. 27.

"Elm." *Polemic,* XI (Winter, 1966), p. 31.

"The Great Scarf of Birds." *The New Yorker,* November 10, 1962, pp. 48-49.

"Handkerchiefs of Khaibar Khan." *The New Yorker,* November 25, 1961, p. 172.

"Insomnia the Gem of the Ocean." *The New Yorker,* September 16, 1972, p. 40.

"I Want a Lamp." *The American Courier,* July 1, 1949, p. 11.

"Jack." *The New Yorker,* October 19, 1957, p. 134.

"The Lament of Abrashka Tertz, A Russian Song Rendered by John Updike." *The Leader,* January 17, 1966, p. 3.

"Marching Through a Novel." *Saturday Review,* July 3, 1971, p. 24.

"Martini." *Contact,* I (February, 1960), pp. 52-53.

"Memories of Anguilla, 1960." *New Republic,* November 11, 1967, p. 21.

"Notes." *The New Yorker,* January 26, 1957, pp. 28-29.

"Old Faces of '56." *The New Yorker,* October 27, 1956, p. 36.

"On an Island." *Saturday Review,* November 7, 1970, p. 29.

"Parable." *Contact,* I (February, 1960), pp. 52-53.

"Reflection." *The New Yorker,* November 30, 1957, p. 216.

"Sand Dollar." *The Atlantic,* March, 1972, p. 43.

"Scansion from Exalted Heights." *The New Yorker,* February 9, 1957, pp. 28-29.

"Simple Life." *The New Yorker,* January 18, 1958, p. 108.

"Skyey Developments." *New Republic,* March 8, 1969, p. 28.

"Solid Comfort." *The New Yorker,* February 18, 1956, p. 93.

"Song in American Type." *The New Yorker,* March 30, 1957, p. 30.

"South of the Alps." *Commonweal,* October 17, 1969, p. 72.

"Sunday." *The American Scholar,* XLI (Summer, 1972), p. 389.

"Sunday Rain." *Saturday Review,* April 17, 1971, p. 59.

"To a Waterbed." *Harper's Magazine,* December, 1972, p. 66.

Translator of "Ballad about Nuggets" by Evgenil Aleksandrovich Evtushenko. *Life,* February 17, 1967, p. 38.

Translator of "The Labyrinth" by Jorge Luis Borges. *The Atlantic,* April, 1969, p. 72.

Translator of "Restaurant for Two" by Evgenil Aleksandrovich Evtushenko. *Life,* February 17, 1967, p. 33.

Translator, with Albert C. Todd, of "America and I Sat Down Together" by Yevgeny Yevtushenko. *Holiday,* November, 1968, pp. 38-42.

"Upon Shaving Off One's Beard." *The New Yorker,* May 16, 1970, p. 37.

"Vision."   *The New Yorker*, January 7, 1961, p. 77.
"Wind."   *Commonweal*, January 21, 1972, p. 373.
"Yonder Peasant."   *Contact*, I (February, 1960), pp. 52-53.
"Young Matrons Dancing."   *Saturday Review*, January 29, 1972, p. 6.

Book Reviews

THE CARPENTERED HEN (1958)

Dorn, Norman.   "An English Accent Is Heard in the New Modern Poetry."   *San Francisco Chronicle*, November 23, 1958, p. 13.

McCord, David.   "Trivia of Life."   *Saturday Review*, August 9, 1958, p. 32.

McDonald, Gerald D.   "Poetry."   *Library Journal*, LXXXIII (June 15, 1958), p. 1938.

"Updike, John. The Carpentered Hen, and Other Tame Creatures; Poems."   *The Booklist and Subscription Books Bulletin*, LIV (April 15, 1958), pp. 470-471.

"Updike, John. The Carpentered Hen."   *Bulletin from Virginia Kirkus' Service*, XXVI (January 15, 1958), p. 59.

THE POORHOUSE FAIR (1959)

Adams, Phoebe.   "The Poor and Unselfish."   *The Atlantic*, February, 1959, pp. 100-101.

"As They Wait to Die."   *Newsweek*, January 12, 1959, p. 90.

Balliett, Whitney.   "Writer's Writer."   *The New Yorker*, February 7, 1959, pp. 139-140.

Barr, Donald.   "A Stone's Throw Apart."   *The New York Times Book Review*, January 11, 1959, p. 4.

Betts, Doris.   "Fine Novel by Updike."   *Virginian Pilot*, January 25, 1959, p. 6F.

Buchanan, Leigh M.   "John Updike, *The Poorhouse Fair*."   *Epoch*, IX, No. 4 (Spring, 1959), pp. 252-254.

Butcher, Fanny.   "1st Novel Talented, Tho Haphazard."   *Chicago Sunday Tribune Magazine of Books*, January 11, 1959, p. 4.

Chase, Mary Ellen. "John Updike's Wise, Moving First Novel." *New York Herald Tribune Book Review,* January 11, 1959, p. 3.

Coleman, John. "Various Formalities." *Spectator,* March 13, 1959, p. 380.

Diebold, Michael. "Updike Outwits Himself." *Pittsburgh Press,* January 11, 1959, Sec. 3, p. 6.

"Do-gooders Undone." *Time,* January 19, 1959, p. 92.

Fitelson, David. "Conflict Unresolved." *Commentary,* March 3, 1959, pp. 275-276.

Gilman, Richard. "A Last Assertion of Personal Being." *Commonweal,* February 6, 1959, pp. 499-500.

Hicks, Granville. "Novels in Limbo." *Saturday Review,* January 17, 1959, p. 58.

Hughes, Riley. "The Poorhouse Fair, by John Updike." *Catholic World,* May, 1959, p. 162.

Hutchens, John. "Poorhouse Fair." *New York Herald Tribune,* January 16, 1959, p. 38.

Johnson, Pamela Hansford. "Other New Novels." *New Statesman,* March 28, 1959, p. 453.

Klausler, Alfred P. "Steel Wilderness." *Christian Century,* February 22, 1961, pp. 245-246.

Murchland, Bernard G. "Critics' Choices for Catholic Book Week." *Commonweal,* February 27, 1959, p. 581.

O'Leary, Ted. "Satires on the Welfare State." *Kansas City Star,* January 24, 1959, p. 6.

Podhoretz, Norman. "Style and Substance." *Reporter,* January 22, 1959, pp. 42-44.

Price, Martin. "Intelligence and Fiction: Some New Novels." *Yale Review,* XLVIII (March, 1959), p. 464.

Salmon, Peter. "A Slice of Life." *New Republic,* January 12, 1959, p. 20.

Serebnick, Judith. "Updike, John. The Poorhouse Fair." *Library Journal,* LXXXIV (January 1, 1959), p. 123.

————. "New Creative Writers." *Library Journal,* LXXXIV (February 1, 1959), p. 499.

Sherman, Thomas. "Reading and Writing." *St. Louis Post-Dispatch,* March 1, 1959, p. 4B.

"Updike, John. The Poorhouse Fair." *The Booklist and*

Subscription Books Bulletin, LV (January 15, 1959),
p. 260.

"Updike, John. The Poorhouse Fair." *Bulletin from Virginia Kirkus' Service,* XXVI (November 1, 1958), p.
830.

"Ways of the World." *The Times Literary Supplement,*
March 20, 1959, p. 157.

THE SAME DOOR (1959)

B., R. "First Steps of Involvement." *Christian Science Monitor,* August 20, 1959, p. 7.

Cassidy, Thomas E. "The Enchantment of the Ordinary."
Commonweal, September 11, 1959, p. 499.

"Collections of Short Stories." *The Times Weekly Review,*
June 21, 1962, p. 10.

"Cool, Cool World." *Time,* August 17, 1959, p. 98.

Crane, Milton. "Young People with Time to Explore Their
Souls." *Chicago Sunday Tribune Magazine of Books,*
August 16, 1959, p. 3.

De Bellis, Jack. "The Group and John Updike." *Sewanee Review,* LXXII (Summer, 1964), pp. 531-536.

Flory, Claude R. "The Same Door, by John Updike."
English Journal, XLIX, No. 2 (February, 1960), p.
143.

"Fragments of America." *The Times Literary Supplement,*
April 27, 1962, p. 277.

Healey, Robert C. "John Updike with A Packet of Stories."
New York Herald Tribune Book Review, August 16,
1959, p. 3.

Hutchens, John. "Same Door." *New York Herald Tribune,*
August 17, 1959, p. 13.

Keown, Eric. "New Fiction." *Punch,* May 2, 1962, pp.
697-698.

Lodge, David. "Instant Novel." *Spectator,* May 11, 1962,
p. 628.

Mayne, Richard. "Instant Literature." *New Statesman,*
April 27, 1962, pp. 606-607.

"Notes on Current Books." *Virginia Quarterly Review,*
XXXVI (Winter, 1960), pp. xi-xii.

Peden, William.   "Minor Ills That Plague the Human Heart."
    The New York Times Book Review, August 16, 1959,
    p. 5.
Schott, Webster.   "The 'Better' and the 'Best'."   *Kansas City
    Star,* August 29, 1959, p. 6.
Serebnick, Judith.   "Updike, John. The Same Door: Short
    Stories."   *Library Journal,* LXXXIV (August, 1959), pp.
    2376-2377.
Spectorsky, A. C.   "Spirit Under Surgery."   *Saturday Re-
    view,* August 22, 1959, pp. 15, 31.
Tindall, Gillian.   "Short Shrift."   *Time and Tide,* April 26,
    1962, pp. 30-31.
"The World of Neon."   *Newsweek,* August 17, 1959, p. 97.
Yudkin, Vivian.   "More Updike, More Magic."   *Washing-
    ton Post,* August 16, 1959, p. E7.

RABBIT, RUN (1960)

"A Novelist Gets Tough."   *Newsweek,* November 7, 1960,
    pp. 122-123.
Balliett, Whitney.   "The American Expression."   *The New
    Yorker,* November 5, 1960, pp. 222-224.
Boroff, David.   "You Cannot Really Flee."   *The New York
    Times Book Review,* November 6, 1960, pp. 4, 43.
Crane, Milton.   "Rabbit Runs—But Can't Get Away from
    Himself."   *Chicago Sunday Tribune Magazine of Books,*
    November 13, 1960, p. 6.
"Desperate Weakling."   *Time,* November 7, 1960, p. 108.
Didion, Joan.   "Into the Underbrush."   *National Review,*
    January 28, 1961, pp. 54-56.
Diebold, Michael.   "Rabbit Runs As Net Tightens."   *Pitts-
    burgh Press,* November 11, 1960, p. 9.
Edelstein, J. M.   "Down with the Poor in Spirit."   *New
    Republic,* November 21, 1960, pp. 17-18.
"Enemies of Promise."   *The Times Literary Supplement,*
    September 29, 1961, p. 648.
Foster, Richard.   "What Is Fiction For?"   *Hudson Review,*
    XIV (Spring, 1961), pp. 142-149.
Gilman, Richard.   "A Distinguished Image of Precarious
    Life."   *Commonweal,* October 28, 1960, pp. 128-129.

Gorn, Lester H. "New Fiction—Three Novelists View Today's Times with Despair." *San Francisco Chronicle This World Magazine,* November 20, 1960, p. 28.

Hicks, Granville. "A Little Good in Evil." *Saturday Review,* November 5, 1960, p. 28.

Hutchens, John K. " 'Rabbit, Run.' " *New York Herald Tribune,* November 3, 1960, p. 25.

Klausler, Alfred P. "Steel Wilderness." *Christian Century,* February 22, 1961, pp. 245-246.

Lyons, R. "A High E.Q." *Minnesota Review,* I (Spring, 1961), pp. 385-389.

McGuinness, Frank. "In Extremis." *New Statesman,* September 29, 1961, p. 439.

McLaughlin, Richard. " 'Rabbit, Run,' John Updike." *Springfield Republican,* November 20, 1960, p. 5.

Manning, Olivia. "Faces of Violence." *Spectator,* September 15, 1961, p. 361.

Miller, Nolan. "Three of the 'Best.' " *Antioch Review,* XXI, No. 1 (Spring, 1961), pp. 118-128.

"New Fiction." *The Times Weekly Review,* September 28, 1961, p. 14.

O'Leary, Ted. "Satisfying Life Eludes a Runner." *Kansas City Star,* November 5, 1960, p. 6.

Price, R. G. G. "New Novels." *Punch,* September 20, 1961, pp. 443-444.

Reif, Jane. "Unattractive Characters Get Pity." *Virginian Pilot,* January 1, 1961, p. 7B.

Rugoff, Milton. "American Tragedy: 1960." *New York Herald Tribune,* November 6, 1960, p. 7.

Serebnick, Judith. "Updike, John. Rabbit, Run." *Library Journal,* LXXXV (November 1, 1960), p. 4009.

Sinclair, Andrew. "See How He Runs." *Time and Tide,* September 21, 1961, p. 1571.

Southern, Terry. "New Trends and Old Hats." *Nation,* November 19, 1960, pp. 380-383.

Steiner, George. "In a Rut." *Reporter,* December 8, 1960, pp. 81-82.

Thompson, John. "Other People's Affairs." *Partisan Re-*

view, XXVIII, No. 1 (January-February, 1961), pp. 117-124.

"Updike, John. Rabbit, Run." *The Booklist and Subscription Books Bulletin,* LVII (November 15, 1960), p. 180.

W., R. "Rabbit, Run—John Updike." *Tamarack Review,* No. 18 (Winter, 1961), p. 86.

PIGEON FEATHERS (1962)

"Bigger and Better." *The Times Literary Supplement,* February 1, 1963, p. 73.

Bradbury, Malcolm. "New Fiction." *Punch,* February 13, 1963, pp. 247-248.

Chase, Mary Ellen. "But Can He Communicate?" *New York Herald Tribune Books,* March 18, 1962, p. 4.

Chester, Alfred. "Twitches and Embarrassments." *Commentary,* July, 1962, pp. 77-80.

Cook, Bruce A. "A Lesser Form." *Commonweal,* May 11, 1962, pp. 184, 186.

Crane, Milton. "Varied, Accomplished Stories with Unifying Themes." *Chicago Sunday Tribune Magazine of Books,* April 1, 1962, p. 4.

Daniel, John. "Bombardment of Events." *Spectator,* February 8, 1963, p. 172.

Didion, Joan. "Books in Brief." *National Review,* June 19, 1962, p. 452.

Diebold, Michael. "Updike Takes Control." *Pittsburgh Press,* May 15, 1962, p. 22.

Edelstein, J. M. "The Security of Memory." *New Republic,* May 14, 1962, pp. 30-31.

Emerson, Donald. "Three Perceptions." *The Progressive,* August, 1962, p. 35.

Hicks, Granville. "Mysteries of the Commonplace." *Saturday Review,* March 17, 1962, p. 21.

Hogan, William. "The Incandescent Updike at Work." *San Francisco Chronicle,* March 22, 1962, p. 39.

Hutchens, John K. " 'Pigeon Feathers.' " *New York Herald Tribune,* March 23, 1962, p. 19.

Hyman, Stanley E. "The Artist As a Young Man." *New Leader,* March 19, 1962, pp. 22-23.

Lewis, Arthur O., Jr. "John Updike. *Pigeon Feathers and Other Stories." Books Abroad,* XXXVI, No. 4 (Autumn, 1962), p. 435.

"Listen Carefully." *Newsweek,* March 19, 1962, pp. 120-121.

Maddocks, Melvin. "Updike's Stories; Italian Novel." *Christian Science Monitor,* March 22, 1962, p. 11.

Mizener, Arthur. "Behind the Dazzle Is a Knowing Eye." *The New York Times Book Review,* March 18, 1962, pp. 1, 29.

Morse, J. Mitchell. "Fiction Chronicle." *Hudson Review,* XV (Summer, 1962), pp. 302-303.

"New Fiction." *The Times Weekly Review,* February 7, 1963, p. 13.

"Notes on Current Books." *Virginia Quarterly Review,* XXXVIII (Summer, 1962), p. lxxvi.

Novak, Michael. "Critics' Choices for Catholic Book Week." *Commonweal,* February 22, 1963, p. 577.

Parker, Dorothy. "Book Reviews." *Esquire,* June, 1962, pp. 66-67.

"Poetry and Short Stories." *Wisconsin Library Bulletin,* LVIII (July, 1962), p. 240.

Poore, Charles. "Books of the Times." *The New York Times,* March 24, 1962, p. 23.

Pree, Barry. "Special Notices." *London Magazine,* April, 1963, pp. 87-88.

"Put and Take." *Time,* March 16, 1962, p. 86.

Reif, Jane. "Pared Prose in Collection." *Virginian Pilot,* April 29, 1962, p. F6.

Ricks, Christopher. "Tennysonian." *New Statesman,* February 8, 1963, p. 208.

Rowland, Stanley J., Jr. "The Limits of Littleness." *Christian Century,* July 4, 1962, pp. 840-841.

Serebnick, Judith. "Updike, John. Pigeon Feathers and Other Stories." *Library Journal,* LXXXVII (February 15, 1962), p. 786.

Stern, Richard G. "The Myth in Action." *Spectator,* September 27, 1963, p. 389.

Terral, Rufus. "Brilliant Disturber of Memories." *St. Louis Post-Dispatch,* April 1, 1962, p. 4C.

"Updike, John. Pigeon Feathers, and Other Stories." *The Booklist and Subscription Books Bulletin,* LVIII (April 1, 1962), p. 522.

"Updike, John. Pigeon Feathers and Other Stories." *Bulletin from Virginia Kirkus' Service,* XXX (January 15, 1961), pp. 71-72.

THE MAGIC FLUTE (1962)

Dalgliesh, Alice. "Stories for the Christmas Season." *Saturday Review,* December 15, 1962, p. 28.

Graves, Elizabeth Minot. "A Selected List of Children's Books: Music and Art." *Commonweal,* November 16, 1962, p. 214.

Lask, Thomas. "Repeat Performance (Juvenile Division)." *The New York Times Book Review,* November 11, 1962, p. 62.

Mitchell, Elizabeth. "Mozart, Amadeus Wolfgang. The Magic Flute; adapt. by John Updike." *Library Journal,* LXXXVII (October 15, 1962), p. 3896.

THE CENTAUR (1963)

"A Mythical Animal." *The Times Literary Supplement,* September 27, 1963, p. 728.

Adams, Phoebe. "Potpourri." *The Atlantic,* February, 1963, pp. 134-135.

Adler, Renata. "Arcadia, Pa." *The New Yorker,* April 13, 1963, pp. 182-188.

Brooke, Jocelyn. "Snaffle and Curb." *The Listener,* October 10, 1963, pp. 577-578.

Buitenhuis, Peter. "Pennsylvania Pantheon." *The New York Times Book Review,* April 7, 1963, pp. 4, 26.

Cook, Eleanor. "Mythical Beasts." *The Canadian Forum,* XLIII (August, 1963), pp. 113-114.

Crane, Milton. "Classic Myth Refurbished." *Chicago Sunday Tribune Magazine of Books,* February 3, 1963, p. 4.

Culligan, Glendy. "Gods Thrive in Pa." *Washington oPst,* February 3, 1963, p. G7.

Curley, Thomas. "Between Heaven and Earth." *Commonweal,* March 29, 1963, pp. 26-27.

Davenport, Guy. "Novels with Masks." *National Review,* April 9, 1963, pp. 287-288.

De Bellis, Jack. "The Group and John Updike." *Sewanee Review,* LXXII (Summer, 1964), pp. 531-536.

Diebold, Michael. "Updike Novel Ambitious." *Pittsburgh Press,* February 3, 1963, p. 8.

Fuller, Edmund. "Reading for Pleasure." *Wall Street Journal,* February 4, 1963, p. 14.

Gardiner, Harold C. "Some Early Spring Novels." *America,* March 9, 1963, pp. 340-341.

Grauel, George E. "Updike, John. *The Centaur.*" *Best Sellers,* XXII (February 15, 1963), p. 423.

Hicks, Granville. "Pennsylvania Pantheon." *Saturday Review,* February 2, 1963, p. 27.

Hill, W. B. "Fiction." *America,* May 11, 1963, pp. 678-679.

Hogan, William. "Greek Myths in a High School Setting." *San Francisco Chronicle,* February 4, 1963, p. 31.

Kirsch, Robert. "National Awards Criticized." *Los Angeles Times,* March 11, 1964, p. 4.

Kluger, Richard. "John Updike: How Most of Us Really Live." *The New York Herald Tribune Book Review,* April 7, 1963, p. 8.

Lewis, Arthur O., Jr. "John Updike. *The Centaur.*" *Books Abroad,* XXXVII, No. 3 (Summer, 1963), p. 340.

Malin, Irving. "Occasions for Loving." *Kenyon Review,* XXV, No. 2 (Spring, 1963), pp. 348-352.

Miller, Jonathan. "*The Centaur* by John Updike." *The New York Review of Books,* I, No. 1, p. 28.

Minetree, Harry. "From Olinger, Pa., to Mt. Olympus." *St. Louis Post-Dispatch,* March 24, 1963, p. 4C.

Murray, James G. "Books." *Critic,* XXI (February-March, 1963), p. 72.

"New Fiction." *The Times Weekly Review,* October 10, 1963, p. 12.

Nordell, Roderick. "An Updike Mythology." *The Christian Science Monitor,* February 7, 1963, p. 7.

"Notes on Current Books." *Virginia Quarterly Review,* XXXI, No. 2 (Spring, 1963), p. xlviii.

Pickrel, Paul. "An Updike Experiment." *Harper's Magazine,* April, 1963, pp. 92-93.

Price, Martin. "Seven Recent Novels." *Yale Review,* LII (Summer, 1963), pp. 601-610.

"Prometheus Unsound." *Time,* February 8, 1963, pp. 86-87.

Roberts, Preston. "Horror Made Habitable." *Christian Century,* April 10, 1963, pp. 463-464.

Sale, Roger. "Gossips and Storytellers." *Hudson Review,* XVI, No. 1 (Spring, 1963), pp. 141-149.

Serebnick, Judith. "Updike, John. The Centaur." *Library Journal,* LXXXVIII (January 15, 1963), p. 238.

Steiner, George. "Half Man, Half Beast." *Reporter,* March 14, 1963, pp. 52-54.

Stern, Richard G. "The Myth in Action." *The Spectator,* September 27, 1963, p. 389.

"The Sustaining Stream." *Time,* February 1, 1963, pp. 82-84.

Taubman, Robert. "God Is Delicate." *New Statesman,* September 27, 1963, pp. 406-407.

"Updikemanship." *Newsweek,* February 11, 1963, pp. 91-92.

TELEPHONE POLES (1963)

Burns, Richard K. "Updike, John. *Telephone Poles and Other Poems.*" *Library Journal,* LXXXVIII (October 1, 1963), pp. 3628-3629.

Callahan, Patrick. "The Poetry of Imperfection." *Prairie Schooner,* XXXIX (Winter, 1965-1966), pp. 364-365.

Fandel, John. "Seven Poets: The Creation of Images to Delight." *Commonweal,* May 8, 1964, pp. 212-213.

Fuller, Edmund. "The Versatile Updike." *Wall Street Journal,* October 31, 1963, p. 16.

Keister, Donald. "Updike's *Telephone Poles* Soars to a Beautiful Climax." *Cleveland Plain Dealer,* September 22, 1963, p. 7H.

Kennedy, X. J. "A Light Look at Today." *The New York Times Book Review,* September 22, 1963, pp. 10, 12.

Lask, Thomas. "End Papers." *The New York Times,* September 21, 1963, p. 19.

"Light Fantastic." *Time,* November 1, 1963, pp. 112, 114.

Moody, Minnie. "Promise Unfulfilled in New Updike Poems." *Columbus Dispatch,* December 8, 1963, p. D23.

Ricks, Christopher. "Spotting Syllabics." *New Statesman,* May 1, 1964, p. 684.

"Rustic and Urbane." *The Times Literary Supplement,* August 20, 1964, p. 748.

Schott, Webster. "Any Idea May Be Shaped into Poetry." *Kansas City Star,* December 2, 1963, p. 28.

Simpson, Louis. "Don't Take A Poem by the Horns." *New York Herald Tribune Book Week,* October 27, 1963, pp. 6, 25.

Spector, R. D. "The Poet's Other Voices, Other Rooms." *Saturday Review,* February 1, 1964, p. 38.

Stitt, Peter. "Let Bobo Be Bubo." *Minnesota Review,* IV (Winter, 1964), pp. 268-271.

Tazewell, William. "Author Updike: A Poet at Play." *Virginian Pilot,* October 6, 1963, p. B6.

THE RING (1964)

Dalgliesh, Alice. "Beautiful Image I See." *Saturday Review,* November 7, 1964, p. 52.

Lask, Thomas. "Repeat Performances." *The New York Times Book Review,* November 1, 1964, p. 63.

M., M. "The Ring." *Christian Science Monitor,* November 5, 1964, p. 8.

Morse, Jane C. "Also of Interest." *Horn Book,* XLI (February, 1965), p. 71.

Sheehan, Ethna. "Children's Books for Christmas Giving: Folklore, Fantasy, Poetry." *America,* November 21, 1964, p. 671.

Wagner, Marjorie K. "Updike, John, adapt. *The Ring;* music by Richard Wagner." *Library Journal,* LXXXIX (December 15, 1964), p. 5012.

VERSE (1965)

Cromie, Robert. "John Updike Poetry Put Into New Volume." *Chicago Tribune,* February 16, 1965, Sec. 2, p. 2.

Fremont-Smith, Eliot. "End Papers." *The New York Times,* February 18, 1965, p. 31.

Hamlin, William. "A Harvest of Updike." *St. Louis Post-Dispatch,* September 5, 1965, p. 4B.

Taylor, Michael. "Collected Poems Now in Paperback." *Nashville Banner,* April 2, 1965, p. 28.

ASSORTED PROSE (1965)

Binns, F. W. "Updike, John. *Assorted Prose.*" *Library Journal,* XC (May 15, 1965), p. 2264.

Fremont-Smith, Eliot. "An Adventurer on Behalf of Us All." *The New York Times,* June 23, 1965, p. 39.

Galloway, David D. "Belfast Blues." *Spectator,* February 4, 1966, pp. 142-143.

"The Gymnast." *Newsweek,* May 17, 1965, pp. 108, 110.

Hicks, Granville. "They Also Serve Who Write Well." *Saturday Review,* May 15, 1965, pp. 25-26.

Kay, Jane H. "Casuals by Updike." *The Christian Science Monitor,* June 26, 1965, p. 9.

Kenny, Herbert. "Updike's Essays Show Variety and Style." *Boston Globe,* May 24, 1965, p. 14.

Mayne, Richard. "Epicures, Etc." *New Statesman,* February 4, 1966, p. 169.

Moraes, Dom. "Professional's Suite." *The Listener,* February 3, 1966, pp. 180-181.

Morgan, Thomas B. "A Casual Collection." *The New York Times Book Review,* June 13, 1965, p. 10.

Newman, Charles. "Journalistic Exercises." *Chicago Tribune,* May 23, 1965, Sec. 9, p. 12.

"On Demand." *Time,* May 21, 1965, p. 113.

"Pick of the Paperbacks." *Saturday Review,* January 21, 1967, p. 40.

"That Long Atlantic Crossing." *The Times Literary Supplement,* February 17, 1966, p. 124.

OF THE FARM (1965)

Aldridge, John W. "Cultivating Corn Out of Season." *New York Herald Tribune Book Week,* November 21, 1965, p. 5.

Berolzheimer, H. F. "Updike, John. Of the Farm." *Library Journal,* XC (December 1, 1965), p. 5303.

Buitenhuis, Peter. "The Mowing of a Meadow." *The New York Times Book Review,* November 14, 1965, pp. 4, 34.

Burgess, Anthony. "New Fiction." *The Listener,* April 21, 1966, p. 589.

Casey, Florence. "Updike's Trap of Freedom." *Christian Science Monitor,* November 18, 1965, p. 15.

Cook, Roderick. "Books in Brief." *Harper's Magazine,* January, 1966, p. 100.

Culligan, Glendy. "Updike is Back on the Farm With a Luminous Novel." *Washington Post,* November 23, 1965, p. A22.

Davenport, John. "The Generation Between." *The Spectator,* April 29, 1966, p. 537.

Enright, D. J. "Updike's Ups and Downs." *Holiday,* November, 1965, pp. 162, 164-166.

Epstein, Joseph. "Mother's Day on the Updike Farm." *New Republic,* December 11, 1965, pp. 23-25.

Fleischer, Leonore. "Forecast of Paperbacks." *Publisher's Weekly,* CXC (November 21, 1966), p. 77.

"Four-Ring Circus." *Newsweek,* November 15, 1965, pp. 129-130.

French, Warren. "Updike Turns Back from Ambitious Mythology." *Kansas City Star,* November 14, 1965, p. 10F.

Hicks, Granville. "Mothers, Sons, and Lovers." *Saturday Review,* November 13, 1965, pp. 41-42.

Klein, Marcus. "A Mouse in the Barn." *Reporter,* December 16, 1965, pp. 54-60.

Kort, Wesley. "A Confession of Debt." *Christian Century,* January 19, 1966, p. 82.

Lindroth, James R. "Of the Farm." *America,* November 27, 1965, p. 692.

Moore, Harry T. "Static Exercise in Technique." *Pittsburgh Press,* December 5, 1965, p. 12.

"Mother's Boy." *The Times Literary Supplement,* April 14, 1966, p. 321.

"Narrowing Compass." *Time,* November 12, 1965, p. 118.

Poore, Charles. "Joey at 35, The House of Knopf at 50." *The New York Times,* November 20, 1965, p. 33.

Seward, William. "Reunion at Farm Attracts Ghosts Too." *Virginian Pilot,* November 21, 1965, p. B4.

Sullivan, Richard. "A Quartet of Tangled Actors." *Chicago Tribune,* November 28, 1965, Sec. 9, p. 6.

Sullivan, Walter. "Updike, Spark and Others." *Sewanee Review,* LXXIV (Summer, 1960), pp. 709-716.

Taubman, Robert. "Updike." *New Statesman,* August 12, 1966, p. 233.

Thompson, John. "Matthiessen and Updike." *The New York Review of Books,* December 23, 1965, pp. 20-21.

Weeks, Edward. "The Duel on the Farm." *The Atlantic,* December, 1965, p. 138.

THE MUSIC SCHOOL (1966)

Adams, Robert Martin. "Without Risk." *The New York Times Book Review,* September 18, 1966, pp. 4-5.

Appel, David. "Updike Vignettes, Perelman Parodies." *Philadelphia Inquirer,* September 18, 1966, Sec. 7, p. 7.

Bergonzi, Bernard. "Updike, Dennis, and Others." *The New York Review of Books,* February 9, 1967, pp. 28-30.

Braybrooke, Neville. "'Meditations." *Spectator,* June 23, 1967, p. 744.

"Brief Reviews." *Critic,* XXV (October-November, 1966), p. 116.

Casey, Florence. "Tiny Happenings of Near-events." *The Christian Science Monitor,* September 22, 1966, p. 11.

Cook, Roderick. "Books in Brief." *Harper's Magazine,* September, 1966, pp. 113-114.

Dilts, Susan. "Updike in a Deep Rut." *Baltimore Sunday Sun,* October 2, 1966, p. D9.

"Fiction." *The Booklist and Subscription Book Bulletin,* LXIII (October 15, 1966), p. 238.

Hicks, Granville. "Domestic Felicity?" *Saturday Review,* September 24, 1966, pp. 31-32.

Hill, W. B. "Fiction." *America,* May 6, 1967, p. 702.

Hubler, Richard. "Updike Dazzles Until It's Boresome." *Los Angeles Times,* September 25, 1966, p. 28.

Jacobsen, Josephine. *"The Music School:* John Updike." *Commonweal,* December 9, 1966, pp. 299-300.

"John and Bruce." *Newsweek,* September 26, 1966, p. 116.

Kauffmann, Stanley. "Onward with Updike." *New Republic,* September 24, 1966, pp. 15-17.

Light, Carolyn M. "Updike, John. *The Music School."* *Best Sellers,* XXVI (October 1, 1966), p. 240.

Macaulay, Robie. "Cartoons and Arabesques." *World Journal Tribune Book Week,* September 25, 1966, p. 4.

McNamara, Eugene. "The Music School." *America,* October 15, 1966, p. 462.

"Madrigals from a Rare Bird." *Time,* September 23, 1966, pp. 105-106.

Meinke, Peter. "Yearning for Yesteryear." *Christian Century,* December 7, 1966, p. 1512.

Minerof, Arthur. "Updike, John. *The Music School."* *Library Journal,* XCI (September 15, 1966), p. 4137.

Morse, J. Mitchell. "Where Is Everybody?" *Hudson Review,* XIX (Winter, 1966-1967), pp. 673-682.

Newman, Charles. "Top Talent Taking It Easy." *Chicago Tribune,* September 11, 1966, Sec. 9, p. 8.

Price, R. G. G. "New Novels." *Punch,* June 21, 1967, p. 924.

Samuels, Charles T. "A Place of Resonance." *Nation,* October 3, 1966, pp. 328-329.

"Updike, John. *The Music School*." *Choice,* III (February, 1967), p. 1130.

Weeks, Edward. "He and She." *Atlantic Monthly,* November, 1966, pp. 154, 156.

Wells, Joel. "Updike Runs . . . On and On." *Extension,* LXI (October, 1966), pp. 54-55.

Zane, Maitland. "An Updike Collection: Emotions Laid Raw." *San Francisco Chronicle,* September 18, 1966, p. 38.

COUPLES (1968)

Archer, William H. "Couples." *Best Sellers,* XXVIII (April 15, 1968), pp. 32-33.

Bradley, Van Allen. "Mr. Updike's Fakery." *Chicago Daily News Panorama,* March 30, 1968, p. 10.

Broyard, Anatole. "Updike's Twosomes." *New Republic,* May 4, 1968, pp. 28-30.

Cayton, Robert F. "Updike, John. *Couples*." *Library Journal,* XCIII (March 15, 1968), p. 1164.

"Community Feeling." *The Times Literary Supplement,* November 7, 1968, p. 1245.

Gordon, David J. "Some Recent Novels: Styles of Martyrdom." *Yale Review, LVIII* (October, 1968), pp. 112-126.

Greenfeld, Josh. "A Romping Set in a Square New England Town." *Commonweal,* April 26, 1968, pp. 185-187.

Griffin, C. W., Jr. "Updike's Tarbox." *Reporter,* May 30, 1968, pp. 43-44.

Hicks, Granville. "God Has Gone, Sex Is Left." *Saturday Review,* April 6, 1968, pp. 21-22.

Hill, William B. "Couples." *America,* June 8, 1968, p. 757.

———. "Fiction." *America,* May 4, 1968, p. 622.

Hope, Francis. "Screwing in Turn." *New Statesman,* November 8, 1968, pp. 639-640.

Kazin, Alfred. "Couples." *Choice,* V (July, 1968), p. 628.

———. "Updike: Novelist of the New, Post-pill America." *Chicago Tribune Book World,* April 7, 1968, pp. 1, 3.

Kort, Wesley. "Desperate Games." *Christian Century,* October 23, 1968, pp. 1340-1342.

Maddocks, Melvin. "John Updike's Uptown Peyton Place." *Life,* April 5, 1968, p. 8.

Murray, Michele. "*Couples* All Surface: 'Updike Has Narrowed His Vision to the Bed'." *National Catholic Reporter,* May 1, 1968, p. 11.

"Notes on Current Books." *Virginia Quarterly Review,* XLIV (Summer, 1968), p. xcvi.

Novak, Michael. "Son of the Group." *Critic,* XXVI (June-July, 1968), pp. 72-74.

Shaw, Russell. "Couples." *Sign,* XLVIII (September, 1968), p. 58.

Sokolov, Raymond A. "Musical Beds." *Newsweek,* April 8, 1968, pp. 125-126.

Stern, Richard. "Men, Women and Lovestuff: All About It." *Chicago Sunday Sun-Times Book Week,* April 7, 1968, pp. 1, 9.

Thompson, John. "Updike's Couples." *Commentary,* May, 1968, pp. 70-73.

Trilling, Diana. "Updike's Yankee Traders." *The Atlantic,* April, 1968, pp. 129-131.

Yglesias, José. "Coupling and Uncoupling." *Nation,* May 13, 1968, pp. 637-638.

MIDPOINT AND OTHER POEMS (1969)

Adams, Phoebe. "Short Reviews: Books." *The Atlantic,* June, 1969, p. 118.

"Answers to Questions Unasked." *The Times Literary Supplement,* January 29, 1970, p. 104.

Brownjohn, Alan. "Dualities." *New Statesman,* March 6, 1970, p. 332.

Demos, John. "*Midpoint and Other Poems.*" *Library Journal,* XCIV (April 1, 1969), p. 1504.

Gates, Anne. "John Updike—Wearing His Poet's Hat." *Christian Science Monitor,* August 15, 1969, p. 9.

BOTTOM'S DREAM (1969)

Heyen, William. "Sensibilities." *Poetry,* CXV (March, 1970), pp. 428-429.

Heins, Paul. "John Updike, Adapter: *Bottom's Dream*" *Horn Book,* XLV (December, 1969), p. 667.

McConnell, Lynda. *"Bottom's Dream." Library Journal,* XCV (April 15, 1970), p. 1643.

Magid, Nora L. "Clear the Stage for a Repeat Performance." *The New York Times Book Review,* Pt. 2, November 9, 1969, p. 65.

BECH: A BOOK (1970)

Algren, Nelson. "Bech: A Book." *Critic,* XXIX (November-December, 1970), pp. 84-86.

Broyard, Anatole. "All the Way with Updike." *Life,* June 19, 1970, p. 12.

Davenport, Guy. "On the Edge of Being." *National Review,* August 25, 1970, pp. 903-904.

Edwards, Thomas. "Bech: A Book." *The New York Times Book Review,* June 21, 1970, pp. 1, 38.

Gold, Ivan. " 'You Really Gets'." *Nation,* June 29, 1970, pp. 791-792.

Kramer, Hilton. "Portrait of the Artist as a Jewish Intellectual." *Chicago Tribune Book World,* July 19, 1970, p. 3.

Kuehl, Linda. "The Risks in Putting On a Put-On." *Christian Science Monitor,* July 23, 1970, p. 7.

"The Lion That Squeaked." *Time,* June 22, 1970, pp. 82-83.

Murray, John. "Bech: A Book." *Best Sellers,* XXX (July 15, 1970), pp. 159-160.

Murray, Michele. "Profile of a Literary Hustler." *National Catholic Reporter,* July 24, 1970, p. 13.

Nelson, Barbara. *"Bech: A Book." Library Journal,* XCV (June 1, 1970), p. 2183.

"On Not Rocking the Boat." *The Times Literary Supplement,* October 16, 1970, p. 1183.

Ozick, Cynthia. "Ethnic Joke." *Commentary,* November, 1970, pp. 106-114.

Raban, Jonathan. "Talking Head." *New Statesman,* October 16, 1970, p. 494.

Richardson, Jack. "Keeping Up with Updike." *The New York Review of Books,* XV (October 22, 1970), pp. 46-48.

Schickel, Richard. "Books in Brief." *Harper's Magazine,* July, 1970, p. 102.

Seelye, John. "Notable." *New Republic,* July 11, 1970, p. 27.

Sokolov, Raymond A. "Gentile Parody." *Newsweek,* June 15, 1970, p. 106.

RABBIT REDUX (1971)

Allen, Bruce D. "Of A Linotype Operator at the Edge of Obsolescence." *Library Journal,* XCVI (November 1, 1971), p. 3640.

Davenport, Guy. "Even As the Heathen Rage." *National Review,* December 31, 1971, pp. 1473-1474.

Gill, Brendan. "Notes on Current Books." *Virginia Quarterly Review,* XLVIII (Spring, 1972), p. xlviii.

————. "A Special Case." *The New Yorker,* January 8, 1972, pp. 83-84.

————. "Unsentimental Education." *The Times Literary Supplement,* April 7, 1972, p. 385.

Gordon, J. "Updike Redux." *Ramparts,* X (April, 1972), pp. 56-59.

Heidenry, John. "Back to Pennsylvania." *The Economist,* CCXLIII (April 8, 1972), p. 12.

————. "The Best American Novel in a Decade." *Commonweal,* January 7, 1972, pp. 332-333.

Hill, William B. "Fiction." *America,* May 20, 1972, p. 550.

Howes, Victor. "Rerun Rabbit Run." *Christian Science Monitor,* November 18, 1971, p. 11.

Kennedy, Eileen. "Rabbit Redux." *Best Sellers,* XXXI (December 15, 1971), pp. 429-430.

Lindroth, James. "Rabbit Redux." *America,* January 29, 1972, pp. 102, 104.

Locke, Richard. "Rabbit Redux." *The New York Times Book Review,* November 14, 1971, pp. 1, 2ff.

Lodge, David. "The Lost American Dream." *The Tablet,* April 15, 1972, pp. 349-350.

Murray, Michele. "Rabbit Runs in Circles." *National Catholic Reporter,* December 10, 1971, p. 13.

Oldsey, Bernard. "Rabbit Run to Earth." *Nation,* January 10, 1972, pp. 54-56.

Ricks, Christopher. "Flopsy Bunny." *The New York Review of Books,* XVII (December 16, 1971), pp. 7-9.

Samuels, Charles Thomas. "Updike on the Present." *New Republic,* November 20, 1971, pp. 29-30.

Sheppard, R. Z. "Cabbage Moon." *Time,* November 15, 1971, p. 89.

Theroux, Paul. "A Has-been, 10 Years Later." *Chicago Tribune Book World,* November 14, 1971, pp. 3, 10.

Trevor, William. "All Right, Sort Of." *New Statesman,* April 7, 1972, pp. 462-463.

MUSEUMS AND WOMEN (1972)

Grumbach, Doris. "Suburban Middle Age." *New Republic,* October 21, 1972, pp. 30-31.

Kennedy, Eileen. "Museums and Women." *Best Sellers,* XXXII (November 15, 1972), p. 392.

Prescott, Peter S. "Following Through, Sadly." *Newsweek,* October 23, 1972, pp. 109, 112.

Rohrbach, Peter T. "Museums and Women and Other Stories." *America,* December 16, 1972, pp. 535-536.

Skow, John. "Sliding Seaward." *Time,* October 16, 1972, p. 91.

Tanner, Tony. "Museums and Women." *The New York Times Book Review,* October 22, 1972, pp. 5, 24.

Wood, Michael. "Great American Fragments." *The New York Review of Books,* XIX (December 14, 1972), pp. 14, 16.

Critical Essays on John Updike

Adams, Mildred. "El escritor John Updike: ¿Cuento o novela?" *Revista de Occidente,* I (August, 1963), pp. 198-202.

Aldridge, John W. "John Updike and the Higher Theology," in *The Devil in the Fire.* New York: Harper and Row, 1972.

————. "The Private Vice of John Updike," in *Time to Murder and Create: The Contemporary Novel in Crisis.* New York: David McKay, 1966.

Alley, Alvin D. "Centaur: Transcendental Imagination and Metaphoric Death." *English Journal,* LVI (October, 1967), pp. 982-985.

Alley, Alvin D. and Hugh Agee. "Existential Heroes: Frank Alpine and Rabbit Angstrom." *Ball State University Forum,* IX (Winter, 1968), pp. 3-5.

Alter, Robert. "Updike, Malamud, and the Fire This Time." *Commentary,* October, 1972, pp. 68-74.

Arnavon, Cyrille. "Les Romans de John Updike." *Europe,* XLIV, No. 446 (June, 1966), pp. 193-213.

Bellow, Saul. *Recent American Fiction.* Washington: Library of Congress, 1965.

Brenner, Gerry. "Rabbit, Run: John Updike's Criticism of the Return to Nature." *Twentieth Century Literature,* XII (April, 1966), pp. 3-14.

Brüning, Eberhard. "Tendenzen der Persönlichkeitsgestaltung im amerikanischen Gegenwartsroman." *Zeitschrift für Anglistik und Amerikanistik,* XVI, No. 4 (1968), pp. 390-401.

Burchard, Rachael C. *John Updike: Yea Sayings.* Carbondale: Southern Illinois University Press, 1971.

Burgess, Anthony. "Language, Myth, and Mr. Updike." *Commonweal,* February 11, 1966, pp. 557-559.

Busha, Virginia. "Poetry in the Classroom: 'Ex-basketball Player'." *English Journal,* LIX (May, 1970), pp. 643-645.

Cimatti, Pietro. "Burroughs e Updyke." *La Fiera Letteraria,* April 29, 1962, pp. 3, 4.

Cowley, Malcolm. "Holding the Fort on Audubon Terrace." *Saturday Review,* April 3, 1971, pp. 17, 41-42.

de Rambures, Jean-Louis. "Le Coeur secret de l'Amérique." *Réalités*, No. 266 (March, 1968), pp. 99-103.

Detweiler, Robert. "Four Spiritual Crises in Mid-Century American Fiction." *University of Florida Monographs, No. 14*. Gainesville, Florida, Fall, 1963.

————. *John Updike*. New York: Twayne, 1972.

————. "Updike's *Couples:* Eros Demythologized." *Twentieth Century Literature*, XVII (October, 1971), pp. 235-246.

Ditsky, John. "Roth, Updike, and the High Expense of Spirit." *University of Windsor Review*, V, No. 1 (Fall, 1969), pp. 111-120.

Dommergues, Pierre. *Les U.S.A. à la recherche de leur identité: Rencontres avec 40 écrivains américains*. Paris: Editions Bernard Grasset, 1967.

Doner, Dean. "Rabbit Angstrom's Unseen World," in *New World Writing 20*. Edited by Stewart Richardson and Corlies M. Smith. Philadelphia: J. B. Lippincott, 1962.

Doyle, Paul A. "Updike's Fiction: Motifs and Techniques." *Catholic World*, September, 1964, pp. 356-362.

Ducharme, Edward R. "Close Reading and Teaching: 'Shillington.'" *English Journal*, LIX (October, 1970), pp. 938-942.

Duncan, Graham H. "The Thing Itself in 'Rabbit, Run.'" *English Record*, XIII, No. 4 (April, 1963), pp. 36-37.

Elistratova, A. "Tragiceskoe zivotnoe—celovek: o dvux romanax Dzona Apdajka." *Inostrannaja Literatura*, IX, No. 12, pp. 220-226.

Enright, D. J. "The Inadequate American: John Updike's Fiction," in *Conspirators and Poets*. London: Chatto and Windus, 1966.

Eshelman, William R. "Updike Lauds National Medalist E. B. White." *Wilson Library Bulletin*, XLVI (February, 1972), pp. 489-490.

Finkelstein, Sidney. "Acceptance of Alienation: John Updike and James Purdy," in *Existentialism and Alienation in American Literature*. New York: International Publishers, 1965.

Fisher, Richard, E. "John Updike: Theme and Form in the Garden of Epiphanies." *Moderna Sprak,* LVI (Fall, 1962), pp. 225-260.

Flint, Joyce. "John Updike and *Couples:* The WASP's Dilemma." *Research Studies* (Washington State University), XXXVI (December, 1968), pp. 340-347.

Gado, Frank. "Conversation with John Updike." Schenectady, New York: Union College, 1971.

Galloway, David Darryl. *The Absurd Hero in American Fiction: Updike, Styron, Bellow, Salinger.* Austin: University of Texas Press, 1970.

————. "The Absurd Man as Saint: The Novels of John Updike." *Modern Fiction Studies,* X (September, 1964), pp. 111-127.

Gasca, Eduardo. *Literatura de la tierra baldía: John Updike.* Caracas: Ediciones de la Biblioteca Universidad Central de Venezuela, 1969.

Gass, William H. "Cock-a-doodle-doo," in *Fiction and the Figures of Life.* New York: Alfred A. Knopf, 1970.

Geller, Evelyn. "WLB Biography: John Updike." *Wilson Library Bulletin,* XXXVI (September, 1961), p. 67.

Gilman, Richard. "Fiction: John Updike," in *The Confusion of Realms.* New York: Random House, 1969.

Gratton, Margaret. "The Use of Rhythm in Three Novels by John Updike." *University of Portland Review,* XXI (Fall, 1969), pp. 3-12.

Guyol, Hazel Sample. "The Lord Loves A Cheerful Corpse." *English Journal,* LV (October, 1966), pp. 863-866.

Haas, Rudolf. "Griechischer Mythos im Modernen Roman: John Updikes *The Centaur,*" in *Lebende Antike: Symposion für Rudolf Sühnel.* Edited by Horst Meller and Mans-Joachim Zimmermann. Berin: E. Schmidt, 1967.

Hainsworth, J. D. "John Updike." *Hibbert Journal,* LXV (Spring, 1967), pp. 115-116.

Hamilton, Alice. "Between Innocence and Experience: From Joyce to Updike." *Dalhousie Review,* XLIX (Spring, 1969), pp. 102-109.

Hamilton, Alice and Kenneth. *The Elements of John Up-*

dike. Grand Rapids, Michigan: William B. Eerdmans, 1970.

————. *John Updike: A Critical Essay.* Grand Rapids, Michigan: William B. Eerdmans, 1967.

————. "John Updike's Prescription for Survival." *Christian Century,* July 5, 1972, pp. 740-744.

————. "Metamorphosis Through Art: John Updike's *Bech: A Book.*" *Queen's Quarterly,* LXXVII (Winter, 1970), pp. 624-636.

————. "Theme and Techniques in John Updike's *Midpoint.*" *Mosaic: A Journal for the Comparative Study of Literature and Ideas,* IV, No. 1, pp. 79-106.

Hamilton, Kenneth. "John Updike: Chronicler of 'The Time of the Death of God.'" *Christian Century,* June 7, 1967, pp. 745-748.

Harper, Howard Morrall, Jr. *Desperate Faith—A Study of Bellow, Salinger, Mailer, Baldwin and Updike.* Chapel Hill: The University of North Carolina Press, 1967.

Hertzel, Leo J. "Rabbit in the Great North Woods." *University Review* (Kansas City), XXXIII (December, 1966), pp. 143-147.

Hicks, Granville. "Generations of the Fifties: Malamud, Gold, and Updike," in *The Creative Present: Notes on Contemporary American Fiction.* Edited by Nona Balakian and Charles Simmons. Garden City, New York: Doubleday, 1963.

————. "John Updike," in *Literary Horizons: A Quarter Century of American Fiction.* New York: New York University Press, 1970.

Hill, John S. "Quest for Belief: Theme in the Novels of John Updike." *Southern Humanities Review,* III (Spring, 1969), pp. 166-175.

Howard, Jane. "Can A Nice Novelist Finish First?" *Life,* November 4, 1966, pp. 74, 74A, 74C, 74D, 76, 79-82.

Hyman, Stanley Edgar. "Chiron at Olinger High," in *Standards: A Chronicle of Books for Our Time.* New York: Horizon Press, 1966.

Kort, Wesley A. "The Centaur and the Problem of Vocation," in *Shriven Selves.* Philadelphia: Fortress Press, 1972.

Kretzoi, Charlotte M. "Témakeresés a modern amerikai irodalomban. John Updike." *Valágirodalmi Figyelö,* IX, pp. 293-299.

La Course, Guerin. "The Innocence of John Updike." *Commonweal,* February 8, 1963, pp. 512-514.

Le Vot, André. "Le Petit monde de John Updike." *Les Langues Modernes,* LXIII (January-February, 1969), pp. 66-73.

————. "Updike Poète, ou le Mythe d'Antée." *Les Langues Modernes,* LIX (November-December, 1965), pp. 50-55.

Lodge, David. "Post-Pill Paradise Lost: John Updike's *Couples,"* in *The Novelist at the Crossroads, and Other Essays on Fiction and Criticism.* Ithaca: Cornell University Press, 1971.

Logu, Pietro de. "La Narrativa di John Updike." *Studi Americani,* X (1964), pp. 343-368.

Mailer, Norman. "Norman Mailer vs. Nine Writers." *Esquire,* July, 1963, pp. 63-69, 105.

Matson, Elizabeth. "A Chinese Paradox, But Not Much of One: John Updike in His Poetry." *Minnesota Review,* VIII, No. 2 (1967), pp. 157-167.

Mizener, Arthur. "The American Hero as High School Boy: Peter Caldwell," in *The Sense of Life in the Modern Novel.* Boston: Houghton Mifflin, 1964.

Muradian, Thaddeus. "The World of Updike." *English Journal,* LIV, No. 7 (October, 1965), pp. 577-584.

Murphy, Richard W. "In Print: John Updike." *Horizon,* IV, No. 4 (March, 1962), pp. 84-85.

Myers, David. "The Questing Fear: Christian Allegory in John Updike's *The Centaur." Twentieth Century Literature,* XVII (April, 1971), pp. 73-82.

Nichols, Lewis. "Talk with John Updike." *The New York Times Book Review,* April 7, 1968, pp. 34-35.

Novak, Michael. "Updike's Quest for Liturgy." *Commonweal,* May 10, 1963, pp. 192-195.

O'Connor, William Van. "John Updike and William Styron: The Burden of Talent," in *Contemporary American*

Novelists. Edited by Harry T. Moore. Carbondale: Southern Illinois University Press, 1964.

Peter, John. "The Self-Effacement of the Novelist." *Malahat Review,* No. 8 (October, 1968), pp. 119-128.

Petillon, Pierre-Yves. "Le désespoir de John Updike." *Critique* (Paris), XXV (1969), pp. 972-977.

Petter, H. "John Updike's Metaphoric Novels." *English Studies, L* (April, 1969), pp. 197-206.

Podhoretz, Norman. "A Dissent on Updike." *Show,* III (April, 1963), p. 49. Reprinted in Podhoretz, Norman. *Doings and Undoings: The Fifties and After in American Writing.* New York: Farrar, Straus, 1964.

Reising, R. W. "Updike's 'A Sense of Shelter'." *Studies in Short Fiction,* VII (Fall, 1970), pp. 651-652.

Rhode, E. "Grabbing Dilemmas: John Updike Talks about God, Love, and the American Identity." *Vogue,* February 1, 1971, pp. 140, 184-185.

Rotkirch, Kristina. "Den otillfredsställde amerikanen." *Nya Argus,* LVII (1964), pp. 142-144.

"Run from Rabbit." *America,* November 19, 1960, pp. 257-258.

Rupp, Richard H. *Celebration in Postwar American Fiction 1945-1967.* Coral Gables, Florida: University of Miami Press, 1970.

Samuels, Charles Thomas. "The Art of Fiction XLIII: John Updike." *Paris Review,* XII (Winter, 1968), pp. 84-117.

————. *John Updike.* Minneapolis: University of Minnesota Press, 1969.

Seelbach, Wilhelm. "Die antike Mythologie in John Updikes Roman *The Centaur.*" *Arcadia,* V, No. 2 (1970), pp. 176-194.

Sheed, Wilfrid. "John Updike: *Couples,*" in *The Morning After.* New York: Farrar, Straus and Giroux, 1971.

Sissman, L. E. "John Updike: Midpoint and After." *The Atlantic,* August, 1970, pp. 102-104.

Sokoloff, B. A. *John Updike: A Comprehensive Bibliography.* Folcroft, Pennsylvania: Folcroft Press, 1972 [Limited Edition].

Standley, Fred. *"Rabbit, Run:* An Image of Life." *Midwest Quarterly,* VIII (July, 1967), pp. 371-386.

Stubbs, John C. "The Search for Perfection in *Rabbit, Run." Critique,* X, No. 2 (1968), pp. 94-101.

Suderman, Elmer F. "Art as a Way of Knowing." *Discourse,* XII (Winter, 1969), 3-14.

————. "The Right Way and the Good Way in *Rabbit, Run." University Review* (Kansas City), XXVI (October, 1969), pp. 13-21.

Tanner, Tony. "The American Novelist as Entropologist." *London Magazine,* X (October, 1970), pp. 5-18.

————. "A Compromised Environment," in *City of Words: American Fiction 1950-1970.* New York: Harper and Row, 1971.

Tate, Judith M., Sister, O.S.B. "John Updike: Of Rabbits and Centaurs." *Critic,* XXII (February-March, 1964), pp. 44-51.

Taylor, C. Clarke. *John Updike: A Bibliography.* Kent, Ohio: Kent State University Press, 1968.

Taylor, Larry E. *Pastoral and Anti-Pastoral Patterns in John Updike's Fiction.* Carbondale: Southern Illinois University Press, 1971.

"View from the Catacombs." *Time,* April 26, 1968, pp. 66-68ff.

Waldmeir, Joseph J. "Only an Occasional Rutabaga: American Fiction Since 1945." *Modern Fiction Studies,* XV (Winter, 1969/70), pp. 467-481.

Ward, J. A. "John Updike: *The Centaur." Critique: Studies in Modern Fiction,* VI, No. 2 (Fall, 1963), pp. 109-114.

————. "John Updike's Fiction." *Critique: Studies in Modern Fiction,* V, No. 1 (Spring-Summer, 1962), pp. 27-40.

Wyatt, Bryant N. "John Updike: The Psychological Novel in Search of Structure." *Twentieth Century Literature,* XIII (July, 1967), pp. 89-96.

Yates, Morris W. "The Doubt and Faith of John Updike." *College English,* XXVI (March, 1965), pp. 469-474.

INDEX

RAINSTORMS AND FIRE

Death, 8, 45-46, 177-178
Detweiler, Robert, 52-53, 69, 135
Dewey, John, 23
"A Dying Cat," 23

Eastlake, William, 104, 105
Eccles *(Rabbit, Run)*, 59-60, 64, 70-71, 72, 75
Edge, Miss *(Concluding)*, 49-50
Eliade, Mircea, 77, 78
Eliot, T. S., 81

"Fanning Island," 10, 22
The Fixer (Malamud), 83
The Floating Opera (Barth), 47
For Whom the Bell Tolls (Hemingway), 79, 137, 167
Forester, Gene *(A Separate Peace)*, 47-48
Forster, E. M., 17
Fox, Elizabeth (Foxy) *(Couples)*, 128-129, 131, 132, 133, 137, 138, 144-145
Franklin, Tommy *(The Poorhouse Fair)*, 38
Friedman, Melvin J., 11

Galloway, David D., 53, 54-55, 86
Gates of Horn, The (Levin), 173
Gilman, Richard, 4
Green, Henry, 49-50
Gregg *(The Poorhouse Fair)*, 29, 32, 43

Hamilton, Kenneth, 44-45, 120-121
Hanema, Angela *(Couples)*, 128, 145
Hanema, Piet *(Couples)*, 128, 129, 130, 131, 132, 133-134, 138, 139-141, 142-143, 145-147
"Happiest I've Been, The," 29
Harper, Howard Morrall, Jr., 113
Hawthorne, Nathaniel, 134, 174
Heinemann, Elizabeth *(The Poorhouse Fair)*, 37-38
Hemingway, Ernest, 79, 137

Hicks, Granville, 82
Hook *(The Poorhouse Fair)*, 29-33, 35, 39, 40, 45-46
Hovey, Neil, 29
Hutchens, John K., 54

"In Central Park," 17

James, Henry, 18-19
Jamiesson, Mrs. *(The Poorhouse Fair)*, 38
Jill *(Rabbit Redux)*, 158-159, 161
Johnson, Pamela Hansford, 4
Jordan, Robert *(For Whom the Bell Tolls)*, 79, 137
Joyce, James, 81

Kern, David ("Packed Dirt"), 22-26, 118
Knowles, John, 47-48
Kruppenbach *(Rabbit, Run)*, 71-72

Lady Chatterley's Lover (Lawrence), 137
Lawrence, D. H., 137
Levin, Harry, 173
"Lifeguard," 15, 16
little-Smith, Harold *(Couples)*, 141
Love, 9, 56
  Couples, 133
Lucas *(The Poorhouse Fair)*, 29

Mailer, Norman, 4
Malamud, Bernard, 83, 160
Memory, 9
Mendelssohn *(The Poorhouse Fair)*, 36-37, 46
"Midpoint," 7
Mr. Sammler's Planet (Bellows), 160
Mizener, Arthur, 102
Mortis, Amy *(The Poorhouse Fair)*, 32, 43, 46
Motes, Hazel *(Wise Blood)*, 11, 100
Museums and Women, 5
"Music School, The" 125-127